1966

MR

TWENTIETH CENTURY VIEWS

The aim of this series is to present the best in contemporary critical opinion on major authors, providing a twentieth century perspective on their changing status in an era of profound revaluation.

Maynard Mack, *Series Editor*
Yale University

DANTE

A COLLECTION OF CRITICAL ESSAYS

Edited by
John Freccero

Prentice-Hall, Inc.  *Englewood Cliffs, N.J.*
A SPECTRUM BOOK

Contents

CONTENTS

DANTE

Introduction

by John Freccero

After seven hundred years, the poetic reputation of Dante Alighieri remains undisputed, in spite of the fact that few of his admirers can any longer give more than momentary assent to what he considered to be the substance of his poem. Ever since the Renaissance, readers of the *Divine Comedy* have become increasingly uneasy about the poem's "system," its "medieval structure," which they can no longer take seriously as theology, any more than they can accept the poem's cosmology as physics. The "unity" of the poem (if by that term is meant the harmony of poetic form with its theological content) is for such readers an abstraction handed down by tradition; they experience a series of lyric fragments strung together only by their own patience or self-discipline.

The duality of form and content (or, as others have put it, the conflict between poetry and belief, poetry and theology, *poesia* and *non poesia*) is the fundamental problem to which critics in our day have directed their attention. For most of them, poetry (however defined) remains the timeless constant to which that *other* polarity (however named) must somehow be adjusted in order to bring the work into proper focus. Perhaps the most famous of such "adjustments" was that proposed by Benedetto Croce, who made of lyricism (*poesia*) an absolute, and relegated all that was conceptually or dramatically meaningful in the poem to the category of *non poesia*. This amounted to blaming our astigmatic vision not on history, but on a distortion inherent in the work itself, thus accounting for the experience of the casual reader, without doing anything to challenge that experience or enrich it. Serious readers, however, found Croce's simplistic solution unacceptable, not only because it denigrated Dante's achievement, but also because by dividing poetry from meaning Croce divorced it from the fullness of the poet's personality. Luigi Pirandello's answer, included in this anthology, constitutes a defense, not only of Dante's poetry, but also of his humanity, seen through the poem, in all of its vital historicity.

T. S. Eliot's attempt at a resolution of the dichotomy took the form of a meditation on the relationship of poetry to belief. In a now famous essay, written with great respect for Dante and for history, Eliot suggested that we distinguish the philosophical "belief" necessary for the writing of the poem from the poetic "assent" necessary for an understanding of it. While we are reading the poem, we give momentary assent to the poet's beliefs in the same way that we give momentary assent to the reality of the journey. The broader question of belief or disbelief simply does not arise in a strictly "literary appreciation." Eliot was not completely satisfied with this tentative formulation, for he recognized that the detached "understanding" of a reader deriving a purely literary satisfaction from Dante's poem is quite different from the "understanding" of a reader spiritually engaged, for whom *full* understanding terminates with belief. The first "understanding," founded upon poetic assent, is all that Eliot as critic could concede; at the same time, however, Eliot the poet recognized Dante's right to expect something more of his readers. In Eliot's reading, the "unity" of Dante's poem remains as transitory as the poetic assent upon which Eliot would found it. When we have finished our "appreciation" the illusion is shattered and we return to a world hopelessly separated from Dante's, moved by his poetry, but untouched and unaltered by the fervor of his convictions.

Dante expected more of his readers because for him literature was at once much less and much more than it is for us. It was less, in a sense, because it was not considered an autonomous form existing in a void somehow detached from both reader and writer, the object of aesthetic worship; rather it was indissolubly linked to the experience which gave rise to it and to which it was intended to bear witness. On the other hand, it was much more than literature is for a contemporary formalist because no appreciation of it could be purely literary. It exerted a powerful influence over its readers for good or for evil and hence was profoundly social. Francesca da Rimini's "appreciation" of the novels of chivalry was more than literary—it was an experience which led to her damnation, as Renato Poggioli demonstrates in an essay which is reprinted here. Similarly, in the *Purgatorio* Statius attributes both his poetic vocation and his religious conversion to his reading of Virgil: "Per te poeta fui, per te cristiano." For Dante, then, both poetry and what we have called "theology" were rooted in the structure which alone gave them meaning; the structure of his experience, of which the poem bears exemplary witness, a *testament* for other men.

Dante considered his poem to be a relationship between his experience and the experience of his readers, not simply a literary object. He knew as well as any modern aesthetician that pure experience is not directly communicable, being by definition unique. For this reason it had to be generalized and staged in dramatic, public terms. In the first canto of the *Paradiso,* as the pilgrim looks into the eyes of Beatrice, the poet compares him to the fisherman Glaucus, who became a god:

Trasumanar significar *per verba*
non si porià; però l'essemplo basti
a cui esperienza grazia serba.

[To go beyond the human cannot be signified in words;
therefore let the example suffice to those for
whom Grace reserves the experience.]

The gloss on this simile may be extended to refer to the whole poem—itself an extended *exemplum* of *esperienza piena* (*Inf*. XXVIII, 48) made possible, in Dante's terms, by grace. It is in the experience that we must believe, not in the *exemplum*, the poem itself, which is his compromise, his expression of what for us is out of reach. Nor does he ask us to believe in the poem's theology or its Christianity, the commitments to which his experience led him, for these are inseparable from the dramatic representation and, like it, depend upon an experience which we must believe precisely because we cannot know it. To both the *exemplum* and the theology we give the same assent that we give to the reality of the journey, with the conviction that, had *we* had a similar incommunicable experience it might well have led us elsewhere and therefore called for a very different *exemplum*. Of course it is Dante's conviction that the poetic record of his conversion will prepare the way for the conversion of others, as Virgil prepared it for him. Nevertheless, this is *his* act of faith, not ours, and it would have been presumptuous of him (in terms of his own beliefs) to expect to do more than prepare the way. To say that he actually expected his readers to share his Christianity, without the experience (*grazia*) which led him to it, is to accuse him of mistaking preparation for perfection, of not being content with the role of a Virgil, but usurping that of Beatrice as well. On the contrary, the fact that Beatrice calls him by name at the top of the mountain implies that each man's *esperienza* is his alone and that each man is free to accept or evade it.

The duality sensed by many of Dante's readers resides in his *exemplum* precisely because the *exemplum* was chosen to be a testament of the poet's *esperienza* to his contemporaries, from whom we are separated by seven centuries. In Dante's cultural context, such a "testament" could not fail to be Biblical. Charles Singleton has demonstrated that Dante's journey is the record of a spiritual development, written in the allegorical mode of theologians, in imitation of "God's book." In a series of studies (of which perhaps one of the lesser known is reprinted here) Singleton has demonstrated that the theological *allotria* (i.e., that which is alien) decried by Croce in fact gives meaning to the poetry and, thanks to an "effort of the historical imagination," gives poetic life to the exegetical materials that, in the hands of others, often degenerated into the static allegory of "this for that." Singleton's great contribution thus far to the history of Dante studies has been not only to bring us closer to the poet's intention through scholarship, but also, through criticism of a new kind, to help us see poetry where before we had seen only antiquated dogma.

It is through an effort of the historical imagination that scholarship in recent years has managed to span the distance that for the ordinary reader separates Dante's antiquated theology from the poetry whose immediacy has not diminished with time. In particular, the analysis of Canto XIII of the *Inferno* by Leo Spitzer minimizes the strangeness of Dante's *exemplum* to us by emphasizing how closely it is related to the poetics that we have always admired, whether or not we knew anything of the culture of which it was a most intimate expression. There is a sense, however, in which scholarly acts of the historical imagination, with their momentary "suspensions of disbelief," transfer the duality sensed by less sophisticated readers from the poem to the reader himself, for, while they reestablish the unity of the author's spirit in history, they truncate the spirit of the reader, whom they ask to surrender his most intimate convictions and *his* place in history for the sake of a literary experience. In other words, the objectivity of the scholar, so necessary to his discipline, runs the risk of encouraging indifference in his reader.

We have however suggested that the poem is a relationship between Dante's experience and that of his readers. The ultimate unity of any *reading* of the poem is therefore not in the poem itself, but in our relationship to it, and requires not only that we see the spirit of the author as a unity in his poem, but also that we maintain our own human integrity while viewing it. It is not enough to go back to the poem in history in order to understand the *exemplum* as a literary artifact; the experience to which it testifies must also be brought to us so that, interpreted in phenomenological terms, without reference to theological abstractions whose validity we no longer take for granted, it may be accepted without compromise. It is to that experience that we must now direct our attention.

To capture the essence of one's experience and then to dramatize it in terms that are intelligible to others is to write a spiritual autobiography, a novel of the self. In one of the essays in this anthology, Gianfranco Contini suggests that Dante's previous attempt at such a "unification" of the self in a retrospective poetic structure, the *Vita Nuova,* was only a partial unification because its purpose was not definitive autobiography but rather preparation for a new, more sublime period, the period of the *Divine Comedy.* It was intended to close one stage in the poet's life in order to begin a new period, with the resolve to write some day of Beatrice "that which has never been written of any other lady."

The title of Dante's first novel of the self hints at the subject matter of all such novels: the profound experience to which, ever since Plato, men have given the name of "conversion." The Dante who *is* tells the story of the Dante who *was,* which is to say that the "little book" marks the break in the spiritual continuity between the former life and the new, while the poem recapitulates the whole of the poet's life in retrospect and constitutes a hymn of praise to Beatrice and a witness of the power of grace. To state the matter in this way, however, is to give the impression that the poem is merely a vehicle for a testament which might equally well have been rendered in the form of a fable, a myth or, more directly, a propaganda tract. It should be stressed, however, that the distinction we have made between an experience and the expression of that experience is purely logical and serves the purpose only of clarifying our own beliefs with respect to the poem. Ontologically, or even phenomenologically, they are one. The experience of conversion for Dante is at the same time the experience of writing the novel of the self, just as the novel of the self depends for its very existence on the conversion which is its subject matter. In other words, Dante might well have addressed to Beatrice the words which Statius addressed to Virgil, "per te poeta fui, per te cristiano," because for him these were not separable vocations.

Conversion in Pauline terms was a burial of the "old man" and a putting on of the new. Similarly, this detachment of the self that *was* from the self that *is* constitutes the first requirement of any literature of the self that pretends to sincerity. This is most apparent in some of the modern forms of the literature of the self which end not in synthesis, but in infinite regression—a series of attempts to grasp the truth about oneself which are constantly being replaced by fresh attempts: the novel, the journal on the novel, the journal on the journal. In such cases there is no real detachment, no gap between *persona* who was and author who is. Because of the essential continuity of subject and object, of observer and the self which is observed, there is no place to stand from which the flow of consciousness can be measured, let alone judged, because both subject and object are swept along by the flow of time. Only death can close the series, lock the door of the self so that inventory may be taken. Death being what it is, however, it is impossible for the self to "take stock" of itself. It is the anguish of the novelist that he can know himself with sufficient detachment only when he is all that he can ever be, at which point he ceases to know anything at all. For this very simple reason bad faith and self-deception seem built into the genre, and modern "confessions" usually wind up in protestations of innocence.

For St. Augustine, the first novelist of the self, the death and resurrection requisite for authentic confession could only be a gift of grace. To make one's confession—or to write one's "confessions"—was for this reason primarily a theological matter. Both the detachment of the novelist and the "new life" of the Christian required a perspective which was logically impossible, a vantage point from which the former self could be judged with the certainty that comes only from organic continuity and with the detachment and finality that can come only with death. In short, a "present moment" (*Confessions* XI) in which time is fixed into an eternity here and now, a release from time within the flow of time. Augustine's *Confessions*, the record of the death of his former self and the birth of the new, were in his view made possible by their subject matter: his conversion by grace. What is more, they were also intended to serve as a "confession" in the more primitive sense: that is, to attest to the experience of conversion, a "confession of faith" for other men.

This is the pattern of Dante's poem, as it is of every "confession," because the novel of the self must of necessity be either a lie or the record of the detachment which in Dante's day was known as a conversion. If the record of Dante's conversion takes a Biblical form it is because the pattern itself is Biblical—a fall and a subsequent redemption, made possible by Christ's death and resurrection. To remember the fall and yet be sure of redemption, to know his former self and yet to be detached from it, Dante needed an Augustinian *present,* a place to stand from which he could see himself, precisely the duration which Farinata tells us that the damned in Hell do not possess (*Inf.* X, 100 ff). The conversion makes the poem possible in the eyes of the poet, for this "present" becomes his through grace and spans the necessary gap between the being of his *persona* and the knowing of the poet. Without the detachment which is a product of his conversion, Dante's dramatic representation would be mere portraiture or image-projection, self-deception of the type that we have come to expect in the genre of "confessions" ever since the nineteenth century. On the other hand, the experience remains incommunicable without the generalized statement whose allegorical conventions made it meaningful to his contemporaries. Thus the poet's experience is the structure of his poem, at once its subject matter and mode of being, without which it could not have been written, except in bad faith. At the same time, the poem (the writing of it) is in itself a creative *askesis* and is part of that experience; while the theological mode in which it is cast provided Dante with what he took to be a rational basis for his experience, a generalized dimension which pointed to the ways in which that intensely personal experience could be made to enter into history and into society, as part of the redemptive scheme of Providence. Experience and *exemplum* are thus dialectically related as the flesh and the word respectively of what we may call, in the term of René Girard, Dante's *incarnation romanesque.*

At the last vision, Dante sees the exemplary timelessness within time in the form of the *Incarnation.* Apart from being the central mystery of Christianity, this also marks the most important moment in the poem, for it is the point of transition between the pilgrim who *was* and the poet who *is,* at once the point of departure and the point of arrival of the poem which we read. Pilgrim and poet converge at the vision which from the beginning has been their goal. The vision is therefore no mere theological intrusion but is the mystery which makes possible both the transition from pilgrim to poet and the poem which is the witness of that transition. It is analogous to the ending of Proust's novel of the self, which ends with the decision to write the novel that we have just finished reading, and the Augustinian "present" which it bestows upon Dante (pilgrim and poet) can be designated in more current terms as "le temps retrouvé." In order to *know*, Dante requires the timeless perspective of the author and a metaphysical structure: in other words, the principle of intelligibility which is his *word*, the plot of the dramatic representation which made of the poem an *exemplum* instantly recognizable to his contemporaries. By itself, however, this *logos* is not enough, for intelligibility runs the risk of abstraction, the static and transparent allegory of "this for that" or, in contemporary terms, the risk of the hack novel, where the outcome is blatantly clear to the reader as it is to the writer because neither is involved in the characters who move like puppets following an inexorable destiny. On the other hand, pure experience cannot be recorded in words. When an attempt is made to convey a flesh and blood reality without perspective, without plot, one runs the risk of unintelligibility, the "private world" of the *nouveau roman*, signifying nothing. Dante as pilgrim cannot see the objective designated for him by the author except in retrospect, when his pilgrimage, his evolution, is over. At that final moment, however, the Incarnation of Christ reveals his own timeless form to him and is joined by the here-and-now reality of his flesh—"la *nostra* effige" (*Par.* XXXIII, 131). The author, who has for us heretofore been an abstract voice, takes upon himself the humanity of his former self. The vision of the Incarnation is therefore a squaring of the circle, a union of Word and flesh, which makes possible the incarnation of the novel, a union of *exemplum* and *esperienza* in the synthesis which, for a believer, was comparable only to the union of the Bible's meaning to its letter, or of Christ's divinity to his humanity.

The poem's ending is therefore, as György Lukács would have it, the transcendent made immanent, but for Dante, not for us. The poem bears witness of his experience in its example, which in turn becomes an element of *our* experience. This is all that the poet wished, for he writes "for the good of the world, which lives with evil" (*Purg.* XXXII, 103). When his vantage point is attained, not only has the demon of his own subjectivity been exorcised by the fulfillment of the desire which is in human terms insatiable, but his view of history and of the world in which he lives has also been purged of the distortions of private perspective, without however being detached from the humanity which joins him to all other men in "*nostra* vita." Thereafter, whatever duality remains in the dialectic between his experience and ours waits upon our own private synthesis in order finally to be resolved.

Dante's Works

The *Vita Nuova,* the story of Dante's love for Beatrice, in verse and
prose
The *Rime:*

    I. Consisting mainly of poems taken from the *Vita Nuova*
   II. Other poems written at the same time, including several verse epistles
  III. The *Tenzone,* or debate in verse, with the poet Forese Donati
  IV. Allegorical and doctrinal poems, including the three long *canzoni,* or
      doctrinal poems, included in the *Convivio*
    V. Other love poems and verse epistles
  VI. The *Rime Petrose,* or "Stony Verses," a collection of love poems which
      tell of the cruelty of a "lady of stone"
 VII. Various verses written during Dante's exile

The *Convivio,* an unfinished philosophical work in four parts, consisting
  of an introduction and three allegorical explications of three long
  canzoni
De Vulgari Eloquentia, a theoretical work on "the common language"
De Monarchia, a treatise on Monarchy and its relationship to the Church
Epistles and *Eclogues* in Latin, as well as a scientific treatise, the *Quaestio
  de Aqua et Terra*
The *Divina Commedia:*

    I. *Inferno*
   II. *Purgatorio*
  III. *Paradiso*

The Survival and Transformation of Dante's Vision of Reality

by Erich Auerbach

Here we shall not speak in the usual sense of Dante's influence on posterity. Neither the few insignificant poets who have imitated the *Comedy,* nor the highly problematic influence of Dante's ideas and teachings, nor the far more important "history of his fame"—in short, no part of what is known in Italy as *la fortuna di Dante*—can have any bearing on the present study. Here we are concerned with something he created and which remained living and effective, quite regardless of whether those in whom we find it followed his doctrines or not, of whether they loved or hated him, or, for that matter, of whether they were even familiar with his work. For the land he discovered has not been lost; many have entered upon it, some have explored it, though the fact that he was first to discover it has been largely forgotten or ignored. The something of which I am speaking, the discovery that remained alive, is Dante's testimony to the reality that is poetry, to the modern European form of artistic mimesis which stresses the actuality of events.

Stefan George[1] speaks of tone, movement, and Gestalt—it is they, he says, that make Dante the father of all modern literature. And perhaps not only of literature. Dante discovered the European representation (Gestalt) of man, and this same representation made its appearance in art and historiography. Dante was the first to configure what classical antiquity had configured very differently and the Middle Ages not at all: man, not as a remote legendary hero, not as an abstract or anecdotal representative of an ethical type, but man as we know him in his living historical reality, the concrete individual in his unity and wholeness; and in that he has been followed by all subsequent portrayers of man, regardless of whether they treated a historical or a mythical or a religious subject, for after Dante myth and legend also became history. Even in

[1] Preface to the *Dante Uebertragungen.*

portraying saints, writers have striven for truth to life, for historical concreteness, as though saints too were a part of the historical process. As we have seen, Christian legend came to be treated as an immanent historical reality; the arts have striven to represent a more perfect unity of spirit and body, spun into the fabric of man's destiny, and despite changes of taste and differences in artistic technique, this striving has endured, through many perils and darkenings, down to our day.

In the present work, we have tried to show that this immense conquest did not spring full-blown from Dante's intuition, but that his creative powers were kindled by his subject, which compelled him, once he had undertaken to set forth the divine judgment, to unearth the complete truth about individual historical men, and consequently to reveal the whole character and personality. As we have repeatedly stressed, his poetic genius was inseparably bound up with his doctrine. But his doctrine did not endure. The *Comedy* represented the physical, ethical, and political unity of the Scholastic cosmos at a time when it was beginning to lose its ideological integrity: Dante took the attitude of a conservative defender, his battle was an attempt to regain something that had already been lost; in this battle he was defeated, and his hopes and prophecies were never fulfilled. True, ideas of a Roman World Empire survived down to the Late Renaissance, and indignation over the corruption of the Church led to the great movements of the Reformation and Counter Reformation. But those ideas and movements have only certain superficial characteristics in common with Dante's view of the world; they originated and grew independently of it. Some were fantastic dreams, some were great popular uprisings, some acts of practical politics, and still others had something of all three: but none possessed the depth and universal unity of Dante's Thomist world view, and their consequence was not the worldwide *humana civilitas* for which Dante hoped, but an increasing fragmentation of cultural forces; it is only after the imperial ideology and the Christian-medieval conception of the world, shaken by intestine struggles, were swept away by the rationalism of the seventeenth and eighteenth centuries that a new practical view of the unity of human society began to take form. Thus Dante's work remained almost without influence on the history of European thought; immediately after his death, and even during his lifetime, the structure of literary, cultured society underwent a complete change in which he had no part, the change from Scholastic to Humanistic thinking, and that transformation undermined the influence of so rigorously committed a work as the *Comedy*. The radical shift in values that has taken place is made clear by the example of Petrarch, who was only forty years younger than Dante. Petrarch was not actually of a different party, he was not opposed to Dante's strivings; but what moved Dante, the whole attitude and form of his life, had grown alien to him. He is distinguished from Dante above all by his new attitude toward his own person; it was no longer in looking upward—as Orcagna portrayed Dante in his fresco of the Last Judgment in Santa Maria Novella—that Petrarch expected to find self-fulfillment, but in the conscious cultivation of his own nature. Although far inferior to Dante in personality and natural endowment, he was unwilling to acknowledge any superior order or authority; not even the authority of the universal world order to which Dante submitted so passionately. The autonomous personality, of which Petrarch was to be the first fully typical modern European embodiment, has lived in a thousand forms and varieties; the conception takes in all the tendencies of the modern age, the business spirit, the religious subjectivism, the humanism, and the striving for physical and technological domination of the world. It is incomparably richer, deeper, and more dangerous than the ancient cult of the person. From Christianity, whence it rose and which it ultimately defeated, this conception inherited unrest and immoderation. These qualities led it to discard the structure and limits of Dante's world, to which, however, it owed the power of its actuality.

Accordingly, even if it is agreed that Dante's creation is closely bound up with his subject matter, that his poetry is inseparable from his doctrine, he seems to be a special case that has never been repeated and hence tells us nothing about the nature of the poetic process. For the art of imitating reality continued to develop quite independently of the presuppositions which seem to have been at the base of Dante's work. No poet or artist after Dante required an ultimate, eschatological destiny in order to perceive the unity of the human person: sheer intuitive power seems to have enabled subsequent writers to combine inner and outward observation into a whole.

But that argument does not take in the whole truth. Its proponents neglect or underestimate the part played in the creative drive by the residues of older intellectual forces and fail to discern such residues beneath superficial changes in consciousness. It is generally acknowledged that the Renaissance represents a unit in the history of European culture and that the decisive element of its unity was the self-discovery of the human personality; and it is also generally recognized that, despite Dante's medieval view of the world, the discovery began with him. Thus there would seem to be reason to believe that something in the structure of the medieval world view was carried over into the new development and made it possible. In the history of modern European culture, there is, indeed, a constant which has come down unchanged through all the metamorphoses of religious and philosophical forms, and which is first discernible in Dante; namely, the idea (whatever its basis may be) that individual destiny is not meaningless, but is necessarily tragic and significant, and that the whole world context is revealed in it. That conception was already present in ancient mimesis, but carried less force, because the eschatological myths of the ancients lent far less support than Christian doctrine and the story of Christ to the conviction that the individual is indestructible, that the life of the individual on earth is a brief moment of irrevocable decision. In the early Middle Ages the historical sense had been dulled—the image of man was reduced to a moral or spiritualist abstraction, a remote legendary dream, or a comic caricature; in short man was removed from his natural, historical habitat. With Dante the historical individual was reborn in his manifest unity of body and spirit; he was both old and new, rising from long oblivion with greater power and scope than ever before. And although the Christian eschatology that had given birth to this new vision of man was to lose its unity and vitality, the European mind was so permeated with the idea of human destiny that even in very un-Christian artists it preserved the Christian force and tension which were Dante's gift to posterity. Modern mimesis found man in his individual destiny; it raised him out of the two-dimensional unreality of a remote dreamland or philosophical abstraction, and moved him into the historical area in which he really lives. But that historical world had to be rediscovered; and in a spiritualist culture, where earthly happening was either disregarded or looked upon as a mere metaphorical existence leading up to man's real and final destiny, man's historical world could be discovered only by way of his final destiny, considered as the goal and meaning of earthly happening. But once the discovery was made in that way, earthly happening could no longer be looked upon with indifference. The perception of history and immanent reality arrived at in the *Comedy* through an eschatological vision, flowed back into real history, filling it with the blood of authentic truth, for an awareness had been born that a man's concrete earthly life is encompassed in his ultimate fate and that the event in its authentic, concrete, complete uniqueness is important for the part it plays in God's judgment. From that center man's earthly, historical reality derived new life and value, and even the *Comedy* where, not without difficulty, the turbulent new forces were confined within an eschatological frame, gives us an intimation of how quickly and violently they would break loose. With Petrarch and Boccaccio the historical world acquired a fully immanent autonomy, and this sense of the self-sufficiency of earthly life spread like a fructifying stream to the rest of Europe— seemingly quite estranged from its eschatological origin and yet secretly linked with it through man's irrevocable bond with his concrete historical fate.

By that I do not mean that literature and art began to concern themselves exclusively with subjects drawn from real life and history, and no such statement would be in keeping with the facts. Mythical and religious subjects continued to be treated, and indeed more penetratingly than before. For they too were drawn into the historical vision we have described; the traditional fable lost its emblematic rigidity, and from the rich material, which had been largely obscured beneath dogmatic and spiritualist symbols, the author was now enabled, by his insight into the unity of character and fate, to select the perceptions that seemed to offer the fullest evidence and the most essential truth. And another form of literature, which is perhaps the most significant of all in modern Europe because it has permeated all others, namely the lyrical self-portraiture initiated by Petrarch, was rendered possible only by the discovery of the historical world. For it was only in that area that the diverse levels of feeling and instinct, the entire unity and variety of the personality, could unfold, that the empirical person, the individual with his inner life, could become an object of mimesis.

This current created rich new possibilities and grave dangers for mimesis. To discuss them is not the purpose of the present book, in which I have tried to grasp Dante's work as a unity, rooted in the unity of his subject matter. It has seemed to me that this approach offered the only hope of representing Dante's historical reality in such a way that "the words may not be diverse from the fact."

The Poetry of Dante

by Luigi Pirandello

Under this title, Benedetto Croce has recently published an essay which, "in order to forge another link in the chain of intellectual progress," attempts once more to establish that *better* approach to Dante criticism begun, according to him, with the great four-volume monograph on the *Commedia* by Karl Vossler, his noted German disciple. Before Vossler, others had already said something about what Croce calls the preliminary, if not precisely the central, problem in the criticism of Dante: that of the *Commedia's* duality. To Bouterweck, that duality presented itself as a distinction and a divergence between the poem's "system" and its poetry; to De Sanctis, as a contrast between allegorism and poetry, between heaven and earth or, as many other earlier critics would have it (less exactly, according to Croce), between Dante the theologian and Dante the poet.

De Sanctis' solution does not seem very happy to Croce, nor can he ultimately accept Vossler's, although he esteems and praises it highly. Vossler, after refusing to think of the *Commedia* as a work of poetry mixed with philosophy (since "the most powerful works of the human spirit are not hybrid, but pure"), agreeing that the "fundamental tone" of the *Commedia's* style is "essentially lyrical," nevertheless thinks that this vital lyrical principle, when confronted with the epico-dramatic action of the poem, at times intimately transforms it into poetry and at other times does not. According to Vossler, the esthetic criticism of the poem should consist of an examination of this struggle and alternation throughout the three *cantiche;* whereas it seems to Croce that such an examination, insofar as it postulates not a contrast but a relationship between structure and poetry to be determined or resolved in each instance,

"The Poetry of Dante," by Luigi Pirandello. A review of Croce's book *La poesia di Dante* (Bari: Laterza, 1921) published in *L'idea nazionale* (September 14, 1921) and later collected with other essays in a volume edited by Manlio Lo Vecchio-Musti and published by Mondadori in 1939, then in 1952, and finally in 1960. The text was established by the editor from the manuscript, owned by the late Silvio D'Amico. The translation, based on the Mondadori edition of 1960 (*Saggi, poesie e scritti vari,* pp. 331-341. Copyright © 1960 by *Arnoldo Mondadori Editore*) is by Gian Paolo Biasin, and was made with the kind permission of the heirs of Luigi Pirandello.

involves Vossler in inextricable difficulties and leads him to erroneous conclusions.

For Croce, in fact, there is no middle ground: "one can overcome these difficulties and errors only by making a sharp distinction between structure and poetry, placing them to be sure in strict philosophical and ethical relationship and thereby considering them necessary elements of Dante's spirit, but being careful to avoid any idea of a poetical relationship between them. Only in this way is it possible to enjoy all of the poetry of the *Commedia* profoundly, and at the same time accept its structure, with some indifference perhaps, but without aversion and, above all, without derision."

This amounts to saying that for Croce the *Commedia* is not a work of poetry, but rather a work in which there are *some poems* to be "enjoyed profoundly," and nothing else. In short, a return to Bouterweck's theory of the "fragmentary quality" of Dante's poetry; the theory about which Croce says, "Although on the one hand it merely conformed to the judgment of Bettinelli and other eighteenth-century critics of Dante's poetry, on the other hand it anticipated a more liberal way of interpreting and enjoying poetry." The sole innovation is the recognition of a strict philosophical and ethical relationship between structure and poetry, considered as necessary elements of the Dantesque spirit, and the acceptance of the poem's structure without aversion or derision.

And with that the link is forged.

Except that precisely in this single innovation (supposing it were consistently maintained, which, as we shall see, it is not) lies the logical pitfall; an irremediable contradiction is revealed the moment Croce wishes to keep united in *strict* and *necessary* relationship those elements which he then wishes to distinguish sharply, with the result that distinction is impossible (it is in fact asserted but not proven) and the strict and necessary relationship, because of the distinction, is equally impossible (it is in fact asserted but not proven).

Given that structure and poetry are both *necessary* elements of Dante's spirit, and given that Dante's spirit, since it is a unity, like all other spirits, *cannot be other than it is,* how explain Croce's failure to see not only that he himself becomes involved in the difficulties and errors which Vossler wished to avoid by positing a relationship rather than a contrast or sharp distinction, but also that he contradicts himself by maintaining first the necessity of the relationship and then the necessity of the distinction? What can it mean to say that the relationship between structure and poetry is of a philosophical and ethical nature, but not of a poetical nature? If it is a *relationship,* it cannot be one-sided; the structure too must be of a poetical nature; if it were not, how could *poetry* possibly be in a *non-poetical* relationship with structure, but only in a philosophical and ethical relationship? This is absurd. Either poetry is no longer poetry, or the relationship does not exist, in which case we are left only with some fragments and a distinction—so much for the unity of the Dantesque spirit and for the relationship which was supposed to be necessary!

And so in fact Croce leaves it. Even in an oppressive tangle of contradictions he affirms that "the true unity of the poetry is in the poetic spirit of Dante, the Dante of the *Commedia*." The poem has no unity of its own, however, so that he adds, "not in the comprehensive unity of his work." "The comprehensive character of the three *cantiche*" can be grasped only "through the contemplation of the individual poetry which they offer respectively, having a certain distinctive physiognomy in each separate *cantica* perceptible through its variety: a poetry which is no different from, nor greater than that offered by any three books in which one poet has collected his own lyrics, arranging them according to certain affinities." Lyrics, in short, "which stand by themselves," as Croce says elsewhere, without having anything to do with structure. But then he states on the contrary that through this structure "Dante's poetry takes on a character of *absolute necessity*, bursting through the framework" so that, "to those who do not believe in the real and autonomous existence of poetry and consider it something artificial and expendable, there could be offered no clearer example for consideration than this poetic fury of Dante—as theologian and as politician—this torrent urged on by a lofty source which makes its way through rocks and stones and flows on impetuously." "Such is its strength and richness that it penetrates every crevice in the rocks and stones and sweeps with its foaming waves and sheets of water, over mountain scenes," so that often one sees nothing but the movement of its waters. "This poetry of Dante, at the very least, enlivens with freshest fantasy the detailed discussions, didactic passages, narrative devices, and even the many abstruse excursions of the scholar into history, mythology and astronomy, investing them all with its passionate and sublime accent."

Then what is the point, you may ask. The fact is that Croce cannot deny that, for these very reasons, framework and poetry "are inseparable in Dante's work, just as the powers of his soul are inseparable, one conditioning the other and therefore flowing into the other"; nevertheless, he then makes his sharp distinction, and says that philosophy and ethics are rendered in a negative way in Dante's poetry, *as they should be,* "as the account of an experience of ineffable things." And it seems, for some strange reason, that the account should not be considered poetic. Croce states that he accepts it, admittedly somewhat indifferently, but without aversion and above all without derision. This is what he says, but when he is put to the test, talk about aversion and derision! So grossly does he exaggerate that even his faithful German disciple Karl Vossler cannot take him seriously. In order not to show aversion and derision Croce, without paying the slightest attention to what he has asserted elsewhere, says that the structure and framework of the *Commedia* cannot be compared to the frame of a painting, because such a comparison runs the risk of again according to that structure "a quality which is properly aesthetic," since frames are usually "visualized together with the paintings and made so as to form an artistic harmony; the completion, as it were, of the paintings themselves, which is really not so in this case." Good Lord! It even clashes as a picture-frame! Even as a frame! Is it then something that just doesn't fit at all? But what about that famous *strict relationship?* And what about that effectiveness which gives to Dante's poetry "its character of absolute necessity, bursting through the framework"? Nothing remains! A frame that doesn't go with the painting. Not bad for someone who would accept it without aversion, and above all without derision! But that's not all.

Do you know what Dante was doing in his representation of the three realms of the other world? Now pay careful attention! Croce does not deny (though he grits his teeth at the concession) that yes, of course, it is "even evident that Dante furnished us with a *certain* representation of the three realms," a representation, in short, "which is certainly to be found in the *Commedia,* and indeed even seems to support the rest of it"—(am I dreaming?)—well, do you know what Dante was doing with such a representation?

All of you are deceived by the power of a creative imagination which has built a world in which the poet himself appears to your eyes, by the miracle of art, no longer as creator but as actor, a traveler who passes through this fictive world, hesitant, fearful, almost as though he had not himself prepared those surprises, those wonders, those sights. All of you, as a result of that journey of his through the eternity of his world, see the gradual unfolding, from moment to moment, of a life which the power of art fixes in eternal attitudes; and you do not even remember any more that what is transitory in the eternal is transformed in its turn into the eternal by the power of art and is certainly not the same for the poet as it is for you—who see the *action* where he saw and felt his *creation,* still new and warm—because the poet's feeling has become almost a reality outside him, and you see it in terms of the representation he has given of it. You do not realize that the poet's objective sentiment could not have for him the eternal character it has for you, because he still visualized the act of creating it gradually, when his material was still growing inside him. The feeling of the moment is still warm for him when, for example, Farinata just now, with that gesture, rises up from the tomb, from the waist up, and Francesca and Paolo at his affectionate cry come close to him to tell him of their sweet sighs. All of you, were it not for these circles, and were there not a "whirlwind" in one of them, would not see Francesca and Paolo again, and without those tombs in that other circle you would not again see Farinata who exists entirely in his gesture, rising "from the waist up"; gradually as you read you seem to see and touch that world, so great is the power of art with which the poet presents it to you. You will no doubt reply that this representation is not, and cannot be, other than an imaginative creation of prodigious power.

How naïve you are, my dear readers! How you lack "an eye and ear for poetry"!—It is a representation and that cannot be denied. Yes, it is indeed a *certain* representation; a representation which is to be found in the *Commedia* and even seems to support the rest. And yes, Croce, dealing with representation, will feel a little embarrassed in recognizing it, much less defining it, because according to his *Estetica* he ought really to call it art. For heaven's sake what would it be? What would it be? Ah, not art! No Sir! But do you know what it is? Imaginative construction —there you are! Not poetry. Not philosophy. It is the imagination which "intervenes as a demiurge and accomplishes a totally practical work, that is, to mold an object which suggests to the imagination the idea of another world, of the eternal." As I said before, am I dreaming? The imagination which molds an object which suggests to the *imagination itself* the idea of the other world! This is really an idea from the other world, where it may be possible to see such marvels; works of which one cannot say what the devil they are, since they are not poetry, nor even poetry gone wrong, as you would expect from an imagination which, as demiurge, wants to achieve a purely practical work; nor is it a purely practical work, because it is molded by the imagination which in fact molds it for its own use.

If all of this is difficult enough just to put into words, imagine what chance Croce has of proving it. He tries to say it one way and then of course contradicts himself. In the *Introduction* p. 11, he had written: "It must be admitted . . . these doctrines have an *imaginative* rather than a *speculative* basis in the text . . . it is important to know them, but in the same way as one knows a myth, a fable, or any fact, that is, as *elements or parts of poetry, from which, rather than from logic, they receive their imprint and significance.*" Excellent! So that one would expect that the *image* of those thoughts, the *imprint* and *poetic significance* of those *elements* and of those *parts of Dantesque poetry,* being elements and parts of poetry, could not be other than poetry. Not a chance! How can they be poetry? They cannot be because Croce, after saying this, then says that the necessary poetic and creative motive is lacking. And why is it lacking? Listen. Because "if in the powerful soul of Dante the firm belief in the reality and eternity of the life hereafter is united with a feeling for worldly things, if 'both heaven and earth had a hand' in his poem, the obvious consequence is that strictly speaking the representation of the other world, of Hell, Purgatory, and Paradise, could not be the intrinsic subject of his poem nor its creative and dominant motive." Is this a proof? On the contrary, it is easier to see it as a proof of what Croce wants to deny. If heaven only had a hand in his poem, if one found in Dante only the firm belief in the reality and eternity of the life hereafter, without the added feeling in his powerful soul for worldly things, Dante would be an ascetic, a theologian, a Lenten preacher or who knows what. Instead he is simply a poet, the poet who composes a poem in which both heaven and earth have a hand, precisely because, thank heaven, there is in him earth as well as heaven, and his firm belief is joined with a powerful feeling for earthly things.

To say that a representation of the other world would have required an absolute predominance of the feeling of the transcendent over that of the immanent, a disposition peculiar to mystics and ascetics who scorn the world, harsh and fierce, or ecstatic and blessed (such as can be found in Christian hymnography or in some canticles by Jacopone); and to say that the rhythm then would be much accelerated, with images surfacing and vanishing again, sometimes with vigor, at other times vaguely nuanced, as they are alternately sketched in yearning or in terror, urged on from all around by the presence of God—Hell like this, Purgatory like that, and Paradise in such and such a way; all this is to say how he, Benedetto Croce, would have written the *Commedia,* or how it would have been written by a Christian hymn-writer or by Jacopone, but it does not prove that Dante couldn't do it in a different way, his own way, without the absolute predominance of the transcedent, that disposition peculiar to mystics and ascetics, with its rhythm, its images, its own Hell, its own Purgatory and its own Paradise. In the last analysis, it seems to me that his way is quite satisfactory for those of us who do not have "the eye and ear" for poetry which Croce has.

And so there is no proof to the contrary. Yet, still in order to accept this *imaginative construction* without aversion or above all without derision, Croce says that "perhaps one could suitably call it [that "perhaps" is priceless!] a theological or ethico-politico-theological novel, by analogy with the 'scientific' or 'socialistic' novels which have been written in recent times and which are still being written." In other words the *Journey to the Center of the Earth,* or *Around the Moon,* or *Around the Sun* by Jules Verne or Bellamy's *Looking Backward;* but a theological one; that is "with a certain imprint of seriousness," with a fine priest's hat on his head.

The very obvious representation of the three realms of the other world which can practically be seen and touched is not the result of Dante's creating with his art the reality of those three worlds inhabited by his eternal figures; no: it is purely by cold invention, "otherwise one would introduce into Dante's genius too great a mixture of madness and one would fail to give him the respect due to him." No, for Croce Dante is not mad: Dante does it on purpose, "he behaves like all writers of *that type* of theological, scientific or socialistic novels" who are all similarly "precise and meticulous and support what they imagine with reason *because their thesis requires it.*" Do you follow? It is as if to say: Gentlemen, Dante is trying to put one over on you. And Croce does not want to be disrespectful to him. But for him these *imaginative constructions* have "scarcely any importance." Do you know why? Because, above all, "we are preoccupied with other things"!

It seems to me appropriate once more to repeat: am I dreaming? No, gentlemen: here Croce begins to speak ironically of those who perform exercises in logic on what appear to be and are logical contradictions within the representation. But he does not speak ironically in the name of the *irrational* which can be found in every *imaginative creation;* he does so rather because it seems to him ridiculous to take so seriously, as those poor fools do, something which for him has scarcely any importance, that imaginative construction which in his opinion is not born of a poetic motive and which is useful "neither for indicating the particular poetic character, granted that there is one, of each *cantica,* nor for marking the transition from one poetic situation to another." Because for him "the poetry of the three *cantiche* is not derived from the *idea* of the journey through the three realms." Indeed, one could not quarrel with him if we were dealing with the *idea* of a journey. The trouble is that it is a question rather of a *representation* than of an *idea:* of a representation made by Dante, and not of a theologian's idea; in other words, such as Dante was able to make, given what he was, one whole being; and not such as Benedetto Croce would have made, had he been a poet.

But Dante, the one whole being, had the serious fault of not being able to fit into the esthetic theory of Benedetto Croce, the nature and fruits of which are known to all. Dante the poet, as Croce would have him, does not coincide with Dante the critic: "the act of poetic creation and the philosophic meditation of it" are for him two *distinct* and *diverse* acts, you must understand. Even though it is a philosophic meditation *of* the poetic creation, this act is now *distinct* and *diverse,* and one act no longer conditions the other and no longer flows together with the other, as he maintained earlier. With this fine logic, therefore, one must deal with "the poetry of Dante, *not according to Dante,* but according to truth." Which is to say, according to that same esthetic theory.

Dante might reply that indeed, when he intended to write didactic and practical treatises he did so, such as *De Vulgari Eloquentia* and *De Monarchia;* and that if he had wanted to write another one, equally didactic and practical, a treatise which, after one on the common language and another on political government, would deal precisely with morals, he would have done so. And had he wanted then to write many lyrics or lyrical episodes and give them a *non-poetical* structure, he would similarly have done so, as in the *Vita Nuova* or in the *Convivio.* If instead he wrote the *Commedia,* this indicates that he did not want to write a treatise or a work composed of poetical and non-poetical parts; but a poem. For this reason it is absolutely arbitrary to try and see *in his intention itself* two intentions, a duality, two Dantes. He, who was one Dante only, *felt* he could extract poetry from the subject matter he chose to celebrate, which means that he felt his subject poetically, or, more precisely, that this subject matter was his poetic feeling; if it were otherwise, he would have composed a treatise and not a poem.

His fantasy is populated with images and not ideas. But Croce, who is constantly denying what he has already affirmed, says that "that subject matter" in Dante's spirit "is shaped into poetry" and then that it remains subject matter for an allegorico-moral treatise.

Croce begins to speak in the abstract of allegory in order to prove that, in poetry, there is never a place for allegory; that it is indeed discussed but, when one goes to look for it and grasp it, it is not to be found. He suggests three possibilities: first that allegory is united to a poem *ab extra,* by decreeing though an act of will that such and such characters, actions or words in the poem should also signify a certain fact which has happened or will happen, or a religious truth or a moral judgment or anything else; and in this case it is clear—he says—that poetry remains intact and is alone of concern for the history of poetry while everything else belongs to the sphere and history of technique (another pigeon-hole). The second possibility is that allegory does not allow poetry to exist, does not let it be born, and in this case, since there is no poetry there is absolutely no subject of concern for the history of poetry. The third case is that in which there is admittedly allegory but in which it is expressed entirely in images, so that it neither remains outside of poetry, as in the first case, nor destroys and hinders it as in the second, but instead cooperates with and within it. Very well, says Croce, this third case is clearly contradictory since, if allegory exists it is always by definition outside of and contrary to poetry, and if instead it is really within poetry, fused and identified with it, then there is no allegory at all, but only poetic imagery which cannot be confined to material and finite things, but is always spiritual and of infinite worth. In all of these cases, whoever reads poetically does not, cannot, should not ever reach an allegorical meaning because he navigates in other and sweeter waters. And on the other hand it is impossible, no matter how hard one tries, to see two things, one beside the other, when one of them can appear only when the other disappears.

One could object: and what about the fable? It is allegory. Isn't it poetry? Certainly, as long as it functions as a representation; but representation of something which requires a meaning in itself: a moral meaning, desired indeed for itself, but not only for itself, or otherwise one would not be writing a fable but giving a moral precept: hence a precept yes, but one which has become an image, a representation, poetry. And so allegory does not belong to any of the three cases which Croce sets forth. Not outside of, contrary to or within poetry; but the simultaneous, continuous moral implication of the representation. If one wants to play the sophist, there can be no definitions which are valid or invalid *a priori.*

And in any case, it remained to be demonstrated that Dantesque allegory fell within one of these categories.

Whoever intentionally composes an allegory certainly does not believe in the reality of the image which for him is the fictitious form of an idea to be portrayed. In Dante, on the contrary, allegory is always necessary and essential: it is the other world which is the *real* world: not an idea but a *reality* to be created poetically.

Dante believes in the allegorical form of his sentiment, which is to say, he believes in the reality of his representation, and *sees himself* in it, through it, touching everything, describing everything in its marvellous reality. To talk of a novel-allegory, of an intellectual construct, is blasphemy.

The greatest mistake consists in measuring Dante's allegory on the same terms as all other allegories; that is, as an idea which is dressed up, a concept in figurative terms. It is precisely the contrary. Dante moves from earth to heaven, from human to divine. For him, to *enjoy* ONLY *through the senses* is characteristic of an inferior nature. He refuses to make of his figures merely the symbols of ideas, as if they had no reality in themselves. But for him form has a reality precisely because it is a symbol; thus, inasmuch as it signifies something, it is such as it is; and art is the portrayal of this something, by which every form lives in its allegorical essence, not as in a garment, but rather in its authentic reality. It is not Grace which becomes Beatrice; it is Beatrice who lives in her essential form of divine Grace. It is clear that we have here an absolute reversal of the concept of allegory. Whoever does not understand this cannot understand Dante.

Is this Dante's *false poetics?* But what if all this for him is not a way of thinking but of feeling, if all this is not an abstract thought to be treated in verse, but a feeling to be portrayed?

One must not speak of an allegorical framework as of a skeleton. The skeleton is the poem itself, with all its flesh and blood, all its muscles and nerves. Flesh, muscles and nerves are distributed in varying proportions throughout: here the flesh is bleeding, there a muscle is flexed. At one point the nerves quiver, at another there is only the hardness of bone and the skeleton can be touched. But all of it is alive, and that skeleton is never death.

The *Vita Nuova*

by T. S. Eliot

All of Dante's "minor works" are important, because they are works of Dante; but the *Vita Nuova* has a special importance, because it does more than any of the others help us to a fuller understanding of the *Divine Comedy*. I do not suggest that the others may be neglected; the *Convivio* is important, and also the *De Volgari Eloquio* [*De Vulgari Eloquentia*]: and every part of Dante's writings can give us some light on other parts. But the *Vita Nuova* is a youthful work, in which some of the method and design, and explicitly the intention, of the *Divine Comedy* are shown. Because it is an immature work, it requires some knowledge of the masterpiece to understand; and at the same time helps particularly toward understanding of the *Comedy*.

A great deal of scholarship has been directed upon examination of the early life of Dante, in connection with the *Vita Nuova*. Critics may be roughly divided into those who regard it as primarily biographical, and those who regard it as primarily allegorical. It is much easier for the second group to make a good case than for the first. If this curious medley of verse and prose is biographical, then the biography has unquestionably been manipulated almost out of recognition to fit into conventional forms of allegory. The imagery of much of it is certainly in a very ancient tradition of vision literature: just as the scheme of the *Divine Comedy* has been shown to be closely similar to similar supernatural peregrination stories in Arabic and in old Persian literature—to say nothing of the descents of Ulysses and Aeneas—so there are parallels to the visions of the *Vita Nuova* such as the *Shepherd of Hermas* in Greek. And as the book is obviously not a literal statement, whether of vision or delusion, it is easy to make out a case for its being an entire allegory: for asserting, that is, that Beatrice is merely a personification of an abstract virtue, intellectual or moral.

I wish to make clear that my own opinions are opinions founded only upon reading the text. I do not think that they are such as can either be

"The *Vita Nuova*." The final part of the essay "Dante" from *Selected Essays* by T. S. Eliot, new edition (New York: Harcourt, Brace & World, 1950). Copyright 1950 by Harcourt, Brace & World. Reprinted by permission of Harcourt, Brace & World and Faber & Faber, Ltd.

verified or refuted by scholars; I mean to restrict my comments to the unprovable and the irrefutable.

It appears likely, to anyone who reads the *Vita Nuova* without prejudice, that it is a mixture of biography and allegory; but a mixture according to a recipe not available to the modern mind. When I say the "modern mind," I mean the minds of those who have read or could have read such a document as Rousseau's *Confessions*. The modern mind can understand the "confession," that is, the literal account of oneself, varying only in degree of sincerity and self-understanding, and it can understand "allegory" in the abstract. Nowadays "confessions," of an insignificant sort, pour from the press; everyone *met son cœur à nu*, or pretends to; "personalities" succeed one another in interest. It is difficult to conceive of an age (of many ages) when human beings cared somewhat about the salvation of the "soul," but not about each other as "personalities." Now Dante, I believe, had experiences which seemed to him of some importance; not of importance because they had happened to him and because he, Dante Alighieri, was an important person who kept press-cutting bureaus busy; but important in themselves; and therefore they seemed to him to have some philosophical and impersonal value. I find in it an account of a particular kind of experience: that is, of something which had actual experience (the experience of the "confession" in the modern sense) *and* intellectual and imaginative experience (the experience of thought and the experience of dream) as its materials; and which became a third kind. It seems to me of importance to grasp the simple fact that the *Vita Nuova* is neither a "confession" nor an "indiscretion" in the modern sense, nor is it a piece of Pre-Raphaelite tapestry. If you have that sense of intellectual and spiritual realities that Dante had, then a form of expression like the Vita Nuova cannot be classed either as "truth" or "fiction."

In the first place, the type of sexual experience which Dante describes as occurring to him at the age of nine years is by no means impossible or unique. My only doubt (in which I found myself confirmed by a distinguished psychologist) is whether it could have taken place so *late* in life as the age of nine years. The psychologist agreed with me that it is more likely to occur at about five or six years of age. It is possible that Dante developed rather late, and it is also possible that he altered the dates to employ some other significance of the number nine. But to me it appears obvious that the *Vita Nuova* could only have been written around a personal experience. If so, the details do not matter: whether the lady was the Portinari or not, I do not care; it is quite as likely that she is a blind for someone else, even for a person whose name Dante may have forgotten or never known. But I cannot find it incredible that what has happened to others should have happened to Dante with much greater intensity.

The same experience, described in Freudian terms, would be instantly accepted as fact by the modern public. It is merely that Dante, quite reasonably, drew other conclusions and used another mode of expression, which arouses incredulity. And we are inclined to think—as Remy de Gourmont, for once misled by his prejudices into the pedantic attitude, thought—that if an author like Dante follows closely a form of vision that has a long history, it proves that the story is mere allegory (in the modern sense) or fake. I find a much greater difference in sensibility between the *Vita Nuova* and the *Shepherd of Hermas* than Gourmont did. It is not at all the simple difference between the genuine and the fraud; it is a difference in mind between the humble author of early Christian times and the poet of the thirteenth century, perhaps as great as that between the latter and ourselves. The similarities might prove that a certain *habit* in dream-imagery can persist throughout many changes of civilization. Gourmont would say that Dante borrowed; but that is imputing our own mind to the thirteenth century. I merely suggest that possibly Dante, in his place and time, was following something more essential than merely a "literary" tradition.

The attitude of Dante to the fundamental experience of the *Vita Nuova* can only be understood by accustoming ourselves to find meaning in *final causes* rather than in origins. It is not, I believe, meant as a description of what he *consciously* felt on his meeting with Beatrice, but rather as a description of what that meant on mature reflection upon it. The final cause is the attraction toward God. A great deal of sentiment has been spilt, especially in the eighteenth and nineteenth centuries, upon idealizing the reciprocal feelings of man and woman toward each other, which various realists have been irritated to denounce: this sentiment ignoring the fact that the love of man and woman (or for that matter of man and man) is only explained and made reasonable by the higher love, or else is simply the coupling of animals.

Let us entertain the theory that Dante, meditating on the astonishment of an experience at such an age, which no subsequent experience abolished or exceeded, found meanings in it which we should not be likely to find ourselves. His account is then just as reasonable as our own; and he is simply prolonging the experience in a different direction from that which we, with different mental habits and prejudices, are likely to take.

We cannot, as a matter of fact, understand the *Vita Nuova* without some saturation in the poetry of Dante's Italian contemporaries, or even in the poetry of his Provençal predecessors. Literary parallels are most important, but we must be on guard not to take them in a purely literary and literal way. Dante wrote more or less, at first, like other poets, not simply because he had read their works, but because his modes of feeling and thought were much like theirs. As for the Provençal poets, I have not the knowledge to read them at first hand. That mysterious people had a religion of their own which was thoroughly and painfully extinguished by the Inquisition; so that we hardly know more about them than about the Sumerians. I suspect that the difference between this unknown, and possibly maligned, Albigensianism and Catholicism has some correspondence with the difference between the poetry of the Provençal school and the Tuscan. The system of Dante's organization of sensibility—the contrast between higher and lower carnal love, the transition from Beatrice living to Beatrice dead, rising to the Cult of the Virgin, seems to me to be his own.

At any rate, the *Vita Nuova,* besides being a sequence of beautiful poems connected by a curious vision-literature prose, is, I believe, a very sound psychological treatise on something related to what is now called "sublimation." There is also a practical sense of realities behind it, which is antiromantic: not to expect more from *life* than it can give or more from *human* beings than they can give; to look to *death* for what life cannot give. The *Vita Nuova* belongs to "vision literature"; but its philosophy is the Catholic philosophy of disillusion.

Understanding of the book is greatly advanced by acquaintance with Guido Guinicelli, Cavalcanti, Cino, and others. One ought, indeed, to study the development of the art of love from the Provençal poets onward, paying just attention to both resemblances and differences in spirit; as well as the development of verse form and stanza form and vocabulary. But such study is vain unless we have first made the conscious attempt, as difficult and hard as rebirth, to pass through the looking-glass into a world which is just as reasonable as our own. When we have done that, we begin to wonder whether the world of Dante is not both larger and more solid than our own. When we repeat

Tutti li miei penser parlan d'Amore

we must stop to think what *amore* means—something different from its Latin original, its French equivalent, or its definition in a modern Italian dictionary.

It is, I repeat, for several reasons necessary to read the *Divine Comedy* first. The first reading of the *Vita Nuova* gives nothing but Pre-Raphaelite quaintness. The *Comedy* initiates us into the world of medieval imagery, in the *Inferno* most apprehensible, in the *Paradiso* most rarefied. It initiates us also into the world of medieval thought and dogma: far easier for those who have had the college discipline of Plato and Aristotle, but possible even without that. The *Vita Nuova* plunges us direct into medieval sensibility. It is not, for Dante, a masterpiece, so that it is safer for us to read it, the first time, for the light it can throw on the *Comedy* than for itself.

Read in this way, it can be more useful than a dozen commentaries. The effect of many books about Dante is to give the impression that it is more necessary to read about him than to read what he has written. But the next step after reading Dante again and again should be to read some of the books that he read, rather than modern books about his work and life and times, however good. We may easily be distracted by following up the histories of Emperors and Popes. With a poet like Shakespeare, we are less likely to ignore the text for the commentary. With Dante there is just as much need for concentrating on the text, and all the more because Dante's mind is more remote from the ways of thinking and feeling in which we have been brought up. What we need is not information but knowledge: the first step to knowledge is to recognize the differences between his form of thought and feeling and ours. Even to attach great importance to Thomism, or to Catholicism, may lead us astray, in attracting us too much to such differences as are entirely capable of intellectual formulation. The English reader needs to remember that even had Dante not been a good Catholic, even had he treated Aristotle or Thomas with skeptical indifference, his mind would still be no easier to understand; the forms of imagination, phantasmagoria, and sensibility would be just as strange to us. We have to learn to accept these forms: and this *acceptance* is more important than anything that can be called belief. There is almost a definite moment of acceptance at which the New Life begins.

What I have written is, as I promised, not an "introduction" to the study but a brief account of my own introduction to it. In extenuation, it may be observed that to write in this way of men like Dante or Shakespeare is really less presumptuous than to write of smaller men. The very vastness of the subject leaves a possibility that one may have something to say worth saying; whereas with smaller men, only minute and special study is likely to justify writing about them at all.

Introduction to Dante's *Rime*

by Gianfranco Contini

Rather than speak of Dante's *canzoniere,* as have scholars since Charles Lyell (1835), it is more prudent to speak of his *rime.* Ever since the experience of Petrarch, one involuntarily associates the sixteenth-century sense of the word "canzoniere" with the idea of a unified work, the organic experience of a soul. Hence when used of Dante the word tends to transport back to the thirteenth century the exigency of a conscious psychological construction enclosed with a transparent story, in which style is precisely and above all a perennial effort of simplification and elimination. In the work of Dante there were indeed efforts toward unification, most obviously that of the *Vita Nuova:* but this was a unification that was superimposed, made up of facts from the past viewed in retrospect from the end of youth and intended to resolve one period lyrically in order to prepare the way for another more splendid ("io spero di dicer di lei quello che mai non fue detto d'alcuna . . . [I hope to write of her what has never been written of any other]"). It is therefore a partial, episodic unification, presupposing multiplicity. It is at the same time a transcendent unification, sought after in a system of synopses (*razos*) and a narrative scheme. Aside from other spontaneous groupings (that designated by *Parole mie* is deliberate), we find in the *Convivio* a far less solid attempt at unification which is moreover interrupted. In this collection of difficult allegorical *canzoni* the intention is constantly and unequivocally to create beautiful forms in celebration of the great moral virtues. Thus the so-called *canzoniere* of Dante dispenses with the *Vita Nuova,* and is composed of the remainder of the *rime* and the experiments which succeeded the period of the "dolce stil novo," the "sweet new style." It may be defined as a most proud collection of occasional pieces (*estravaganti*).

The history of Italian lyric poetry from its origins is still conceived of according to Dantesque categories, corresponding to general critical exigencies of the times, to be sure, but, in fact, existing only after Dante's efforts (for example, critical concepts such as "the Sicilian School," "the sweet new style," or the "Sicilian limitations" of Guittone d'Arezzo): and this is true *a fortiori* of the history of his own lyrics. This is not just a question of semantic definition of such terms as *nove rime* [new verses], *Loda* [poetry of praise], *bello stile* (patterned after Virgil's "high tragedy" ["the beautiful style which has done me honor"—*Inf.* I, 87]), or *canzoni* (which are in effect individual applications of the tragic style); above all, Dante's judgment of his predecessors and his contemporaries, from the Provençal poets to Cino, is a function of his own particular poetics. The principles of that Dantesque literary history are of course contained in a theoretical work such as the *De Vulgari Eloquentia,* which serves as a kind of justification of the *bello stile,* although they are not adhered to when the organic nature of the poem definitively replaces the *fragmenta* of the tragic style; but an equal number of principles are found in the *Commedia,* which is also a rich encyclopedia of style. If we consider how essential to the *Convivio* is its defense of the vernacular and its justification of the ideal banquet which, replacing the juvenile unity of the *Vita Nuova,* joins the allegorical *canzoni* in a more mature unity, it will be clear to us how one of the constants of Dante's personality was a perpetual meditation on technique as it played upon his poetry, an association of the concrete act of writing poetry with stylistic awareness. This confers on Dante's work its apparent periodicity or even discontinuity in rhyme: in him there is never peace, but the torment of dialectics. Precisely because Dante seems to stand outside his work, it is less inappropriate in his case than it might be with other poets to attempt to recognize in his whole work the traces of an ideal chronology. He views his own style objectively, not as an absolute (as did the humanist Petrarch and the poets of the Platonic Renaissance), but as an *ad hoc* attempt. He has a sense not so much of a general limitation of form as of the particular limits of the styles of various schools and it is characteristic of him to use a preceding experience as an element of a new experience, not as something final in itself. In this sense his *estravaganti* have a linear unity, for each becomes a point of departure for the next in the poet's restless striving. Hence, the *canzoniere* is fragmentary, not only because it lacks unity of inspiration, but also because the series of attempts is never ended to the poet's satisfaction.

Dante's teachers and friends had already displayed a noteworthy latitude of technique and of taste. . . . His own poetic variety, however, has a different purpose and meaning. There is never in him the slightest suspicion of skepticism. His light touches are far from the centers of inspiration; for, basically, there is in Dante a terrible seriousness: all the "imitations" are distilled to the extreme (several Sicilian elements remain indelibly in the *rime*), but they never deviate toward the slightly cynical amplification of parody. In reality, technique is with him something of a sacred order, his means of ascetic exercise, indistinguishable from the

thirst for perfection. On one hand he seeks a *delicate* technique to conceal effort, resolving it in a gently modulated flow, corresponding to the
world of the *Vita Nuova:* the renunciation of earth and dedication to
a lady who is more real as she gives less of herself to the poet, as she
withdraws from him, until she refuses him even her greeting and her
glance, becoming most real when she is physically dead; the same climate in which the struggle with sin, the effort to achieve a victory over
sin, tends to lose its exceptional quality and becomes normalized in
the daily acceptance of an ideal. On the other hand (to distinguish
rather summarily between these two extreme poles of inspiration), his
harsh technique underscores the effort, accentuating the salient points of
the rhythm, particularly in rhyme—this corresponding to the sentiment
of love and the sense of a difficult life, of the obstacle and of the overcoming of the obstacle. Essentially, the technical "means" is simply the
instrument for the search into the self. More exactly, it is that same religious thirst in action. In practice, to be sure, this does not rule out
frequent lapses into abstract technical virtuosity. At first the correspondence between Dante's techniques and his particular moments of inspiration seems to suggest a lack of that artistic detachment from experience
characteristic of Dante's colleagues, leaving his poetry merely a chapter
in the history of customs, or in his own moral autobiography. On second
thought, the technical variation seems rather to reflect a spiritual evolution in process, thus relevant to poetic form.

We continually have recourse to the poets of his age when we speak
of Dante's lyric poetry, not because of the superstition of the literary
historian, nor because of the usual pedagogical artifice of defining by
differentiation and antithesis, but rather because their interrelationship
is fundamental. The "sweet style" denotes that school of poetry most
gracefully and strongly aware of collaborating in the creation of an objective poetry; in other words, the school which has the greatest sense of
being a school. It is both inadequate and inexact to think of it as a common stylistic ideal accepted by each practitioner; there are also in the
"sweet style" all the emotional premises of a common undertaking, and
above all the ideal of friendship which recalls in these former aristocrats
and highly cultured *bourgeois* the equality and solidarity of medieval
French knights. The sonnet "Guido, i'vorrei" is usually interpreted correctly as a typical product of this taste, not, however, because it embodies
the motif of enchanted escape to distant exotic places (in which we can
easily recognize Provençal and *jongleuresque* traditions), but because that
escape toward an unreal world is accomplished in the company of intimate and affectionate friends with their ladies. In this intimacy, the more
warm for its fanciful nature, desire remains one and the wish to be together increases. The absolute separation from the real, converted into
friendship, is the content of the poem; friendship is the definitive emotional element of the *stil nuovo*. In poetic practice, the poets' tendentious

refusal to differentiate themselves or to underscore their individuality seems foreign to the post-romantic Western mind conditioned to the nineteenth-century exaltation of subjectivity. But we are not dealing here with that involuntary similarity which renders it difficult to attribute anonymous works of the minor Romantics, nor with equivalence in the sentimental or historico-nationalistic meaning of the word, such as we find later in the minor symbolists, or even today among the minor surrealists. Nor are we dealing exclusively with the objective poetics of a "classical" period. . . . We have rather to do with something which is more conscious because, while as a good craftsman the classic poet believes in a canon of *ars,* the *stilnovist* believes in an absolute inspiration and keeps his pen (according to Dante's expression [*Purg.* XXIV, 52 ff]) following closely upon the "dictation" of Love. The frequent interchangeability of manuscripts—the difficulty of attribution on stylistic grounds, in the absence of documentary evidence—is but a pallid external reflection of an essentially theoretical interchangeability. The dividing line between Dante and Cino, for instance (leaving apart for the moment the circumstances which made the confusion possible within the confines of the Middle Ages), is far from sure. To say that our judgments are uncertain is tantamount to saying that property and the individual are nonessential.

Indeed, what Dante tells us in the episode of Bonagiunta to which we have alluded (*Purg.* XXIV, 52 ff.) is the fundamental text for understanding the *dolce stile.* To be interpreted fully, it must be understood that inspiration ("amor mi spira—[Love inspires me]") is not private or momentary, nor is it of an amatory order.[1] (The *De Vulgari Eloquentia* recognizes that the tragic style may even have war for its object, but this would be going beyond the considerations of style in general to those of particular style, technically understood.) Rather, inspiration comes from a transcendent principle, a decisive abandonment to Love. Inspiration is objective and absolute and, therefore, even if the normal content of the *stilnovistic* lyric is amorous fact, minutely analyzed and then hypostasized into its elements, this analysis should be attributed not merely to an individual but to a universal: to the individual as an exemplar of man. Thus, the personality of the new troubadour, far from affirming itself, is dissolved in a chorus of friendship which, besides being the general dimension of such a poetry, even provides an initial poetic motif. A counterpart to the motif of the chorus of the poet's friends is the choral background of women from which the *Beatrice* is set off as queen and as source of their honor and fount of their beauty. In the climate of this terrestrial paradise, anterior to history, Adam exists side by side with several men of flesh and blood, while the somewhat smaller feminine group has the sole function of underscoring the pres-

---

[1] In the *Vita Nuova* (XXV, 6) Dante puts forward arguments "against those who make rhymes on other than amatory material."

ence of Eve and lives as metaphor analogous to the friends who surround the poet. The result is that, like the poet, the character who speaks
in the first person, who is "the absolute individual," the woman too
loses every historical attribute, every personal idiosyncrasy. Extending
gradually the field of observation, one notes that the entire experience
of the *stilnovist* is depersonalized, transferred to a universal order: specific
occasions are forgotten and experience immediately crystallized. This
has been revealed in a more or less elementary and empirical way (but
empiricism is precisely the point of departure), by T. S. Eliot when he
denies that the "Dantesque novel" can have the significance of a modern
confession:

> It is difficult to conceive of an age (of many ages) when human beings
> cared somewhat about the salvation of the "soul," but not about each other
> as "personalities." Now Dante, I believe, had experiences which seemed to
> him of some importance; not of importance because they had happened to him
> and because he, Dante Alighieri, was an important person who kept press-
> cutting bureaus busy; but important in themselves; and therefore they seem
> to him to have some philosophical and impersonal value.[2]

We must be aware of our modern romantic education—brought up as
we are in the aesthetic cult of untransformed subjective reactions—in
order to measure how much more, in comparison, the *stilnovist* projected
such reactions into representations or into figures. A plastic system of
relationships among things is for him the only means of expressing the
objects of his dreams in orderly fashion; what recent and somewhat
eccentric Anglo-Saxon readers, inspired by the premises quoted above,
have expressed as the "objective correlative." Insofar as these imaginative
interpreters are concerned only that the figure be "related" while caring
little for its significance, the concrete "super-sense," their exegesis is
inadequate; in practice, however, a transliteration of the objective figuration of *stilnovistic* poets into the subjective romantic representation might
serve, at least pedagogically, to demonstrate the significance of this incarnation in plastic terms. When in the sonnet "Sonar bracchetti" Dante
allows his preoccupation with love (the "gabbo") to reprove him as
though it were a demon, for having substituted bourgeois satisfactions for
the pursuit of his courtly duty, the *joie d'amour,* the external "action"
represents an internal remorse; instead of the contemporary myths of consciousness, we have a minute "religious drama." (We must bear in mind
that, from this point of view, a general characteristic of medieval art is
its intimate dramatic quality, or even theatricality.) And when elsewhere
(in the sonnet "De gli occhi de la mia donna [My lady's eyes]") Dante
returns to the most "dangerous pass" of all (*E tornomi colà dov'io son
vinto*) and, before the very eyes of his lady, closes his own eyes as desire

---

[2] T. S. Eliot. *Dante,* p. 63 of the original edition; reprinted in this volume.

dies, this spatial and multiple figural action might be translated as "to accede to temptation and to succumb." A man tries to shut out dark thoughts unworthy of his manhood, is unable to do so, and only by reflecting upon his amorous desire does he succeed in identifying that unrest as a momentary intimation of the mortality of his beloved: this is the sense of the sonnet "Un dì si venne a me Malinconia [One day Melancholy came to me]," but it misses the essential quality of the poem, the concretization of a premonition, its private manifestation in a vision —in other words, the reality of the angel. A last example will be both the most clear and the most obviously narrative: that of "Lisetta," the record of a strong man's victory over temptation. Desire is so great that it finally wanders into a vague zone of longing, but it cannot overcome a moral decision. Given the mentality which underlies medieval poetics, it is clear that the sonnet is not concerned with physical fact, with an authentic Lisetta who is rejected. Indeed, at this point, what is most evident is the profit which Dante derived from the typically Sicilian theme of the separation of the woman from her image painted in the heart of the lover. Lisetta is real (not from an absolute and irrelevant point of view, but in terms of the poet's initial consciousness) insofar as she is an image in the mind of Dante. For this reason, the laborious and discordant efforts of some scholars to identify and distinguish among Dante's so-called "beloved" ladies (when not directed simply toward the isolation of several poetic experiences) are not only superfluous from the standpoint of Crocean esthetics (*allotria*) but are also extraneous to Dante's own poetics. Another consequence of importance follows from this in the order of tonality: having once separated himself from his spiritual adventures and having set them aside, the poet can wipe away the frown that self-obsession produces in the romantic (tending toward ultimate evasion via the grotesque), he can undergo a series of tender moments or bewilderments, of recoveries and smiles (*Cf.* verses such as "Prendo vergogna, onde mi ven pesanza [I am ashamed and become downcast]"; "Amore lo mira con pietà [Love looks upon him with pity]"; " 'Che hai, cattivello?' ['What ails you, poor boy?']"). Thus in Dante, who is most serious as far as his method is concerned, there is outlined the possibility of a certain "irony."

The lack of "lyricism" in Dante's poetry, as we have described it, explains how from a general historical point of view there is no clear and distinct stylistic "development" perceptible within it, but rather a permanent process of restlessness. The first development that can be described in a formula is constituted by the *nove rime*. One cannot speak of an abandonment of Guittone d'Arezzo's position for the *dolce stil nuovo* in any strict sense, because from the point of view of the school, Dante's "Guittonian" rhymes are simply *divertissements,* gallantries, *peccata iuventutis,* and the supposed conversion is only a drifting from one group of friends to another. . . . From the standpoint of poetic practice, however, the Dante of the "Guittonian" mode, who splits words such as "parla" in several ways in order to multiply equivocal rhymes, who rhymes two words, "Ch'amato," with the rare word "camato" and indulges in verbal echoes ("ciò che sentire Doveano a ragion senza *veduta,* Non conobber *vedendo* [That which they should have felt without having seen, they did not know when they saw]"), leaves a few traces in the Dante of the *Commedia,* who, after years of abstention from similar undertakings in the "tragic" climate of the *canzoni,* will for example place "non ci ha" in the mouth of Mastro Adamo in order to rhyme with "oncia" and "sconcia" (*Inf.* XXX, 83-87) and will make Pier della Vigna lament over the whore who so "inflamed" (*infiammò*) all minds against him that "those who were inflamed in turn inflamed Augustus" (*infiammati infiammarono, Inf.* XIII, 67-68) and, in a warm peroration, will pray Virgil and pray again so that the prayer will be worth a thousand (*priego—ripiego— priego, Inf.* XXVI, 66). The commentators repeat, correctly, that the counterfeiter Adamo is cursing his tremendous immobility ("potessi in cent'- anni andare un'oncia [If only I could move an inch in a hundred years]") and an extension of ridiculous proportion in human terms spreads out frightfully before him, up to the anguish of the broken rhyme ("e men d'un mezzo di traverso non ci ha [and it is no less than half across]"); they repeat, with equal justice, that Pier, the minister of Frederick II, speaks fittingly as a princely *dittatore,* displaying an up-to-date rhetorical elegance even in prayer. Thus the commentators show that Dante the Guittonian is no longer on his own, but is rather confined and put to work within the Dante of the *Commedia.* This new Dante, in speaking of Guittone with scorn, in fact speaks of an earlier moment within himself, now completely surpassed. The Guittonian poet who existed in a pure, unskilled state is now subordinated and tamed, and serves a purpose very different from that of abstract exercise. The Guittone of abstract exercise must certainly be distinguished from Guittone himself as well, and the historian, who must be reasonably respectful toward great men who have fallen in the battle for glory, has an obligation to recognize that something else, far more essential, passes from Guittone through Dante into the general consciousness and tradition of Italian letters. The doctrinal meditation takes its point of departure, culturally speaking, from Frate Guittone. The eloquent and energetic vein which runs from "Poscia ch'Amor [Since Love]" to "Doglia mi reca [Grief brings me daring]" lies along the same line as his moral *canzone.* Dante's lack of gratitude toward the old master, not very different from the anti-D'Annunzian attitudes of several of our Italian contemporaries, is precisely the sign of his having also beaten the old poet on his own ground, of a final victory, of having absorbed and surpassed his supreme ambition.

If, as we have said, *stilnovism* is for Dante essentially fidelity to the "dittatore" and thus is the poetics of the objectification of feelings, its culmination and at the same time its renewal is achieved when the organization of the "faithful company of Love" [*fedeli d'amore*] becomes complete, even to the point of providing the justification for the poetry. The myth is certainly among the most beautiful in the history of poetics (*Vita Nuova* XVIII): if happiness no longer in the least resides in something exterior to the beloved, in the salutation of his lady, which up to this point was the final cause of life within him, it exists in something permanent, in "those words which praise the lady"; and since—this is the theme both of the feminine "chorus" and of the "objectification" of remorse—the gentle ladies reprove him for having used words other than those which praise her, he proposes "to take for the subject of his material" forever after "that which is praise of this most gentle lady." What moves the mind of Dante and determines the *nove rime* is therefore the necessity for unity and totality (the *razo* of "Donna ch'avete" likewise enables us to be present at the conjunction between inspiration, the voice of God within [*est deus in nobis*] from which the poem has its origin ("Allora dico che la mia lingua parlò quasi come per se stessa mossa [So I say that my tongue was moved as if by itself]") and the work itself, the thought of "alquanti die [Several days]." This same exigency inspires the extension of the techniques of amorous poetry to moral poetry and brings forth from the *nove rime* the *bello stile.* Such a transition is allegorized in the sonnet "Due donne in cima de la mente mia [Two ladies uppermost in my mind]" in which the univocal quality of love is first divided into beauty and virtue, and is then reunited. All of this is proclaimed, it should be noticed, by Love, the "fount of gentle speech" (*fonte del gentil parlare*) that is, the "dittatore." Nevertheless, this unity may be still shattered; the risk of allegorical poetry. Until this point there was no question of allegorism in the usual (dualistic) sense of the word, for we have rather been dealing with an objective poetics which is almost the opposite of allegorism, being preoccupied with unity: the objective presentation of internal facts. Allegorism begins with a divorce of the things signified; thus, in the *Convivio,* the allegorical *canzone* "Voi che 'ntendendo [You Intelligences who move]" closes with the pathetic exclamation, "Notice *at least* how beautiful I am," and the *Convivio* (II, xi, 4) will gloss it in these terms: "the goodness and the beauty of each type of speech are diverse and distinct; for goodness is in the meaning and beauty is in the ornament of words; and both are pleasing, although goodness is especially pleasing." On the one hand, therefore, a plurality of meanings, an overlapping of levels which interfere with each other, never blending perfectly; on the other hand, the possibility that philosophical explication, "prose" itself, according to the definition of the idealists, might remain squalid and diverced from the poetry. The extreme case is presented by another *canzone* of the *Convivio,* "Le dolce rime." At the time of that *canzone,* Dante, in order to justify the varied and progressive isolation of his moral themes, constructed a whole mythology based upon the abandonment, at least for the moment, of love, in its sweet and delightful sense. But Love in the deeper sense remains always the fountainhead of all good and beauty is "formed by virtue alone." Of these the *canzone* "Doglia mi reca" will speak: the poet of righteousness emerges from the poet of love. And this abandonment of the poet by love becomes also an abandonment of love by the poet; that is, human love finds a competitor in the love of virtue. The competition is objectified and represented as a rivalry between ladies, so that initially there is the possibility of an exegetical ambiguity, a hesitation between literal interpretation and allegorical interpretation. (One need only think of the case of the "pargoletta [the little girl]": Is she a real woman? a symbol?) The confusion of the commentators has validity only with respect to that moment of poetic "transition."

In Dante's moral verses there exists the zeal of the neophyte who has just entered into the disputations of philosophers. We find an equal enthusiasm in Dante the lover of poetry and the student of literature, the product of these same years. (The moral and scientific enthusiasm is contemporary with the enthusiasm for Provençal poetry in the *De Vulgari*.) As a young man, Dante had known a Provençal poetry which was second-hand: very specialized, or mannered. . . . So indirect an influence could only be relevant to abstract themes, could only be ritualistic. "If we search the *langue d'Oc* of the past 150 years," says Dante in the *Vita Nuova* (XXV, 4), "we do not find things of importance said before the present time." And in this period there is indeed no great exterior variety to be found, for the Provençal mind concentrates on subtly plying its trade. But if Dante dedicated himself precisely to extracting from it its essential teaching—style—he had nevertheless to work back along that course of a century and a half in order to differentiate the generations from each other. His was a philology at the service of poetry. For this reason Dante's Provençalism becomes first-hand in the encounters with the Golden Age troubadours of the *Commedia:* Guiraut de Bornelh, Bertran de Born, Folguet, Sordello (this last one not in chronological order, as a peripheral author); above all Arnaut Daniel. Within the *rime* this authentic Provençalism is represented by the "Stony Verses" (*rime petrose*), echoes of which remain in the *Commedia* as the verbalization of a difficulty, the taking possession of a restless reality. Our continuous interpretive recourse to the *Commedia* is no mere didactic artifice, nor is it an attempt to retrace the past and previous poetical materials retrospectively in terms of a poetry subsequently attained. It is rather due to the essential contingence of those immobile lyrics, to their lack of complete autonomy. The current, legitimate admiration[3] for this series of suggestive poems should make it nevertheless clear that, apart from the fragments of the *rime petrose* in the *Commedia* (for example in the circle of traitors), the inspiration of the *rime petrose* themselves seems radically fragmentary.

---

[3] Some reservations are expressed by Croce, *La poesia di Dante*, pp. 46-7.

Along with the feeling of subjective reality as object, difficult in itself, such as we find in the *rime petrose,* the "debate" *(tenzone)* with Forese Donati offers a reality known through a whole spectrum of resentment and distortions approaching caricature. And the representation of it is vivid and witty. . . . We are far from the ascetic leveling (and, as in the case of every *askesis,* renunciation) of the *Vita Nuova,* and the new sense of the real postulates a richer fabric, complements and components which cannot be found in the earlier period. Once more, having seen that first *stilnovistic* unity shattered (which now in retrospect seems always to have been provisional), we find ourselves in the presence of extremely respectable fragments, which certainly conspire toward a unity; but that unity is external; only in the *Commedia* does it come into actuality.

Nevertheless, the poetics of resentment seems grafted with particular aptness onto the poetics of the moral life when that resentment becomes disdain for the cowardice of the present generation, and the virtues become women who are torn and despised, like Lady Poverty in the canto of San Francesco. Their ill-treatment guarantees Dante's fidelity to them, but also and above all, it guarantees their own poetic existence: and through that ill-treatment, moral life acquires a figurative reality, just as the hyperbolic conventions of the cult of love unrequited, or rather, self-requited, had their figurative reality. The poet of righteousness and the avenger of the self live together in harmony with the practiced designer of symbolic compositions in the *canzone* "Three Ladies" *(Tre Donne)*, the great canzone of Dante's exile. Here we find the moral illness of a whole century, disaster precisely in the etymological sense ("e dolgasi la bocca De li uomini a cui tocca [let it grieve the mouths of men whom it befits]"), coinciding with personal exile ("E io, che ascolto nel parlar divino . . . [And I, who listen to the divine voice]"). Our rapid sketch of the development of Dante's poetry would seem thus to close with "Tre Donne"; but the divergence of the two chronologies, ideal and real, seems once more to be verified, since a slight trace of the preoccupation with biography left in us causes us to note that this *canzone* is believed to belong to the earliest period, indeed, the earliest months of Dante's exile. Now that the astronomical argument has dated the *rime petrose* out of the canon of the *rime* of exile, those *rime* seem to lack a stylistic organic unity. We will not speak of the correspondence with Cino, . . . nor of the sonnet for Lisetta, which is truly and deliberately archaic (its mood is at any rate very light and the poem is basically a *divertissement*), which was attributed to this period by the merest hypothesis. But historic reasons prove that the two great canzoni, "Doglia mi reca [Grief brings me daring]" and the *Montanina*, "Amor da che convien [Love, since I must grieve]," are later than "Tre Donne," although the first is reminiscent of the doctrinal *rime* of the *Convivio*, and the second . . . undoubtedly betrays the experience of *rime petrose*, yet, throughout a large section of the poem and in its over-all tone (the painting of the image, the distinction between the woman and the image of her), Dante seems to fall back on a Sicilian manner devoid of the old merits of ingenuity. Strictly speaking, then, are we not still at the beginning of our task? Here the conflict of ideal and real chronologies becomes a decisive indication of the fundamental crisis of the *Rime* when they are just about to end. One of the most acute of those critics who would furnish us with an ideal chronology, and certainly one of the most elegant, Ferdinando Neri, declares: "this *canzone* [the *Montanina*] is a problem that even I give up trying to explain to myself: there is in it some courtly love, a certain movement reminiscent of Cino, others of the *rime petrose.*"

Anecdotes aside, the problem, however, is the same general one of the incapacity of the *Canzoniere* to justify itself, of its inexplicability according to its own principles. The *Montanina* is the only lyric by Dante to which we are successful in attributing a relatively late date and it is situated along an involuted line of development, almost along a line of error. In conclusion, can there be a better argument to show that an obsession with the *Commedia* on the part of the critic of the *rime* is not simply a vain ideal stimulated by the *Commedia's* greater artistic merit? Only according to this canon can one see the exploratory workings of Dante's mind and the feverishness of his efforts.

Dante and Medieval Culture

by Bruno Nardi

It is said that the importance of Dante's philosophical thought has been somewhat exaggerated, as has the degree of originality attributed to him. I would venture on the contrary to affirm that the fault lies in the other direction; that is, in maintaining, as so many do today, that Dante's philosophy is substantially that of the "good brother Thomas Aquinas." Dante's Thomism has now become a legend which is diffused through many commentaries and accepted as obvious in most literary handbooks. If this legend, as I believe, has its source in the inexact and approximate knowledge which Dantists had of medieval philosophical doctrines, then it gained credit from the zeal with which it was spread by certain neo-Thomists who show an apologetic intent which is quite out of place, as if Dante's faith would have been less firm, or the religious spirit of the *Commedia* less pure, had he been less faithful to the philosophy of Thomas Aquinas. This would be like saying that Manzoni's religious feeling was less sincere because he dared to write that the famous *Disquisitiones Magicae* of the inquisitor Martin Del Rio, "having become the most authoritative and indisputable text, was for more than a century the standard and the powerful stimulus for lawful, horrible and uninterrupted massacres."

Before passing judgment on the importance and originality of the philosophy of our poet (who boasted of being *vir philosophiae domesticus*), I propose a more modest task, with a mind free of any sectarian prejudice which might tend to make of Dante a rebellious precursor of Luther or a spokesman for the Counter Reformation and for Thomism. This task, which seems to me nevertheless of some importance if we are to understand that mighty mind, is to determine with the greatest critical exactitude what Dante thought of the philosophical problems on which he meditated. Afterwards, if necessary, we shall draw whatever conclusions have to be drawn.

Meanwhile, it seems to me, a few conclusions have already begun to be obvious: the poet shows that he has explored certain problems more profoundly than his contemporaries, and his solutions often appear more complex and daring than theirs.

"Dante and Medieval Culture." The introduction to *Dante e la cultura medievale* (Bari: Laterza Editore, 1942) by Bruno Nardi. Translated by Yvonne Freccero, with the kind permission of the author. Reprinted by permission of the author.

Thus, while one recognizes that the general scheme of his metaphysics is that of Christian Scholasticism, nevertheless he has surely introduced into it certain characteristic details, such as the doctrine *à propos* of the lunar spots, in order to explain the derivation of the many from the one; such as that of the mediate creation of the lower world; and that too of the empyrean as the intellectual seat of the sensible world, and the doctrine concerning the origin of the human soul resulting from the collaboration of the creative act with the work of nature, which was restored to favor by Rosmini.

Thus in his reflections on the nature of language Dante starts from the Aristotelian concept of the natural mutability of languages in order to vindicate the precedence of the vernacular over "grammatica," and even goes so far as to refute the old theological prejudice concerning the incorruptibility of the language of Adam.

Similarly in the discussions concerning the nature of love which were kindled among the Italian poets of the thirteenth century, there seems to have been a dialectical development comparable to the discussion of Plato's *Phaedrus;* so that from the rhetorical exercises which call to mind the discourse of Lysias we arrive with Dante at the rediscovery of the divine origin of Eros. It is in the poetic representation of the ascent of the soul beyond the heavens, celebrated in the second discourse of Socrates, and in the vision of Er at the end of the *Republic,* rather than in the humble visions of the Middle Ages, that the fertile seed of the philosophy and poetry of the *Commedia* can really be found. To the objection that the Florentine poet had no knowledge of those two works of the Athenian philosopher, we may reply that Platonic thought spread in countless rivulets and by then was inspiring a vast literature which, at least in part, was already well known to Dante. But even without this, great geniuses, in order to understand each other, do not need the means usually required by more superficial minds. The spirit is diffused through hidden subterranean ways. And minds accustomed to meditation communicate with each other all the more easily, even across distances of place and time, the more they immerse themselves in the depths of consciousness, where the light of truth is kindled. And so it is useful to note that even the last thesis of the *Phaedrus*—that true eloquence is the sincere expression of the feelings of the soul—finds a perfect echo in the verses of the poet:

> I' mi son un, che quando
> amor mi spira, noto, ed a quel modo
> ch'e' ditta dentro vo significando;
> [I am one who takes note when love
> inspires me and signify it after the
> manner in which it is said within me.]

since the subject of love, as Richard of St. Victor said, "aut tota intus est aut nusquam est," so that "solus de ea digne loquitur qui, secundum quod cor dictat, verba componit" [Love is completely within or it is nowhere . . . he alone speaks of it worthily who writes according to what the heart says] (*De grad. charit.,* ch. I).

But the most serious problem afflicting Dante's mind is that concerning the "cagion che il mondo ha fatto reo"—"the cause of the world's evil." At first he believed that he had found that cause in the egotism of the cities and particular principalities, because their greed had not been curbed by their master, the human will; and he wrote the *Monarchia.* The vigorous affirmation in this work of the unity of the human race is remarkable. It is deduced from the Averroistic principle that all men tend toward a single end, which is that by means of a common will the potential of the possible intellect be at all times completely realized. From the unity of the human race he then deduced the necessity of universal monarchy, and from this he defended its independence against the invading ecclesiastic power, assuming as the basis of this independence the autonomy of reason as opposed to faith. Later he discovered that the reason for the evils which afflicted Christianity went deeper: not only had the moderating authority of the Empire decreased, but even the Church, by allowing itself to become involved in the affairs of this world, had betrayed its evangelic mission and was setting an example of bad conduct for Christians. Thus to re-establish order on earth it was necessary not only to restore imperial authority but also to carry out a religious reform which would lead the Church back onto the straight path.

Whoever judges this utopia of Dante from the point of view of political history or the history of political doctrines inevitably finds it too unreal to be of assistance in changing the course of events. But the fault lies precisely in judging it from a political rather than a moral point of view. It was the aim pursued by the juridical tradition of Bologna that was political, even when it exploited the ideal of religious reform in order to strengthen the thesis that, in temporal matters, no one gives orders to the Emperor. Dante goes beyond the imperialistic thesis and corrects the monastic ideal of reform with a vision of a "beatitudo huius vitae," to be realized on earth thanks to the complete actualization of the reason "que per phylosophos tota nobis innotuit"—"which is completely revealed to us through the philosophers."

We once looked at medieval philosophy the way one looks at the vague outline of distant mountains, veiled in mist, on the furthest horizon. But if the traveler draws near them he can begin to distinguish ridges and summits separated from the valleys, of varying height and appearance. Some are green with woods, others barren and rocky. If he then penetrates those valleys and tries to climb those peaks, he discovers, to his great surprise, more and more of them, and he discerns chains jutting out at various points from the main axis of the range. This is the way the philosophy of the Middle Ages seems today to one who is not content to look at it from a distance: Augustinianism, Thomism, Scotism, Averroism are merely those which have been ignored least among the many different tendencies which the practised eye can distinguish amid the complexity of thirteenth-century thought. Around them are others no less worthy of recognition, such as that which gets its inspiration from Albertus Magnus, from whose doctrine Dante drew so extensively.

Returning to the images I have used, I would venture to say that Dante's thought stands among many chains and ridges like a rugged peak of the Dolomites, rising above them, shining in the sun, inviting and tempting: whoever endures the strain of the ascent is rewarded at the summit with the enjoyment of the great panorama and the sound of the celestial harmony which charms the ear of all who have learned to rise above the earthly world of the senses.

The Mind in Love:
Dante's Philosophy

by Kenelm Foster, O.P.

My aim, in this paper,[1] is a rather ambitious one; and to give the argument plausibility, I shall have to focus attention on a few fundamental Dantean topics, neglecting all the rest. I shall use particularly the unfinished prose treatise, the *Convivio*, and of course the *Divine Comedy*; and take philosophy in the widest sense, as including theology. Were my subject Dante's views about philosophy, as it was M. Gilson's in his excellent *Dante et la philosophie*, I should have to concentrate on those passages where the poet explicitly or implicitly distinguishes philosophy from the natural sciences or theology, and compares one discipline with another; and in that case, like M. Gilson, I should have to attend as much to the *Monarchia* as to the *Convivio*. But these are minor works, after all. Moreover, within the *Divine Comedy* itself, I do not think that the technical distinction between philosophy and theology is of primary importance. What we enter, as readers of the *Comedy*, is the continuous spiritual movement of a mind seeking God; and what I want to do, though it would be presumptuous to promise success, is to show the fundamental factors in that mind and search, to disclose Dante's central and governing idea. By so narrowing my range I shall, I venture to hope, increase my chance of saying something interesting: and if I thereby also increase the risk of talking unintelligibly, I can only plead in advance that the risk seems to me worth taking.

It will be clear that I am not concerned here either with Dante's sources or with "placing" him historically. I shall not attempt to prove that he was a Thomist or a near-Thomist, a Neoplatonist or an Averroist. This historical question has been much discussed in recent years, and I have my modest opinion on it. But here I am concerned with what Dante

"The Mind in Love: Dante's Philosophy," by Kenelm Foster, O.P. A paper read to the Aquinas Society of London in 1956 (Blackfriars, 1956). Reprinted by permission of the publisher.

[1] All references to Dante are to the "testo critico" of the Società Dantesca Italiana (Florence 1921). The translations are my own, with a little help from J. D. Sinclair's version of the *Divine Comedy* (London, John Lane, 1939-1946). [K. F.]

thought, not with how far his thought resembles or depends on that of other men. I know that one cannot understand the terms that a man uses without a knowledge of their history; but I beg to be credited with enough history for my purpose, remembering the Aristotelian tag, so convenient to lecturers, *oportet addiscentem credere.*

But before going on perhaps I ought to face more squarely the question whether one may properly speak of Dante's philosophy at all. The man was obviously first and foremost a poet, and poets do not write like philosophers, if the method of philosophy is dispassionate analysis. Poetry is not dispassionate, and if it expresses ideas, it does not stop to analyze them. You cannot properly philosophize in a poem. It is true that Dante's poetry exhibits a certain amount, an unusual amount, of analysis and argument. But even Dante did not consider his poems expressed ideas in a rationally satisfying way; otherwise he would not have subjoined so much prose commentary, in order, as he says somewhere, "to explain the meaning of the text." [2] He was indeed an indefatigable self-explainer. The *Vita Nuova* explains the youthful lyrics; the *Convivio* was planned as an explanation of poems written in the years that followed; and the *Comedy* itself, if the Can Grande letter is authentic, was succeeded by a fragment of prose commentary which might have grown into a volume had the poet lived longer.

But no one familiar with the bulk of Dante's prose, and able to recognize a philosopher at work, would call it philosophical without qualification. To write philosophy it is not enough to have genuine insight and intellectual enthusiasm; one must display a steadily dispassionate consideration of the arguments for and against whatever conclusions one eventually arrives at: and such methodical impartiality, though perhaps within Dante's capacity, is not conspicuous in his practice. M. Gilson has paid tribute to what he calls the "remarkable vigor and inventive richness" of the poet's dialectic in Book I of the *Monarchia,* and to the "marvellous density" of the final chapter of Book III.[3] But these merits hardly suffice to put Dante in the front rank of political philosophers, though they certainly suffice to make the *Monarchia* a profoundly interesting document. The *Convivio* again, an earlier work and in some ways a less mature one, is chiefly remarkable for some profound introspective insights and in general as the expression of a wonderful intellectual and moral vitality, rather than for any calm procedure of analysis and proof. To quote M. Gilson once more, it is a work "full of philosophical and indeed theological ideas written by one who is not technically either a philosopher or a theologian." [4]

One might press for a definition of what is meant by "technically a philosopher," but it is clear enough that if one is to call Dante a philoso-

---

[2] *Convivio* 4, 1, 11.

[3] *Dante et la Philosophie* (Paris, 1939), pp. 179 and 195.

[4] *Op. cit.,* p. 86.

pher, it is not in virtue of his technique. This technique was a normal scholastic one: many terms and distinctions from Aristotle (especially from the *De Anima* and the *Nicomachean Ethics*) transmitted through the Arabs and St. Albert and especially St. Thomas Aquinas; a special Neoplatonist influence from the *Liber de Causis;* much dexterity in the use of the syllogism; a good knowledge of the science of the period, especially of its astronomy. The technique, shall we say, of a well-informed amateur. This may seem an understatement when we remember the *range* of Dante's mind and its passionate profundity; remembering too his rich and various literary culture and easy familiarity with the whole Vulgate Bible. But on the philosophical side his equipment was not extraordinary. The wonder in any case is that he became as learned as he did. He had, as he freely admits, to sweat for it. Consider his circumstances. He only began his deeper studies at about the age of twenty-five, after the death of Beatrice, when he was already married, with a growing family. His philosophical reading began with Boethius and Cicero, and at first he found it hard going. "I set myself," he tells us, "to read that not very well known work of Boethius (the *Consolatio*) . . . and hearing that Cicero had written a book treating of the consolation of Laelius for the death of his friend Scipio . . . I set myself to read that also. And though I found it hard at first to penetrate their meaning, in the end I got into it as far as the knowledge of Latin, which I already had, and a little natural intelligence permitted; which intelligence had already brought me to see many things in a dreamy sort of way, as appears in the *Vita Nuova.* . . . And as it may happen that a man looking for silver accidentally hits on gold . . . so I, seeking consolation (for the death of Beatrice) found not only a remedy for my sorrow but the language of authors and sciences and books; reflecting on which I judged that philosophy—the lady of these authors and sciences and books—was a very great thing. And I imagined it as a noble lady, whom I could not represent to myself in any attitude but one of compassion; with the result that my sense of truth ("lo senso di vero") was so drawn to her that I could not take my eyes off her. And with this image in mind I began to frequent the places where she displayed herself as she truly is, in the schools of the religious and at the disputations of philosophers: so that within a short space of time, perhaps thirty months, I began to find such delight in her company that her love drove out and destroyed every other thought." [5]

This revealing text shows us, if we needed showing, that young Dante was a poet before he became a philosopher, and a poet in the courtly love tradition of the period. If philosophy was a lovely thing, it had to be imagined as a woman. We may note also, with a view to later developments, the implied distinction between image and truth: the "immagine" gazed at by the "senso di vero" leads the young man back to school, where

---

[5] *Convivio* 2, 12, 2-7.

it then begins to show its true significance, "veracemente." Notable too is the seriousness of this amateur: two and a half years seem to him a short philosophical novitiate. Dante, we see, began with a lofty idea of the sublimity of philosophy: a point to be borne in mind.

Through the 1290s Dante laid the foundations of his philosophical and scientific culture, though without abandoning his earlier literary interests; his astonishing artistic originality only fully revealed itself later, but it was not dormant now. Toward the turn of the century, however, practical affairs increasingly engaged his attention as the political state of Florence was convulsed by the strife of the Black and White factions of the ruling Guelf party. Dante was a prior of the city in 1300, ambassador to the pope in 1301, and then, by the victorious Blacks, banished from Florence early in 1302. During the next few years he wandered much in central and northern Italy, suffering from poverty and fretted by a burning sense of injustice. The unsettled existence of one who knew by experience

> . . . come sa di sale
> lo pane altrui, e com' è duro calle
> lo scendere e 'l salir per altrui scale,[6]

could hardly have favored study. But Dante was a great in more ways than one: he did not yield to misfortune. And in the event the bitterness of exile served Dante's genius—not only by intensifying with new urgency and moral energy his tremendous poetic gift, not only by enlarging that experience of men and places which was to crystallize in the *Divine Comedy,* but also by focusing and deepening his contemplative intelligence. But before trying to sound the depths of that intelligence, let us turn back to a passage in the *Convivio,* in praise of philosophy, with a view to seeing how Dante envisaged his own intellectual vocation, his attitude to the general ideal of wisdom, in the years preceding the *Comedy.*

The third book of the *Convivio* is all an impassioned praise of wisdom. "How great [he writes] was the desire which love put in me to see her can be neither conceived nor expressed. . . . O how many nights there were when the eyes of others were closed in sleep and my own gazed fixedly at the dwelling of my beloved!" [7] But when this erotic metaphor is combined with that of friendship, it clearly becomes more than a residue of the courtly love tradition. For friendship is understood in terms of Aristotle's analysis in the *Ethics,* which permits a simultaneous affirmation of intellectual humility and intellectual ambition. The

---

[6] *Paradiso* XVII, 58-60: "how salty is the taste of another man's bread, and how hard the way up and down another man's stairs."

[7] *Convivio* 3, 1, 3.

analogy of friendship supported both attitudes. Dante seems to himself far from wise, full of ignorance and confusions. But he has learned from Aristotle that friendship between unequals is still possible, if a "proportion between them . . . somehow reduces their dissimilarity to a similarity."[8] Now this proportion is found in the will, in desire: Dante knows far less than his beloved who, as wisdom, knows everything; but he loves far more than he knows; and his love is a power to transcend actual understanding. So he seizes eagerly on the Pythagorean definition of philosophy as *love* of wisdom: "this Pythagoreas, being asked whether he thought himself wise, disclaimed the title, saying he was not wise but only a lover of wisdom." Philosophy, insists Dante, is a term "not of arrogance but humility." Yet the aim it implies is not humble at all, but as high as truth itself. Indeed, no lesser aim would be worthy of the situation; for it would mean a return to the subjective limitations of the lover. The friendship-analogy makes this clear too. There are three sorts of friendship: for utility, for pleasure, and for the *bonum honestum,* "per onestade," i.e., a friendship based on a mutual appreciation of virtue; and this third sort is the only true sort. So the conclusion is drawn:

> As true friendship . . . has for its subject a knowledge of virtuous action ("de l'operazione buona") and as its form a love of the same, so philosophy, considered in itself . . . has for its subject the understanding, and as its form a quasi-divine love of the intellect. And as of true friendship the efficient cause is virtue, so of philosophy the efficient cause is truth. And as the end of true friendship is the noble delight of living together in a way worthy of men, that is to say rationally . . . so the end of philosophy is the supreme delight that admits of no defect or interruption, the true bliss that is attained in the contemplation of truth.[9]

So exalted a conception of philosophy naturally leaves room for distinctions; and, first of all, between life on earth and life in heaven, natural reason and reason glorified. A few pages further on Dante will tell us that the speculative felicity of pure knowing is not perfectly to be found on this side of eternity; here below happiness is only found in the life of moral virtue, with a limited satisfaction for speculative reason (in those who are free to use it) in the various sciences. For on earth the mind is limited by its instrument the imagination, and so by the body.[10] The distinction, from now on, will be rather emphatically drawn by Dante between the life of moral virtue and the life of speculation, between life that ends with the death of the body and life that goes on into eternity.[11]

[8] *Convivio* 3, 1, 7. Cf. *Nic. Ethics,* 1163b 30.
[9] *Convivio* 3, 11, 7-15.
[10] *Convivio* 3, 15, 6-10; cf. 3, 4, 9 and *Paradiso* IV, 40-42.
[11] *Convivio,* 4, 17, 9-12; 4, 22, 10-18; *Mon.* 3, 16, 7; cf. *Purgatorio* III, 34-39, *Paradiso* II, 10-2, IV, 40-2.

Since the poet is a Christian, another distinction, between nature and grace, is implied; but this theological distinction, though always present to Dante's mind, tends to be resolved into the philosophers' distinction between action and speculation.[12] The theory of grace, if theory it can be called, is the weak point in Dantean theology.[13] As for philosophy, the term, in the *Convivio*, keeps a certain width and generality. The first thing Dante insists on defining for would-be philosophers is the *motive* that should govern them.

One must not, he means, treat philosophy as either a utility or a pleasure.[14] Pleasure can certainly arouse the mind, as the beauty of a poem is a sort of bait to draw one into the goodness which is its meaning: through a sensuous pattern of sound and imagery reason seeks its own satisfaction. Here the medieval aesthetic appears. Already in Book II of the *Convivio* we have been assured that we can enjoy the poet's song without understanding what it means: "I say that in all discourse goodness and beauty are separate and distinct, for goodness is in the meaning and beauty in the verbal adornment; and both give delight, but the goodness gives the greater delight." So the poet tells his song not to worry if it chance among people who are puzzled over its meaning ("la tua ragione"). Let it say to them,

> If you cannot see my goodness, at least attend to my beauty. Which is to say . . . O you who cannot see the meaning of this canzone, do not reject it on that account; only look at its beauty, which is great, both for the sentence-construction, which interests the grammarians, and for the plan of the discourse, which interests the rhetoricians, and for the numerical relation of its parts, which interests the musicians. These things are clearly beautiful, if attentively considered.[15]

I quote this passage not only for the characteristic touch that a poem's meaning is even more delightful than its beauty, but also as introducing the great traditional order-pattern of ends and means: in which the outward exists for the inward, sense for reason, the sensible for the intelligible, the image for the idea, what is apparent for the sake of what is relatively concealed, what is expressible for what is perhaps inexpressible by man or anyhow only expressible in virtue of a special human disci-

---

[12] I mean that Dante tends to differentiate between the natural life and the super-natural life as two kinds of happiness (*beatitudo*); the latter being the beatific vision. Christianity tends to be characterized as *the way to perfect vision.*

[13] I may return to this matter another time. Here it may suffice to say that I have in mind: (a) the Good Pagans in Dante's Limbo, (b) the rarity of his allusions to the Sacraments. True, there is the impressive allegory of *Purgatorio* IX: but taking the *Comedy* as a whole, there is a lack of emphasis on life in the Body of Christ *on earth*, I think.

[14] *Convivio* 3, 11, 7-11.

[15] *Convivio* 2, 11.

pline or a special divine grace. This pattern—grounded on nature, conse-
crated by Catholic tradition, and reaffirmed in scholastic metaphysics—
is not only presupposed by Dante, it forms the living structure of his
mind, as we shall see in more detail presently. For the moment let us
note those three Arts to which the poet submits, as if for their approval,
the outward form, the beauty of his poem: Grammar, Rhetoric, Music;
and note especially the two last, for we meet them again in the description of philosophy as friendship.

Dante gladly acknowledged the pedagogical function of Rhetoric: it
had introduced him to philosophy, pointing beyond itself as beauty
points to goodness and sense to reason. In a quaint yet far from negligible
section of the *Convivio* each of the Liberal Arts or Sciences of medieval
culture is allotted its own heavenly symbol. Rhetoric's symbol was the
planet Venus; for is not this brilliant planet the loveliest of the stars, and
is not Rhetoric the pleasantest of all the sciences? Since, as Dante adds,
the purpose of Rhetoric is precisely to be pleasant.[16] It is so pleasant that
many people spend all their time on it and its sister science Music, and
shun and fly from other intellectual disciplines. And there is no harm
in that, provided they do not call themselves philosophers. For the other
sciences too are all parts of philosophy. To love wisdom in its rhetorical
or musical aspect only is like loving a friend only for the pleasure you
get from him; it is no more philosophy than that is true friendship.
Dante had been of the bright rhetorical company, and he never lost
touch with it—witness the poets, artists and musicians who turn up in
the *Purgatorio*—; but he would not be tied to it. One is reminded of
another great Italian whose mind in some ways resembled Dante's and in
some ways was so different—Alessandro Manzoni, who once described
himself (in a letter to Victor Cousin) as "un élève de rhétorique qui a
écouté quelquefois et en passant, à la porte de la salle de philosophie." [17]
Dante was less modest, and perhaps more ingenuous.

Yet the gay *letterati* and musicians have more philosophy in them than
those others who study only to acquire money and worldly advantages—
like (and now the whip cracks!) "the lawyers and the doctors and nearly
all the religious." These practical folk are the furthest from the real
thing, because truth as such is simply not their aim at all. In short,
philosophy is the appetite for truth (and this rules out the practical
people), and for truth as transcendentally including everything (and this
leaves the aesthetes far behind).[18]

A reflection suggests itself at this point: that Dante stands out among
poets, not only, or rather not so much, by the range of his intellectual
appetite, as by his passion for discovering *order* within that range, for

---

[16] *Convivio* 2, 13, 13-14.

[17] This letter seems to have been never sent to Cousin, or even finished: it is printed
by P. Fossi in an appendix to his *La Conversione di Alessandro Manzoni*, Bari, 1933.

[18] *Convivio* 3, 11, 7-11.

connecting one truth with another only after each has been distinguished from the rest. Though his poetry is vastly richer and more confident than Manzoni's, he would have agreed with Manzoni's very characteristic remark that "poetry should take truth for its object as the only source of a noble and enduring delight." [19] Dante's wide-ranging poetry is inwardly disciplined by a severity in drawing distinctions no less than Manzoni's, though in Dante this quality has none of the hair-splitting anxiety not to be misunderstood that we feel in the nineteenth-century poet. Dante did not, I think, greatly care whether he was misunderstood or not: but he had to understand himself; and this need to know his own mind was in fact (and here the scholastic discipline played its indispensable part) a concern with the *object*—with the proper natures and distinctions of things.

Through the joy of sheer knowing philosophy introduced him to an objective cosmos, grander than any dream—an immense, unfathomable order of parts in a whole. For a moment knowledge is eclipsed by wonder, the mind is dazzled, almost daunted. This is the moment of "stupore," of noble wonder, of that bewilderment felt by the soul in the presence of "great and wonderful things, which insofar as they seem great reduce the beholder to reverence, and insofar as they seem wonderful set him desiring to understand them." [20] The poet speaks from experience, of course; his capacity for wonder, for admiration, in the full sense of the term, was utterly sincere. But the text echoes also Aristotle's well-known remark that wonder was at the origin of philosophy, and no doubt the allusion was intended.[21] Dante is expressly associating the feeling of "stupore" with adolescence, but in fact it accompanies him at every stage of his penetration of God's creation, from the *Vita Nuova* experience of human beauty to the *Paradiso* experience of divine beauty. Of this process from wonder to wonder, three typical moments are suggested by the *Convivio*: corresponding to an awareness (1) of the body-soul complexity of human nature, (2) of human history, and (3) of the cosmic order revealed by astronomy.[22] In each case what is marveled at is a complexity, what is glimpsed is an order or convergence of parts in a whole, what is praised is a half-concealed wisdom, transcending present understanding, but causing, by the little that is glimpsed of it, a hunger for full understanding. In the *Paradiso* this theme recurs persistently in terms of the question and answer dialectic whereby Dante is raised by Beatrice toward the complete vision. The process becomes explicit at the close of the fourth canto, between the end of one stage of an enquiry (into the human will) and the beginning of the next:

[19] See the *Lettera sul Romanticismo* addressed to Cesare D'Azeglio, in *Opere Varie*, ed. Barbi and Ghisalberti, Milan, 1943, p. 617.

[20] *Convivio* 4, 25, 5.

[21] *Metaph.* 982, b, 10.

[22] *Convivio* 3, 8, 1; 4, 5, 9; 3, 5, 22.

> O amanza del primo amante, o diva,
>   diss' io appresso . . .
>
> Io veggio ben che già mai non si sazia
>   nostro intelletto, se 'l ver non lo illustra
>   di fuor dal qual nessun vero si spazia.
>
> Posasi in esso come fera in lustra,
>   tosto che giunto l'ha; e giugner puollo:
>   se non, ciascun disio sarebbe frustra.
>
> Nasce per quello, a guisa di rampollo,
>   a piè del vero il dubbio; ed è natura
>   ch' al sommo pinge noi di collo in collo.[23]

To which Beatrice answers, echoing his "I see well":

> Io veggio ben sì come già risplende
>   ne l'intelletto tuo l'etterna luce,
>   che, vista, sola e sempre amore accende.[24]

How characteristic are these passages, especially the first! Note that image of the wild animal, resting tired in its lair, "tosto che giunto l'ha"; and the repetition of the verb expressing the effort of reaching forward, of searching—*giugnere*:

> tosto che giunto l'ha; e giugner puollo.

For the effort, though extreme, is assured of success,

> . . . e giugner puollo:
> se non ciascun disio sarebbe frustra.

Such a stress, recurring in dozens of texts, indicates a character extraordinarily predisposed to aim at what is great and arduous, to delight in difficulties for the joy of overcoming them—or more precisely, because difficulties indicate the greatness of the object desired, as the highest mountains are the hardest to climb to the top. One recalls the scholastic

[23] *Paradiso* IV, 118-132: "O beloved of the First Lover, O divine one . . . I see well that our intellect can never be satisfied but with the truth beyond which there is no other truth. There it reposes, like a wild beast in its lair, as soon as it reaches it; and reach it it can, else all desire would be in vain. And from this springs up enquiry like a sapling at the foot of truth—which is nature driving us on from hill to hill."

[24] *Paradiso* V, 7-9: "I see well that already eternal light is reflected in your mind—that light which, once seen, alone and always kindles love."

notion of the "irascible part" of the sense appetite, which aims at an object *quoddamodo elevatum supra facilem potestatem,* and which, tempered by virtue, is the passion of the *magnanimus.*[25] Dante, both in art and thought, reveled in difficulties; you can often see him deliberately placing obstacles in his own way. It came naturally to him to represent in its widest sweep and greatest complexity whatever he set himself to explore and express; and then to go for it like an athlete or a fighter. The *Paradiso* is a sustained attack on the inarticulate; a wrestling match, he calls it in the first canto, and in the twenty-third, a battle:

> . . . ancora mi rendei
> a la battaglia dei deboli cigli.[26]

What then was the spring behind all this effort? What was it that set his mind and art moving so furiously? Surely some glimpse of the end to be reached, conjoined with a keen sense of actual distance from that end: a sense of immense potentialities not yet actualized, but able to be. And how able to be? Here we approach, I think, the center of Dante's mind and the heart of our subject.

Let us turn back to the opening of *Paradiso* V. Beatrice is approving the triumphant declaration of intellectual desire with which canto IV had ended. She says:

> S' io ti fiammeggio nel caldo d'amore
> di là dal modo che in terra si vede,
> sì che de li occhi tuoi vinco il valore,
>
> non ti maravigliar: che ciò procede
> da perfetto veder, che, come apprende
> così nel bene appreso move il piede.[27]

What Beatrice represents here is clear enough: divine wisdom set in relation to the searching human mind of the poet. Essentially she is the same ideal wisdom whom we met in the *Convivio*; this "beloved of the first lover" is that wisdom who dwelt with God "as in an eternal wedlock." [28] More precisely, Beatrice represents perfect vision ("perfetto veder"), both term and cause of the divine love ("caldo d'amore," etc.). In fact, she is the perfection of knowledge and love; she loves all she knows and knows all she loves. A little of her knowledge is now shared by Dante, and it

---

[25] *Summa Theol.* 1a-2ae, xxiii, 1; 2a-2ae, cxxix, 5.
[26] *Paradiso* XXIII, 77-78: "Again I returned to the battle of my weak eyes."
[27] *Paradiso* V, 1-6: "If I flame on you with hot love beyond all earthly experience, so that I overcome your sight, do not wonder; for this comes from perfect vision which, as it apprehends, moves toward the apprehended good."
[28] *Convivio* 3, 12, 13.

makes him desire more. Knowledge breeds desire of knowledge; it *seeds* questions ("dubbio"), as we have seen. Distinctions would be called for here in a less summary treatment, but at present it suffices to say that once intelligence, the truth-faculty, has tasted truth precisely as truth, i.e., as its own correspondence with reality, it cannot help wanting truth whole and entire, i.e., its correspondence with all reality, "di fuor dal qual nessun vero si spazia"; and this because truth, "the good of the intellect," is what the intellect exists to possess.[29] At the touch of truth the whole mind stirs, all its energies awake:

> Io veggio ben sì come già risplende
> ne l'intelletto tuo l'etterna luce
> che, vista, sola e sempre amore accende.[30]

The mind stretches out to vision, to "perfetto veder," because it is in its nature to do so:

> . . . ed è natura
> ch' al sommo pinge noi di collo in collo.

But let us examine more closely this intellectual appetite. The intellect's function as such is simply "to know what things are";[31] which is also its perfection, what it ultimately desires. Now Dante's thought—half-veiled in imagery, never thoroughly analyzed—moves always to and fro between the subject and the object of intellectual desire; stressing now the distinctive nature of the desirer and now the object desired; though each stress implies the other, and the two sometimes draw together, as in the final canto of the *Paradiso*. The subjective stress is strong in the *Convivio*, and especially in a vigorous passage toward the end (IV, 22) which states the final term of human desire as the soul's *use* ("*uso*") of itself. The act of love which must finalize desire is considered as final precisely in the order of the *subject's* activity; so that, while that act is a joyful possession of some object, it is regarded as being, as it were, applied by the subject to and for itself, the possessor: who in this sense is finalized by using himself in using the thing possessed. This way of speaking may seem odd, yet St. Thomas too allows that in a certain sense "using," *uti*, may be considered as the ultimate end. "The term end," he writes, "sometimes denotes a thing possessed, and sometimes the possession itself; as a miser's end is money and the possession of it. Absolutely speaking the ultimate end is a thing (*ipsa res*) . . . but in a relative sense it is the thing's possession; as no miser craves money, except to possess

---

[29] *Convivio* 2, 13, 6; cf. *Inferno* III, 17-18.
[30] *Paradiso* V, 7-9. [See n. 24 above.—Ed.]
[31] *Convivio* 4, 15, 11.

it." Hence insofar as one refers the desired object to one's possession of it, one may be said to find one's ultimate end in a "using" (*uti* or *usus*).[32] This is not however the normal sense of *usus* for St. Thomas; who prefers to reserve *usus* for the application of means to an end, and its companion term *frui*, enjoyment, for the union with end as such.[33] Dante's very emphatic placing, in this text of the *Convivio*, of *uso* at the *end* of purposeful activity suggests a slightly more subjective approach than St. Thomas'; inasmuch as one uses a thing for oneself, but one enjoys a thing for what it is in itself. And the reader finds himself asking how this subjective stress can be connected with the equally strong stress, elsewhere in Dante, on an *object* of desire that transcends the human subject and the limits of the individual.

In the same passage that I am considering, Dante says that human joy essentially comes from the soul's use of its noblest part, because this is the part of itself that the soul naturally loves most; and this part being the intellect, joy must increase in the degree that intellect is active, i.e., is understanding actually.[34] A life entirely occupied in understanding would be entirely joyful. But such a life could only be found apart from the body or where there is no distraction from the body: whence the conclusion that perfect joy must be sought in another life than this.[35] But the point to note here is Dante's insistence that the soul naturally loves most its noblest part. Why should this be so? It is, we learn, because if each part of man has its own goodness, reason or intellect has the distinctively human goodness; and therefore its activity is the most one with or, as Dante likes to say, is the closest to, the human subject as such. You will recognize the traditional recourse to the concept of unity in the philosophy of love.[36] Unity is both the effect of love, since love draws things together, and the cause of love, since love is always a subject's response to some affinity, real or supposed, in an object. Unity governs love at both ends. The doctrine is traditional; but Dante's stress falls where one might have expected it less, on unity as the *cause* of love. I love most what was nearest to me before my loving began—the goodness proper to me, my "propria bontade." Why, ultimately, is this?

The reason is given in a definition of love, to which the philosophical reader of Dante must continually return. Love is spiritual union, "unimento spirituale." [37] And union in *act* is meant: not only because Dante is talking about actual loving, but more deeply because all potentiality metaphysically presupposes actuality. Potency cannot, absolutely, begin

[32] *Summa Theol.* 1a-2ae, xvi, 3.

[33] *Ibid.* 1a-2ae, xi, 3, 4.

[34] *Convivio* 4, 22, 7-10.

[35] *Convivio* 4, 22, 13-18.

[36] E.g. *Summa Theol.* 1a-2ae, xxvi and xxvii. Cf. E. Gilson, *L'Esprit de la philosophie médiévale* (2nd ed., 1944) ch. 14.

[37] *Convivio* 3, 2, 3.

anything. Without working out the metaphysics of the matter, Dante leaps to the conclusion that behind all love and desire is the perfect and perfectly actual unity or self-identity of God. Love, absolutely speaking, *is* God's self-identity. Hence wherever in the universe is self-identity, distinctness in nature and still more in individuality, there is love and there is a trace of God. These three terms—love, unity, likeness of God —are in this sense interchangeable.[38]

But the divine unity is reflected in many creatures, and each of these is only incompletely like it. As a likeness of God's unity, each creature must love itself; as an incomplete likeness, it cannot love only itself, it must love also the greater likeness which it forms together with other creatures. For the likeness in question consists not only in self-identity, understood as the absence of internal division, but in a certain completeness, in a positive coherence of distinguishable modes of being. In short, the unity of the Creator requires, as its likeness, a unity in the created universe. And this is the cosmic order:

> . . . le cose tutte quante
> hanno ordine tra loro, e questo è forma
> che l'universo a Dio fa simigliante.[39]

Let us take another step. The "form" of the cosmos is its order, its total likeness to the totally pre-containing unity of God. And this order obtains between one creature and another. But it already presupposes, and more evidently in the higher creatures endowed with intelligence, an order relating each creature to God. To make this clear we must return to the principle, fundamental in Dante and already touched on, of *causal assimilation*, i.e., that an effect is necessarily like its cause in some way, that to cause is *per se* to transmit a resemblance.[40] Now if the First Cause is fullness of being (as all Christian philosophers hold) we might have expected Dante (certainly a Christian philosopher) to argue, Thomist-wise, that creatures resemble God precisely in respect of their degree of being. And he certainly did not reject this inference. But it is not where he lays his main stress. This stress falls, not on existence, *esse,* but on activity, *operatio*; and chiefly on the activity of knowing and loving, and more particularly on loving. This should become clear if we follow him along two characteristic lines of argument.

1. It is supremely *natural* to God—says Dante, interpreting rather oddly a text from the *Liber de Causis*—it is natural to God to love being,

---

[38] *Convivio* 3, 2, 2-9.

[39] *Paradiso* I, 103-105: "all things cohere in an order, and this is the form by which the universe is like to God."

[40] *Convivio* 3, 2, 5; 3, 6, 11; 3, 14, 2; cf. *Paradiso* VII, 64-81. The common scholastic formula is *omne agens agit sibi simile.*

"volere essere." [41] Therefore the soul naturally desires being, and consequently desires God, the cause of its being. A restatement of the old conception of a "natural desire" for God: but the Dantean touch is clearer in what follows. From that ontological God-love arises love of the manifold "goodness," physical and spiritual, through which God manifests Himself to the soul; and this in the degree that those varieties of goodness appear to it. In the degree that the goodness of reality appears the soul runs to it, impelled by its basic appetite for being. Because reality shines with God's presence, one has only to open one's eyes to love it; and particularly the eye of the mind; which discerns, through the sensible beauty of bodies, the rational beauty of order, the divine design.[42] This theme of a natural attraction through sensible beauty to rational order recurs continually in Dante, especially in the *Comedy*, and particularly in respect of two principal sense-objects: the face of Beatrice and the glory of the stars. And pulling against this attraction from beauty to order goes the reverse movement of egoistic cupidity, whose symbol is the Siren or the Wolf or money or simply "earth." Hence, after Dante's dream of the Siren, half-way up the Mount of Purgatory, sounds the ringing voice of Virgil's imperious reason, the recall to *order*:

> Vedesti', disse,' quell 'antica strega
> che sola sovra noi omai si piagne;
> vedesti come l'uom de lei si slega.

> Bastiti, e batti a terra le calcagne;
> li occhi rivolgi al logoro che gira
> lo rege etterno con le rote magne.[43]

2. But our second line of argument takes us still further—beyond all signs and symbols to the perfect vision. Here we have to trace, not the appetite for being, *essere,* but for activity, *operazione*; and we start from the notion of *joy*. Toward joy every creature is naturally and inevitably orientated, according to the principle that "the deepest desire in everything, and the first given by nature, is to return to its principle," in the sense of what actively originates it.[44] But this return is effected, broadly, in two ways, according as things come to be through secondary causes or by God's direct creation. Plant and animal life turns back to God as to a cause operating in nature, at a remove. But things created directly turn to Him as to an end to be reached by direct contact, "sanza mezzo":

---

[41] *Convivio* 3, 2, 7.

[42] Cf. *Convivio* 1, 4, 3.

[43] *Purgatorio* XIX, 58-63: "You have seen . . . that old witch who alone is cause of the suffering on the mountain above us; you have seen how man gets free of her. Let this suffice! Spurn the earth underfoot: turn your eyes to the lure of the great wheels that the eternal King whirls around you." Cf. *Purgatorio* XIV, 143-151.

[44] *Convivio* 4, 12, 14. Cf. Boethius, *Consol Phil.* III, M.2. Pr. 3.

and of these is the human soul. Issuing immediately from the divine joy, the soul turns then at once toward joy with a quasi-divine appetite which can absolutely not be satisfied save by reunion with the divine joy that caused it:

> ma vostra vita sanza mezzo spira
> la somma beninanza, e la innamora
> di sè sì che poi sempre la disira.[45]

This is the "natural thirst":

> La sete natural che mai non sazia
> se non con l'acqua onde la femminetta
> sammaritana dimandò la grazia.[46]

But how does this appetite show itself? In two ways, differing only as two aspects of the same thirst; the ways of knowledge and love. And Dante's deepest thought bears on the convergence of these two ways. Let us take love first.

(a) Love, we have seen, is spiritual union. The soul loves itself and other things, and increasingly as "goodness" appears to it, in or outside itself, in the ways and degrees suggested. But, in the last analysis, what is goodness but fullness of being? And what, concretely, is this but God, who spans infinity in one act? [47] So we return to our definition of love as spiritual union of soul and thing, soul and self, soul and soul; which, taken up into the absolute, is the pre-containing unity of the divine mind. Hence God is love. Hence the deepest orientation of the created spirit is to no abstract *summum bonum,* but to the primary love itself. When all is said, what the soul finally loves is love; or rather, a Lover; no passive object, but an active ardor that runs to meet us:

> Quello infinito e ineffabil bene
> che la su è, così corre ad amore
> com' a lucido corpo raggio vene.[48]

---

[45] *Paradiso* VII, 142-144: "but your life (i.e., soul) is breathed in directly by the supreme Good, who so enamors it of Himself that evermore it desires Him." Cf. *Purgatorio* XVI, 85-90.

[46] *Purgatorio* XXI, 1-3: "The natural thirst which nothing slakes but that water the Samaritan woman asked for."

[47] *Convivio* 4, 9, 3: ". . . He who is limited by nothing, the first goodness who is God, who alone contains infinity with infinite capacity." Cf. *Paradiso* XIX, 50-51: ". . . that good which has no end and measures itself by itself."

[48] *Purgatorio* XV, 67-69: "The infinite and ineffable good that is above so runs toward love as light to crystal."

I lack space to draw out the Christian implications of this teaching, where they appear perhaps most strikingly, in the noble passage on the Incarnation in *Paradiso* VII and in Piccarda's richly delicate lines (so often sentimentalized) on heaven as the union of the blessed with God's loving will:

> E'n la sua volontade è nostra pace:
> ell' è quel mare al qual tutto si move
> ciò ch' ella cria e che natura face.[49]

(*b*) The way of knowledge runs to the same conclusion, but under a different aspect; not precisely as reunion with all goodness, which is spiritual union, love; but as reunion with all truth, which is that Idea whence all creatures derive at once their existence and variety and the cosmic order they combine to form. This order too is now seen under a slightly different aspect: not as the result of many converging loves, but as the manifold expression of the absolute reality. The key-word is *expression,* connoting mind. The intellect's function is to become true by knowing "what things are" (as we have seen), and also why things are— i.e., to become true by seeing the truth *in* things, their ultimate measure, itself unmeasured or only self-measured, which is their pre-existence, as a simple yet infinitely pregnant idea, in the absolute reality which, as creatures, they express. Dante's effort here is to pass from the notion of truth as reality measuring the human mind to the notion of truth as the divine mind measuring reality.[50] Two texts from the final canto of the *Paradiso* may substantiate this inevitably abstract statement. After Bernard's prayer to our Lady for the grace of Dante's final vision, the description of the vision begins with a concept that will govern it all the way:

> Bernardo m'accenava e sorridea
> perch' io guardassi suso; ma io era
> già per me stesso tal qual ei volea;
>
> chè la mia vista, venendo sincera,
> e più e più intrava per lo raggio
> de l'alta luce che da sè è vera.[51]

---

[49] *Paradiso* III, 85-87: "And in His will is our peace: that will is the sea to which all things flow—all that it creates and nature makes." This last gives the radical distinction between God's direct causing (creation, in the strict sense) and His causing through "nature."

[50] Cf. *Summa Theol.* 1a, xvi, 5, 6.

[51] *Paradiso* XXXIII, 49-54: "Bernard signed to me with a smile to look upwards, but already of myself I was doing as he wished; for my sight, becoming pure, more and more deeply penetrated the great light which is true of itself."

The great light is "true of itself" as the primal thought to which all things must correspond; and this because that thought is itself the absolute primal *thing*:

> Nel suo profondo vidi che s'interna,
> legato con amore in un volume,
> ciò che per l'universo si squaderna:
>
> sustanze e accidenti e lor costume,
> quasi conflati insieme, per tal modo
> che ciò ch' i' dico è un semplice lume.[52]

And this light, the idea behind creation, is the Word, the Second Person of the Trinity. And if it is the loadstone of all intelligence, the "vero in che si queta ogni intelletto," that is because it is the divine *art*, in the Scholastic sense of the term, the idea *in mente artificis*, in the mind of a maker.[53] For every maker loves his work and is loved by it in return.[54] And all these themes—God's art-idea drawing created minds to itself through creation, and God's own eternal attraction to it, so that, as the universal beauty, it centers the love of the Creator and the love of creatures—all this is summarized in the mighty opening of *Paradiso* X:

> Guardando nel suo Figlio con l'Amore
> che l'uno e l'altro etternalmente spira,
> lo primo ed ineffabile Valore,
>
> quanto per mente e per loco si gira
> con tant' ordine fè, ch'esser non puote
> sanza gustar di lui chi ciò rimira.
>
> Leva dunque, lettore, a l'alte rote
> meco la vista, dritto a quella parte
> dove l'un moto e l'altro si percuote:
>
> e lì comincia a vagheggiar ne l'arte
> di quel maestro che dentro a se l'ama,
> tanto che mai da lei l'occhio non parte.[55]

[52] *Paradiso* XXXIII, 85-90: "In its depth I saw contained, bound by love in one volume, the pages of the Universe: substances and accidents and their relations, as it were fused together, so that what I tell of is a simple light."

[53] *Monarchia* 2, 2, 2.

[54] *Convivio* 3, 6, 10; 4, 30, 2. *Monarchia* 1, 13, 1-3.

[55] *Paradiso* X, 1-12: "Gazing at His Son with the Love which the one and the other eternally breathe out, the primal ineffable Power made with such order all that circles through mind or space that he who contemplates it cannot but taste of Him. Lift up then, reader, with me your eyes to the great wheels, directing them on that point where one motion strikes on the other, and there begin to delight in the art of the Master who so loves it in Himself that His eye never leaves it."

With this text's powerful synthesis I end. Enough, I hope, has been said to reveal its meaning to an attentive reader. That meaning is the focal point of all Dante's thought, which all turns and converges upon an insight into the *causal nexus*, the relation between cause and effect. Being is seen as causal and as returning to its cause. The poet's eye saw making—*poesis*—everywhere: and this idea guided his particular expression of the Christian mystery. But to show this in more detail must be left to another occasion; to show in particular how three principal Dantean themes—justice, free will, and the limits of poetic expression—are related to the central insight.

Paolo and Francesca

by Renato Poggioli

. . . Francesca tells her story as if she were reminiscing aloud. One day, Paolo and she were reading together, for their own entertainment, the romance of Lancelot du Lac, and particularly that section of the romance describing how the protagonist was overpowered by his passion for the fair Guinevere. Francesca alludes to all this very succinctly, through the single phrase: "how love seized him" (*come amor lo strinse*), where she uses a violent verb, *stringere*, "to grasp" or "to squeeze," to indicate the violence of the passion mastering the knight's soul. We imagine the two sitting beside each other: one listening, the other, probably Francesca, reading aloud. But the only thing we are told by Francesca is that they were alone, without the company of even the fear of their weakness, or the suspicion of their own selves. It would be impossible to state more concisely the perfidy of temptation, lying in wait to assail two unprepared and defenseless human hearts. The malice of sin threatens and ruins our souls when they yield to self-oblivion, when they abandon themselves, deceitfully, to their own innocence:

> "Noi leggiavamo un giorno per diletto
> di Lancialotto come amor lo strinse:
> soli eravamo e sanza alcun sospetto."

["We were reading one day for delight of Lancelot, how love seized him: We were alone and unsuspecting."]

Francesca's memory rehearses all the unforgettable instants of that fatal moment. They were looking down at the pages of their book, when the suggestive power of the story suddenly raised their gazes toward each other; or, as Francesca says, "that reading made us lift our eyes." This happened more than once: and Francesca seems to lengthen the duration of each of those instants by the dieresis on the word *fiate*,

"Paolo and Francesca" (original title: "Tragedy or Romance? A Reading of the Paolo and Francesca Episode in Dante's *Inferno*"), by Renato Poggioli. From *PMLA*, LXXII, 3 (June 1957). Abridged and reprinted by permission of the Modern Language Association of America.

"times." At every turn, each recognized the same paleness on the other's face. Yet the reading would have perhaps failed to seduce them into sin, if the climax of the tale had not finally broken down all restraints and overcome their resistance:

> "Per piú fiate li occhi ci sospinse
> quella lettura, e scolorocci il viso;
> ma solo un punto fu quel che ci vinse."

["Several times our reading caused our eyes to meet and our faces to pale; But it was one point alone that overcame us."]

The crucial point, the passage by which they were vanquished, is that famous scene in the romance where the noble Gallehaut begs Guinevere to reward the gentle knight Lancelot for loving her so loyally and faithfully, and the Queen complies and kisses Lancelot on his lips. The scene, and the electric effect of its reading, are recalled by Francesca with some of the loveliest lines of the canto:

> "Quando leggemmo il disïato riso
> esser baciato da cotanto amante,
> questi, che mai da me non fia diviso,
>
> la bocca mi baciò tutto tremante."

["When we read how the longed-for smile was kissed by so great a lover, this one, who shall never be parted from me, kissed my mouth, all trembling."]

The transition from a vicarious to a genuine consummation, from the first kiss of Lancelot and Guinevere, which belongs to the realm of imagination, to the first kiss of Paolo and Francesca, which took place in the realm of experience, is beautifully conveyed not only by the change of rhythmical pace, but also by the sudden transformation of Francesca's mode of expression, by the metamorphosis of her language. The lips of Guinevere, the heroine of the romance, are at first marvellously metaphorized into a *disïato riso,* or "longed-for smile." These words are made even more insistently caressing by the dieresis lengthening the adjective and intensifying the radiance of the image. The select choice of words and sounds, as well as the trope itself, by which the curved lips of the loved and loving Queen lose all physical reality, becoming as light and incorporeal as their inviting and wordless smile, tend to give a spiritualized and idealized vision of that imaginary embrace. While the Queen's inviting gesture is re-experienced from the viewpoint of the knight, dazzled by the sight of her seductive smile, the kiss by which Lancelot seals her lips is instead re-evoked from the standpoint of Guinevere, as shown by the passive form of the verb "being kissed" (*esser baciato*), which suggests a feeling of feminine abandon, a gesture of self-offering. As for the complement agreeing with that passive form, "by so great a lover" (*da cotanto amante*), it reveals Francesca's awareness of the personal merits of her partner in passion and sin, and tends to equate his qualities with Lancelot's aristocratic and chivalric virtues. All this implies a process of self-identification: if Francesca sees in her lover the peer of such a worthy as Lancelot, she may also see in herself the equal of his Queen; and she may even think that she had a right to betray Gianciotto, if Guinevere betrayed King Arthur himself. But here the parallelism, and double impersonation, suddenly end. Up to now Francesca has evoked a vision of romantic love through both empathy and sympathy, through the alluring mirror of both sentiment and art. As soon as she deals, not with the fleshless kiss of two fictitious creatures, but with the real one of two living beings, she immediately realizes that she was no Guinevere, and that Paolo was no Lancelot. This realization is evident in the line where she alludes, simply and directly, to her lover. Now she does not refer to him with the usual *costui*, "that one," but with *questi*, "this one," so as to indicate his physical and moral nearness to her. The relative clause following this pronoun (*questi, che mai da me non fia diviso*, "this one who will be never divided from me"), is a cry of possession, where pride mingles with despair. That pronoun and that cry presuppose either a fleeting turn of her eyes, or merely a blind gesture of her hand, as if to assure herself, as well as the two visitors, that her lover still is, and will forever remain, at her side. All this takes but a line, which separates, as a curtain or a barrier, the kiss she once read about from the kiss still alive in the memory of her flesh. Only after having raised such a barrier will she be able to re-evoke, in its loneliness and singularity, their own kiss: which she however catches only in Paolo's gesture. Paolo is described as she saw him at that moment, moving toward her full of trembling and fear. The vision reveals him to us as a weaker and more human vessel than even the timid Lancelot. And we, the readers, see Francesca receiving the kiss not on curved, but on closed and unsmiling lips, to which she refers by using a cruder, singular word. This is what we meant by the transformation of Francesca's language: and such a falling off from the spiritual to the physiological, from the "smile" (*riso*) of Guinevere to the "mouth" (*bocca*) of Francesca, is but the shift or descent from literature to life, from fiction to reality, from romanticism to realism; or more simply, from sentimental fancy to moral truth. Lust and adultery replace for a moment passion and love: a cry of nature breaks forever the mirror of illusion and the veil of self-deceit.

The proof of this is evident in the two statements by which Francesca concludes her tale, each being enclosed in a single line. The first is but an exclamation, ambiguous and significant at the same time. Its clear purport is the acknowledgment, on Francesca's part, of the role which the reading of that famous medieval romance played in their life, as well as the recognition that that role was identical with the one played by Gallehaut in the story they read not too wisely but too well. The ambiguity lies in the mixed tone of the phrase, conveying a double sense of regret for all the bliss and evil of which that hour was the seed: "Galeotto fu il libro e chi lo scrisse"—"Gallehaut was the book and he who wrote it."

By equating the effect of that reading with the action performed by Gallehaut, by identifying the unknown author of the romance with Gallehaut himself, who still preserves a graceful dignity despite the vileness of his services, Francesca treats the book and its author as if she would like to accuse and to absolve them at the same time. She cannot forget the beauty of the story and the glamor of the characters, since that beauty and that glamor still reflect a kind of redeeming light on the sin they committed at the example of Lancelot and Guinevere. While on one side Francesca tries to emphasize in her story all the aspects that may ennoble her experience, she has still too much sense of responsibility to lay more than part of their guilt on others than Paolo and herself. She knows that she has been more sinning than sinned against; hence she dares not call the romance and its writer by the ugly name of panderers. The reader feels nothing more need be added, yet Francesca has something more to say. Strangely enough, she feels it necessary to allude to what happened after the reading had aroused and bared to them their own "dubious desires." To be sure, the allusion is merely negative in character, and takes the form of another reference to the book which they forgot and discarded, as soon as it had led them to their first kiss: " 'Quel giorno piú non vi leggemmo avante. [That day we read no more therein.]' "

At first sight, the final words of Francesca (since these are her final words) seem to be superfluous, and even to lack propriety: they may sound impudent, or at least too complacent, even more than merely unnecessary. What is Francesca's purpose in telling Dante that they did not read in that book any further? Why unveil so deviously, as well as so brutally, those intimate secrets which even a lost woman prefers to keep hidden? Only a harlot, devoid of the last shred not only of modesty, but even of self-respect, would go so far as to speak of her fall in such cynical terms. There is a difference between unchastity and impurity: a woman may be candid without being shameless. In all her behavior Francesca has consistently shown not only great delicacy of feeling, but also tactfulness and good taste. She has given proof of intellectual and moral courage by facing truth in all its nakedness, yet she has constantly avoided the pitfalls of vulgarity and coarseness. If such is the case, we are forced to conclude that her final words must mean something less

plain and obvious than what they seem to suggest. I am unwilling to
follow the example of some interpreters, who take those words at their
face value. The clue we need is perhaps to be found in the very turn of
the phrases by which Francesca opens and closes the story of her fall.
The first and the last line of that story begin with almost identical words:
"one day," "that day" *(un giorno, quel giorno)*. In the second case the
temporal reference appears to be hardly useful or necessary. It would
have been sufficient to say, "and then we read no further." Yet Francesca feels the need to emphasize that they did not read any further
"that day." These two small words cannot be explained away as a mere
pleonasm, as syllables that are there solely to fill the line. They become
pertinent and relevant, and as such, necessary, only if they are supposed to hint or imply that Paolo and Francesca took up again, on other
occasions, the reading of the book which had been "the first root" of their
sin. Why does Francesca wish to suggest these successive readings, after
the one which was interrupted by their first kiss, on the first day of their
love? Such a question may not be answered, yet it must be asked. The
only thing we need to realize is that Francesca wants us to know that the
two lovers returned on other days to the book which once for all has
acted as their go-between. The reason for this, as for Francesca's indirect reference to such a fact, may be seen in a wish not so much to
recapture the wild happiness of the first, fatal moment, as to recover, if
only for an instant, the idealizing and sublimating illusions which literature creates around the realities of sex and lust. It was the worship of
passion, the ideology of love, its idolatry and cult, which had hidden
from their consciences the danger of damnation and the ugliness of sin;
it was the written word, both harmless and harmful, that had spelled
their doom. Yet they tasted the intoxicating sweetness of that worship
or cult not only before, but even after knowing the bitterness of sin.

Now that Francesca has ended her story, the canto goes rapidly toward its end. At this point, Dante has very little to tell us. He merely
observes that while Francesca had been talking, Paolo had been unashamedly weeping, and implies that his tears did not stop even after she
had ceased to speak. From Dante's manner of speaking, rather than from
what he says, we realize that he must never have taken his eyes from
Francesca's face all the while she had been talking to him: and this is
perhaps the first time he has been able to look into the tearful coun-
tenance of her lover. The echoes of Francesca's words, which still fill and
rend his heart, or perhaps, even more, the pitiful spectacle of Paolo's
grief, are too much for Dante, who breaks down under the stress. The
poet suddenly swoons, and falls down like a dead man:

> Mentre che l' uno spirito questo disse,
> l'altro piangea, sí che di pietade
> io venni men cosí com'io morisse;

e caddi come corpo morto cade.

[While one spirit spoke thus the other wept so that out of pity I grew faint and fell as a dead body falls.]

Dante loses his senses out of compassion, while Paolo and Francesca lost their senses out of passion alone: yet, although caused by sentimental participation rather than by moral complicity, his fall parallels their fall. The almost perfect iambic beat of the line seems to reproduce the thud of his body, which for a while will lie on the earth as a lifeless object, as a soulless thing.

. . . The love story which Dante retells in his own way (which coincides, although only in part, with Francesca's way), is "romantic" in the old-fashioned meaning of that term: a meaning fully preserved in the French adjective *romanesque,* but partly surviving even in the epithet "romantic," to which modern usage has given such a broad semantic range. Medieval culture was full of trends which may be defined as "romantic" in the traditional sense; and it expressed those trends in literary forms which, being essentially anticlassical and new, took for their name the word from which both "romantic" and *romanesque* were to derive, that is, "romance." . . . But Dante dares probe the innermost secrets of both passion and lust: and this is why, instead of contemplating "romantic love" from without, he dares to reconstruct the sinful story of Paolo and Francesca from inside, within the framework of the "romance" itself. Yet, as we shall see later, that framework is used not to re-evoke romantic love, but to exorcise it. . . .

The most relevant document which Dante left imbedded in the canto itself [is] Francesca's manner of speaking, the language and diction she employs in telling her story of passion and death. The heroine makes abundant use of the medieval casuistry of love, and her discourse, far from being spontaneous, is rather deliberately constructed. Her words are, and are meant to be, highly conventional, even rhetorical, in character. This conventionalism is so intentional, and so intense, that we cannot certainly apply to her, and to her speech, the definition that Dante gives elsewhere (*Purgatorio,* xxiv. 52-54) of himself, and of his own poetry of love:

> io mi son un che quando
> amore spira noto, ed a quel modo,
> che ditta dentro vo significando.

[I am one who takes note when love inspires me and expresses it as it is written within me.]

By these words Dante means that when a genuine feeling of love truly inspires a poet's heart, it immediately determines the forms of expression best suited to itself. To do so, that feeling must have some purity and innocence, that love must be a matter of the soul, rather than of the senses. The feeling dictating Francesca's fashionable diction is of a very different sort; at any rate, the love of which she speaks in conventional terms is not necessarily identical with the love which bursts forth through the shell of that diction and often breaks it. When she is less self-conscious, Francesca's passion overflows beyond the barriers of convention, and even of convenance; but generally she tries to keep within the limits of a studied elegance, of a stylized modulation of both thought and speech. And this amounts to saying that one of the outstanding critical hypotheses, the one maintaining that Francesca speaks according to the tenets of the *dolce stil nuovo,* is completely wrong. The point may be proved in many ways: for instance, by arguing that no woman was ever a member of Dante's "circle," or that no feminine character ever speaks in the first person in any of the poems written by the poets of that school. It is true that Francesca's speech is full of literary mannerisms, but it is easier to find among them a few peculiar Provençal traits, than any characteristic features of "the sweet new style." The most typical Provençalism to be found in Francesca's speech is *piacer,* nearer, even linguistically, to the original *plazer,* than its equivalent *piacenza,* normally used before Dante's time by the Italian imitators of the Troubadours. As a matter of fact, Francesca uses the term *piacer* or *plazer* in a novel way, by applying it to masculine, rather than feminine, beauty; and this reference to the good looks of her lover contributes to the almost womanly, or at least, unmanly, impression that Paolo seems to produce.

Even so we must still recognize that the first line of Francesca's confession sounds not merely as a reminiscence, but as a repetition of the main belief of "the sweet new style" school, according to which there is an affinity, nay, an identity, between love and a noble heart. That line, which reads: "Amor ch'al cor gentil ratto s'apprende," seems to be an echo, or rather a replica, of the opening words of the famous *canzone* by Guido Guinicelli: "Al cor gentil ripara sempre amore," which the young Dante had paraphrased in the beginning of a famous sonnet of the *Vita Nuova:* "Amore e il cor gentil sono una cosa. [Love is one with the gentle heart.]"

Yet, if my reading of the episode is right, I feel that despite their verbal identities Francesca's statement and the passages just quoted have different, even opposite, meanings. As used by Francesca, *amore* and *cor gentile* signify an experience and a reality that cannot be compared, except in contrast, with the ideals and values those two formulae designate in the language of Guinicelli and Dante. When these two poets connect those two concepts, they intend to say that the spiritual power of love finds its natural abode in a heart made noble by its own merits and virtues. But when Francesca makes the same connection, she means instead that passional love is the calling and destiny of every heart which is noble in this word's literal sense, that is, made such by the gentility of its blood. This is the way Francesca feels, as is proved by the manner in which she speaks about herself and of her own passion and person, or alludes to Paolo, whom she implicitly defines *cotanto amante*, "so great a lover," by so defining Lancelot. One must not forget that the notary Guinicelli, and that Dante, who was officially a member of the medical guild, were respectively citizens of Bologna and Florence, of two free communes, of two democratic commonwealths. Their very conception of love, despite its aristocratic origins, reflects already the cultural awareness of the new burghers' class. The "sweet new style" reacts against the feudal ideology of the Troubadours and their disciples, who believed literally in the doctrine of courtly love, and considered it a privilege of the highly placed and the well born. But Francesca was the member of a family that tried to reduce the city of Ravenna into its own fief, and the pride of her birth and station induces her to prefer the Provençal view. That view had survived the decline of Provençal poetry and culture, and had found new expression in the prose fiction of Northern France, where an equally refined, but less spiritual, sort of love was still considered as the exclusive privilege of knights and dames, of men and women of great breeding and lineage. For Dante and his group love will always remain a matter of election and grace, based on the reciprocal sympathy of two lofty souls; and the poet rephrases this doctrine in a famous passage in the *Purgatorio* (xxii. 10-12), through the following words attributed to Virgil:

> ". . . Amore,
> acceso di virtù, sempre altro accese,
> pur che la fiamma sua paresse fuore;"

[". . . Love by virtue kindled always kindles another, provided only that it show its flame;"]

It has been suggested that these lines are meant as a kind of retractation of the principle embodied in the line where Francesca speaks of the fatality of love, of its refusal to absolve any person being loved from loving in return (*amor ch' a nullo amato amar perdona*); but the hypothesis seems to be groundless. Through the words just quoted Dante qualifies in a higher ethical sense the doctrine of his youth, his own belief in the reciprocity of spiritual love. As for Francesca's statement, no palinode was required, exactly because its equivocal meaning is clarified by the moral lesson contained in the entire episode. No correction was in this case necessary since, despite all appearances, even when using the same verbal expressions, she does not speak the language of Dante, or of all the poets who, as he said in another canto of the *Purgatorio* (xxvi. 99), "rime d'amor usar dolci e leggiadre."

Nor, despite the Provençal mannerisms of her speech, have we any right to deduce that Francesca's manner of speaking is an echo of the diction of the Troubadours. Only Dante himself may help us to find the literary models and the stylistic examples after which he patterned Francesca's discourse. He offers such a help in another part of the canto just mentioned, where he affirms that Arnaut Daniel was the best craftsman of the vernacular word (*Purgatorio,* xxvi. 117-119), and surpassed all his rivals in both "versi d'amore e prose di romanzi."

With this simple line, Dante sums up all the main forms of the literature in the vulgar tongue, as it had developed at that time in Tuscany and in Italy, as well as in Provence and France. He obviously considers only the forms endowed with formal dignity, addressed to a literate and nonpopular audience, dealing in different ways with the same great medieval theme, which, for the intellectual as well as for the social élite, was the theme of love. There is no doubt that Francesca's speech must be patterned on either one of these two main forms. It is true that Francesca's language is highly literary in character, and has very little to do with popular speech: its very sophistication and complexity stand out against the background of the simple style used by Dante in the narrative parts of the canto, and in the whole of his poem. Yet this does not mean that Francesca's manner of speaking is necessarily poetic, especially in the lyrical sense. We have already stated that that language differs from the style which Dante himself called both "sweet" and "new"; and one may add, not too paradoxically, that, although Dante shapes her words and thoughts into the rhythmical and metrical structure of the *Commedia,* she speaks not in verse but in prose. Thus, by making use of the line quoted above, one could say that her forms of expression derive not from the tradition of the poetry of love (*versi d'amore*), either in the *lingua del sì* or the *langue d'hoc,* but from the tradition of love fiction (*prose di romanzi*) in the *langue d'oïl.* After all, the name "Francesca" means nothing else but "French." Dante's heroine translates into her own terms the idiom she has learned from such French literary sources as the romance of Lancelot,[1] hence the formal conventionality, the rhetor-

---

[1] There is no doubt that Dante read the French medieval romances in the original language. As for Paolo and Francesca, they must have read their *libro galeotto* in the same tongue: for, "if an Italian translation of *Tristan* was already extant from the thirteenth century, there is no proof that Lancelot had been granted the same fortune: moreover, and this is what matters most . . . French . . . was then the courtly language par excellence in the Italian North," according to Pio Rajna's statement in his article "Dante e i romanzi della Tavola Rotonda," *Nuova Antologia,* 1157 (1 June 1920). The same problem had been studied before Rajna by Paget Toynbee, in his essay "Dante and the Lancelot Romance," *Fifth Annual Report of the Dante Society of America,* Cambridge, Mass. (1886), and, more fully, in his *Ricerche e Note Dantesche*

ical stylization, of her speech. Almost dialectically, that conventionality and that stylization transform themselves into their very opposites, becoming thus the aptest instrument, the most natural vehicle of which Francesca could avail herself not only to relate her story, but even to idealize and sublimate it.

This general imitation of the tone of the romantic narratives she used to admire so much does not mean that Francesca imitates in any special way the particular language of the romance of Lancelot, nor that, while

---

(Bologna, 1904); after Rajna, by Nicola Zingarelli, in his article "Le reminiscenze dal 'Lancelot,' " in *Studi Danteschi*, 1, 82-90.

All these studies deal in detail not only with the relevant lines in this canto, but also with another famous passage of the *Commedia* connected with the Lancelot romance, to which I have already referred in the present essay. This passage is to be found in *Paradiso*, xvi. 13-15, and reads thus:

> onde Beatrice, ch'era un poco scevra,
> ridendo, parve quella che tossío
> al primo fallo scritto di Ginevra.

[Thereat Beatrice, who was smiling, standing somewhat apart, seemed like her who coughed at Guinevere's first sin written down.]

Here Dante alludes to the same chapter of the Lancelot romance to which Francesca refers in *Inferno*, v; but now he recalls merely a minor incident, preceding the climax of the chapter, which is the kiss exchanged between Lancelot and Guinevere. The one "who coughed" is the Dame de Malehaut, who is also in the grove, during the nightly meeting of the Knight and the Queen. The Dame is still in love with Lancelot, who was once her prisoner, although he pretends to have forgotten it. Pio Rajna (*op. cit.*) explains the reference, and its connection with the present situation, in the following way:

"By coughing, and thus recalling back to herself the attention of Lancelot, the Dame de Malehaut warns him that she is nearby, and makes him understand that the secret he has been so jealously keeping (i.e., his love for the Queen) is no longer a secret for her. Likewise Beatrice, after having withdrawn a little aside, as feeling estranged from the worldly conversation between Cacciaguida and his descendant, with her laughter recalls Dante to the awareness of her presence, so that he may watch himself; and at the same time warns him that the reason of that proud *voi* had not escaped her."

(Dante, who at first addresses his ancestor with "tu," shifts to the more respectful "voi" as soon as he learns Cacciaguida had been knighted before his death.)

I have discussed this passage in detail only to have the opportunity of commenting on the highly interesting closing line of the terzina, "al primo fallo scritto di Ginevra." These words are clearly a definition of the crucial chapter of the Lancelot romance; i.e., of the scene ending with the first kiss of the two lovers. The presence of the adjective *primo* may, in our context, throw some light on one of the most famous lines of *Inferno*, v, which is precisely "quel giorno piú non vi leggemmo avante": and make perhaps more valid my interpretation of that line. Even more significant is Dante's description of the romance itself as a *fallo scritto*, as a "sin written down," exactly because such a description sounds like an explicit replica of the moral judgment about romantic literature which this canto states implicitly, and which Francesca herself sums up in the words: "Galeotto fu il libro e chi lo scrisse."

re-evoking the effect provoked by the reading of that romance, the poet patterned the story of its two readers after the most important episode of the romance itself. Immoral literature may influence life, but not in such a way as to pattern life after itself. When she establishes an apparently perfect parallel between the two "first" kisses, the one exchanged between Lancelot and Guinevere, and the one exchanged between Paolo and herself, Francesca gives the impression of remembering the one as fully as the other: yet Dante knows that she is wrong. The parallelism she implies is partial or relative; and one could say that she unconsciously reshapes the literary kiss to make it better agree with the real one. In other terms, she recollects what she did experience far better than what she did read. Her words mislead the reader (if not the poet) into believing that Lancelot and Guinevere too were "alone and without any suspicion" (*soli e senza alcun sospetto*), while, in their meeting in the grove at night, they were not only accompanied by Gallehaut, but also attended by the Queen's ladies in waiting, who were lingering nearby. What is even more important is that in the book it is the woman, and not the man, who kisses first. As a matter of fact, while the romance fails to mention that the Knight returned the Queen's kiss, Francesca does the same in regard to her response to Paolo's embrace. The parallel is partly one also of contrast, and the implication of this is so obviously suggestive that we do not need to dwell upon it. These details may however point out that Dante cared more for the spirit than for the letter of his text; and this scorn for literalness must be certainly taken into account also in regard to what we have said about his decision to let Francesca speak according to the diction of the love romances.

The very fact that the poet does not adopt the same diction himself, and fails to use it fully in those passages where the character speaking in the first person is not Francesca, but the protagonist of his own poem, clearly shows that even Dante the character avoids involving his own views and values in the language employed by his heroine. The man writing this canto is no longer the young literary enthusiast who once liked so much the French romances so dear to all the Paolos and the Francescas as to define them *Arthuri regis ambages pulcherrimae,* as he did in a famous passage of *De Vulgari Eloquio,* where however the word *ambages* is rather equivocal, and may mean "fancies," as well as "adventures."[2] Here Dante uses the language of the romances almost critically, or rather, as a dramatic device, through which he projects the psychology of Francesca, and within which he encloses her personality as within a shell. Francesco de Sanctis recognized the magnificent total result of Dante's vision and perspective, while ignoring the process or the method by which that result was achieved. In other words, he paid attention to

---

[2] The passage quoted from *De Vulgari Eloquio* may be found in I, x, 2. The double meaning of *ambages* is discussed by Pio Rajna, who prefers interpreting that word in its figurative, rather than in its literal sense.

the natural effects, rather than to the artificial components, of Francesca's speech. It is perhaps for this reason that he was led to interpret the canto in tragic, rather than in *romanesque* terms. Yet this was at least in part a happy mistake, because it saved him from the far more serious error of reading Francesca's words in lyrical key. With his profound insight, the great critic felt that, despite all appearances, Francesca speaks not only outside the frame of reference of "the new sweet style," but in opposition to it. This is what he means when he says that Francesca, "this first-born daughter of Dante," is also "the first truly living woman to appear on the poetic horizon of the modern age." Although readily admitting that such a figure could be created only after "a long elaboration of the feminine ideal in the poetry of the Troubadours and in the very lyrics of Dante," he ends by saying that Francesca is the opposite of Beatrice. Within the poetic tradition from which the latter derives, "man fills the stage with himself; it is he who acts, and speaks, and dreams; while woman remains in the background, named and not represented, like Selvaggia and Mandetta; she stays there as man's shadow, as a thing he owns, as an object he has wrought, as the being issued from his rib, devoid of a separate personality of her own." [3]

. . . The last clue is a negative one: Paolo's silence, and the significance of that silence. Paolo has no existence of his own. He speaks no word during the entire episode; and even when Francesca refers to her lover, the poet pays no attention to him. Dante seems to notice his presence only at the end, and does so only to remark that Paolo must have been weeping for a long time. It was natural for the poet to place Francesca in the foreground of the episode, and Paolo in its background; yet this fails to explain the poet's almost absolute indifference to the lesser of these two protagonists. Such an indifference is not casual, but deliberate. Dante's scorn is not directed toward Paolo as a separate person, but toward what he stands for; and as such it involves all men who, like him, are the slaves, rather than the masters, of love. The passionate man, hardly ever as interesting or suggestive as the passionate woman, is never called hero, while many a woman in love is a heroine. It is said that love exalts the lowly, and humbles the lofty ones; but this is true only in the

[3] This passage . . . is quoted from the most important of all Francesco de Sanctis' Dante essays, and is given as translated by me. De Sanctis originally published that essay in 1869, under the title *Francesca da Rimini secondo i critici e secondo l'arte.* The essay was later included in the collection of his *Saggi Critici.* The text used here is the one reprinted in the 1952 Laterza edition of *Saggi Critici* (VII, 240-256). Though disagreeing with de Sanctis' view, I still feel that his critique of the Paolo and Francesca episode is a masterpiece. Anything the great critic had to say about the *Commedia,* even beyond the famous pages in his *Storia della Letteratura Italiana,* is worth rereading. Such a task can now be easily done, since the Einaudi edition of the *Opere di Francesco de Sanctis,* made under the direction of Carlo Muscetta, has just devoted its 5th volume (Turin, 1955) to the *Lezioni e Saggi su Dante.*

sense that the first is the feminine, and the second the masculine alternative. Especially in love is "the female of the species more deadly than the male." For man, even more than for woman, love is almost always a *liaison dangereuse*. Either one of the two actors or victims of a love story will look pathetic to the eyes of mankind, but while pathos may enhance a woman's personality, it lessens man's stature. A pathetic hero is a contradiction in terms, since he is made to look not only unheroic, but even unmanly. This Dante understood well: so, while raising Francesca to prominence, he reduced Paolo almost to nought. De Sanctis recognized this very well: "Who is Paolo? He is not the man, or the manly type, such as to form an antithesis, to establish a dualism. Francesca fills the stage wholly with herself. Paolo is the mute expression of Francesca; the string trembling at what she says, the gesture accompanying her voice. The one speaks while the other weeps; the tears of the one are the words of the other."

This statement, a perfect aesthetic justification of Dante's conception, implies that the main character of the episode absorbs the lesser one; that its protagonist is this couple of lovers, even more than Francesca herself; that the two lovers form a single personality though such a personality is shaped by its feminine component, rather than by its masculine one. In this very conception Dante shows outstanding originality. No poet went as far as Dante in this reduction to a cipher of the masculine partner of a great passion. Considered alone, Paolo, a bleak pale creature whose only action is weeping, pales nearly to a vanishing point. Love changes man into woman's shadow, and this is true of Paolo not only as the ghost he now is, but as the man he once was. Francesca projects the memory of herself even before the time of her fatal affair, but evokes her lover only during the moment of their sin. And, unconsciously, she fixes him forever in a vision of passive pusillanimity. At least in appearance she describes him in the very moment he acted like a man: when he took the initiative, as he was supposed to do, and kissed her on her mouth. Yet Francesca finds it fit to remember that even in that instant of daring he was trembling in every fiber of his body, like a leaf. Commenting upon the simple and terrible words, *tutto tremante,* by which Francesca recalls the emotions of her lover in that moment of anguish and bliss, Francesco de Sanctis is led to observe that "certainly Paolo's flesh did not tremble out of fright." I am not so sure: I may even be ready to maintain exactly the opposite. Paolo perhaps trembled because he was afraid: of woman and love, or of death and of sin; or simply of the unknown, even of his own fear itself. In this passivity and pusillanimity Paolo strangely resembles the hero to whom Francesca and the poet liken him. In the second of the two romances of which he is the protagonist, *Le Chevalier de la Charrette,* Lancelot is described as willing to look like a coward, and even to risk infamy, merely to pursue his love object; while in *Lancelot du Lac* the Queen kisses him first, as soon as she realizes that he does not dare to do so himself; and, as the text states with comical naïveté, she gives herself the illusion of being the receiver rather than the giver, by taking the knight by his chin: "Et la roine voit bien que li chevaliers n'en ose plus fere; si le prent pour let menton et le base" (xxxi).

All this may suffice to prove not only that Francesca towers above Paolo, but that the poet towers above both. As I have frequently hinted, this cannot be said of Dante the character, whom the author, with great humility and charity, equates with the lesser part of his double creation. This happens at the very ending of the episode, when the reader witnesses at the same time, in two different men, almost the same heartbreak. It is at this point that we suddenly realize that Paolo had been unashamedly sobbing for the entire duration of Francesca's speech; and immediately after this, we learn that Dante has fainted as soon as Francesca has uttered her last word. For a while, at the close of the canto, Dante the character becomes thus the equal of Paolo, and even of Lancelot, who for a while seems to swoon himself, while talking with the Queen of his still unrewarded love. In this brief moment, Dante himself is but a creature of pathos, a victim of pity and self-pity, like Paolo and Lancelot. Dante the poet stops short of the ridiculous, but it is only the timely fall of the curtain which saves the final scene of the episode from an unexpected caricatural effect.

All this amounts to saying that love cannot ever be the tragic passion par excellence. Tolstoy acknowledged as much when he attributed the following words to Konstantin Levin, the masculine protagonist of *Anna Karenina:* "To my mind, love . . . both sorts of love, which you remember Plato defines in his *Banquet,* serve as the test of men. Some men only understand one sort, and some only the other. And those who only know the non-Platonic love have no need to talk of tragedy. . . . In Platonic love there can be no sort of tragedy . . . because in that love all is clear and pure because. . . . But perhaps you are right. Very likely . . . I don't know. I don't know." [4]

Unlike Tolstoy and his hero, Dante was one of those few human beings equally able to understand both kinds of love; and he understood them both as a man and as a poet. He was able to understand the kind of love which stops at the "sweet sighs," and which is generally expressed in lyric form, as well as the kind that experiences the "dubious desires," and manifests itself in romantic fiction. In the same way he understood that neither kind can be tragic. Dante is a moral realist, always subordinating pathos to ethos. So it is improper to interpret the episode of Paolo and Francesca in the light of the romantic view of poetry and life, as de Sanctis did, or according to the decadent view as did Gabriele D'Annunzio in his *Francesca da Rimini.* The latter is not a tragedy, but merely a "poem

[4] Pt. i, Ch. xi (as translated by Constance Garnett).

of blood and lust" (*poema di sangue e di lussuria*), as the author himself so aptly said.[5] In the same way, while using continuously, and almost exclusively, the criterion of tragedy, Francesco de Sanctis gave us an interpretation of the Paolo and Francesca episode far more pathetic than tragic. "Sin is the highest pathos of tragedy, since this contradiction (between the sense of sin and the erotic impulse) is placed not without, but within the two lovers' souls," says the critic, thus reducing the situation to a psychological crisis, even more than to a moral conflict. It is in "the sweet thoughts," even more than in "the dubious desires," that de Sanctis sees "the tragic core of the story, the divine tragedy left unsaid on Francesca's lips, and which only Dante's reverie, so movingly imagined, calls forth and re-enacts," thus showing that he conceives the fall and the ruin of the two lovers in sentimental terms. De Sanctis concludes his analysis by affirming that "pity is the muse of this tragedy, which the poet unfolds only in its main lines, filling the rest with silence and mystery. . . ." But tragedy is made not only of pathos and pity, but also of ethos and terror. A full study of de Sanctis' essay reveals that the critic is reading their episode not in the light of tragedy, but in the light of romantic drama: as a story of love and death, stirring our emotions and feelings rather than our moral sense, as an effusion of sentiment, so pure as to need no catharsis. There is no doubt that this canto is based on an interplay of passion and compassion: yet neither one nor the other, not even their synthesis, can be taken at its face value.

I have already stated that Dante wrote the episode in the key of the love romances, but even this needs qualification, and cannot be taken for granted. In what he did, Dante went beyond not only the form he chose, but also beyond the sentiment which normally inspires or dictates that form. The love romance is primarily, but not exclusively, a medieval genre, so that it recurs even in modern literature, where it changes its style, replacing the convention of fancy with the conventions of realism, and taking the name and the shape of the novel, or of other types of fiction. Yet the new product will remain a love romance if it still expresses sentiment without judging it. This is certainly not the case with such a work as *Anna Karenina,* where the writer condemns his heroine at least by implication, by referring her judgment to the tribunal of God. Such is the sense of the scriptural epigraph that Tolstoy placed at the head of his novel: "Vengeance is mine; I will repay, saith the Lord" (Romans xii.19). Yet the same epigraph would be at least partly improper if placed at the head of this canto, since it would reflect solely the standpoint of Dante the character. In this episode, as in the entire *Commedia,* God has already taken his vengeance, and Dante is a witness of this. Paolo and Francesca have been condemned to everlasting death, to the damnation of their souls: when faced with such a revelation, the

---

[5] In the "Commiato," or "Farewell Song," which precedes the play.

best man can do is silently to bow his head. Yet Dante is not to be satisfied with this, and gives to God's verdict the assent of his own conscience,
even if he does so without words. Though verbally unstated, Dante's
judgment is framed in literary terms; his moral message is implicit in
the situation and the structure of the story, so that no further intervention on the poet's part is required to make it meaningful to us.

Dante achieves this result by a dialectical treatment of the romance
form—by what one might call a double mirror trick. There is no doubt
that the poet derived the idea that the reading of the Lancelot romance
had been "the first root" of the passion and ruin of the two lovers, not
on the authority of any external tradition, but solely on the inner urg-
ings of his own imagination. If the "how" and "why" of Francesca's fall
is an invention of Dante's, then its supposed occasion becomes highly
suggestive and significant. The real kiss of Paolo and Francesca follows
the imaginary kiss of Lancelot and Guinevere, as an image reflecting its
object in a perspective similar and different at the same time. In brief,
the seduction scene fulfills within the entire episode the function of a
play within a play: more properly, of a romance within a romance. This
creates an effect of parody, or, if we prefer to use a less negative term,
something akin to what in modern times has been called "romantic
irony," which in this case operates in an antiromantic sense. This means
that the two romances, one of which may be likened to a frame, and the
other to the picture enclosed therein, react reciprocally in such a way as
to annihilate each other. In his analysis of *Madame Bovary,* starting
from the presupposition that the modern novel is but an offspring of the
ancient romance, and that originally the former was but a love story like
the latter (as proved by the fact that in French both are still called by
the same name), Albert Thibaudet ends by saying that Flaubert's masterpiece is in reality a *contre-roman.*[6] In the same way, the "romance" of
Paolo and Francesca becomes in Dante's hands an "antiromance," or
rather, both things at once. As such, it is able to express and to judge
romantic love at the same time. While Dante the character manifests
his sorrowful regret through the mute eloquence of his bewilderment,
and later of his swoon, so Dante the poet expresses his judgment without
uttering a word, without even a gesture or a sign of reproof or reproach.
Dante does not preach or plead, nor does he need to superimpose an
edifying sermon on the structure of his story. His ethical message may
be easily read not in the spirit, but in the very letter of his tale. It is
Francesca herself that he entrusts with the literary moral of his fable.
This moral is very simple, and could be summed up in the statement
that writing and reading romantic fiction is almost as bad as yielding to
romantic love. This obvious and almost naïve truth is all contained in
the famous line, "Galeotto fu il libro e chi lo scrisse," by which, as Fran-

[6] In his *Réflections sur le Roman,* passim.

cesco D'Ovidio says, the poet confesses his horrified feeling at the thought that he too "could become a Gallehaut to somebody else." [7] But there is no reason for such a fear, since that line helps to destroy the very suggestion on which it is built. It is with traits like this that the poet created this masterpiece, based on the avoidance of tragedy,[8] as well as on the moral sublimation of the romance form.

[7] *Nuovi Studii Danteschi,* II (Milan, 1907), 531.

[8] This concept was first used by Erich Heller, in his article "Goethe on the Avoidance of Tragedy" in *The Disinherited Mind: Essays in Modern German Literature* (Philadelphia, 1952).

Speech and Language in *Inferno* XIII

by Leo Spitzer

The most recent commentary on this canto is that of Grandgent;[1] below are the lines in which he sums up the episode of Pier delle Vigne and treats of the language of the canto:

The style of this canto abounds in curious conceits, such as the

Cred'io ch'ei credette ch'io credesse

[I think that he thought that I thought]

of l. 25, the "infiammati infiammar [The inflamed did inflame]" of l. 68, the double antithesis of l. 69, and the involved paradoxes of the following tiercet. It would seem that meditation over Pier delle Vigne, who dominates the canto, had filled our poet with the spirit of the older school, so that, either purposely or unconsciously, he imitated its artistic processes. Pier delle Vigne's epistolary style is highly artificial and flowery.

The suicide uses his freedom of bodily movement only to deprive himself of it, robbing himself, by his own act, of that which corporeally distinguishes him from a plant. Such a sinner, then, his wicked deed eternalized, may aptly be figured as a tree or bush. Dante's self-slaughterers form a thick, wild forest in the second ring of the seventh circle. There, upon hearing their sentence from Minos, they fall at random, in no predestined spot: they have put themselves outside of God's law, rebelling against his eternal plan. On the Day of Judgment they will return, with the rest, for their earthly remains; but, instead of putting on the flesh again, they will drag their corpses through Hell and hang them on their boughs, where the poor bodies will dangle forever, a torment to the souls that slew them. The pent-up agony of these spirits finds no means of expression until they are broken in leaf or branch; then the voice issues forth with tears of blood.

The like had been seen and heard by Aeneas in a Thracian grove, when, to deck an altar, he unwittingly plucked shrubs from the grave of Polydorus:

"Speech and Language in *Inferno* XIII," by Leo Spitzer. (Dedicated to James Eustace Shaw.) From *Italica* XIX, 3 (September 1942). Copyright 1942 by *Italica*. Reprinted by permission of the publisher and of the author's literary executrix.

[1] For the bibliography, as far as not specifically mentioned, v. Grandgent. I consulted also E. Auerbach, "Dante als Dichter der irdischen Welt"; K. Vossler, "Die göttliche Komödie," 2d ed. (Heidelberg 1925); Croce, "Dantes Dichtung" (translation of Schlosser). I am indebted for various suggestions to my pupils with whom I read the canto in class: A. Bianchini, E. Fenimore, F. J. Powers. [L. S.]

blood trickled from the severed roots, and a voice came forth—not from the tree, as in Dante, but from the mound (Aen., III, 39 ff.):—

> Gemitus lacrimabilis imo
> Auditur tumulo, et vox reddita fertur ad aures:
> Quid miserum Aenea, laceras? Jam parce sepulto,
> Parce pias scelerare manus. Non me tibi Troja
> Externum tulit. Haud cruor hic de stipite manat.

[From beneath the mound is heard a pitiful moan, and a voice from it is carried to my ears: "Alas, why do you tear me, Aeneas? Spare me now in my tomb, spare pollution to your pious hands. Troy bore me; I am not foreign to you, nor is this blood that oozes from the stem."]

In the suicides' wood, an outlet for the mournful voice is afforded by harpies, voracious, filthy birds with maidens' faces, which rend the foliage. They may well represent misgiving or fear of the hereafter—"triste annunzio di futuro danno."

Thus Grandgent (like other commentators, as we shall see) explains the particular devices of style in this canto as due to an association in the mind of Dante with the speech habits to be found in the writings of the historical character Pier delle Vigne. While not denying the existence of such an external association, I shall seek to establish a deeper motivation for Dante's choice of language.

First let us consider the treatment of the main motif: the fate of the suicides who are condemned to assume the shape of plants. As D'Ovidio points out, Dante has borrowed not only from Virgil but also from the author of the *Metamorphoses*: the *uomo-pianta* created by the Christian poet recalls Driope or Lotis or the Heliads (*Uomini fummo, ed or siam fatti sterpi* [We were men and now we are made brush]). This critic, however, points out the difference between an Ovidian and a Dantean metamorphosis, as regards the actual process itself through which metamorphosis is achieved: when, in Ovid, a living person "becomes" a plant (feet stiffening into roots, hair turning into foliage, etc.) there is a continuous identity between the person-as-a-whole and the plant into which he is transformed. But in the case of the suicides treated by Dante, there can, obviously, be no such continuity: it is not the person-as-a-whole, an indivisible unit of body and soul, that becomes a new kind of being; body and soul have been divorced by the act of self-murder and it is the soul alone that survives. These souls bereft of body go to be judged by Minos; wherever they have chanced to fall, there they put out new roots and grow themselves a new body—an ersatz body of meaner stuff to replace the human body from which they have been severed. Thus, in Dante, there is no "development," properly speaking: the soul itself continues to exist without change, while the life of the body is utterly destroyed—its possibility of growth, even into another form, cut off: the second body, the plant-like body, has no ties with the first, but is the product of a new birth that takes place only after death has severed the first body from the soul. Thus, because Dante is dealing here (as, indeed, throughout the *Inferno*) with the fate meted out to the souls of dead men, there can be none of that delicate tracing of transitory intermediate stages in which Ovid delighted, where it is possible to fix that certain moment of perplexity when the living person is no longer human and yet not quite plant or animal; the most famous of all such moments, commemorated by so many artists, is that of Daphne *becoming* a tree (cf. also, in the metamorphosis of Actaeon, the lines "Gemit ille, sonumque,/*Etsi non hominis, quem non tamen edere possit/Cervus* [He moaned in a way which was not human, nor was it the utterance of a deer]").

So much for the process of which the plant-man is the product: what of the product itself and its behavior? Here too Dante differs from Ovid: his *uomo-pianta*, in fact, is a composite of features drawn from both Ovid and Virgil: from the first, obviously, derives the concept of a person being transformed, though by a different process, into a plant (this is not Virgilian: Polydorus does not *become* the myrtle tree[2]); from the second derives the incident in which a plant is stripped of a branch, and a voice, though not that of the tree, protests in pain: from Virgil Dante borrowed a segment of epic activity.[3] These separate borrowings fuse (in an artistic

---

[2] And yet, although no actual metamorphosis is involved in the Polydorus incident, there is a trace of such an idea in the description of the conformation of the myrtle, "*densis hastilibus horrida myrtus* [A myrtle harsh with dense sticks]": this easily suggests a picture of the legendary Polydorus "shot through" with arrows; cf. *hic confixum ferrea texit telorum segetes et iaculis increvit acutis* [Here I am covered and pierced with a harvest of weapons that grow in sharp javelins].

[3] D'Ovidio points out that, in addition to its exterior relationship with the Polydorus episode, this canto reveals an interior association: the guide Virgil, this Dantean character, is at the same time the historic Virgil, author of the *Aeneid*, and it is to his own epic poem that he is referring, when he speaks of *la mia rima:*

> "S'egli avesse potuto creder prima"
> Rispuose il savio mio, "anima lesa,
> Ciò c'ha veduto pur con la mia rima,
> Non averebbe in te la man distesa."

[My sage replied, "O wounded soul, if he might have believed what he had seen only in my verses, he would not have stretched out his hand against you."]

In these lines, which follow upon Dante's act of tearing off the twig, Virgil chides him for his failure to take seriously to heart the account of Polydorus' fate, as found in the *Aeneid:* if only Dante had believed, he would have been forewarned as to the consequences of mutilating the bush. I should add that, in view of the strong medieval tradition concerning the Christian potentialities of the *Aeneid*, we are justified in giving an even deeper meaning to the "lack of faith" for which Virgil upbraids Dante: the latter has failed to realize the implication of the Polydorus incident, that this prefigures the judgment visited upon a sinner by the Christian God (Virgil himself seems, for a moment at least, to have been astounded by the Christian replica of his Polydorus scene

metamorphosis) to give us something unknown either to Ovid or Virgil: a plant that bleeds and speaks. This creature is "very man and very plant": in its growth from a "seed" it has aped the birth and organic growth of a plant; yet this plant not only bleeds (this in itself and other similar phenomena may be found in Ovid), but reveals the anguished workings of a human mind and heart. It represents, then, something quite different from the creations of Ovid, such as Driope and her like: with the latter we have to do only with a plant that was once a human being; there is no painful insistence that this creature, after its metamorphosis, is both plant and human. But the plant-man Piero is described as a vegetal body which is capable of physiological manifestations and in which human consciousness survives unabated: this hybrid creation of Dante is more *monstrously* hybrid than anything to be encountered among the ancients.[4]

—this is the meaning I am tempted to ascribe to the line . . . *la cosa incredibile mi fece indurlo* . . . [the incredible thing made me suggest it to him . . .]).

As to the relationship existing between the pilgrim Dante and his guide, I believe that D'Ovidio puts a false emphasis on the personal vanity which Virgil the author betrays: this is too modernistic an interpretation. Nor am I able to follow this commentator when he would compare Virgil to a professor of medicine, who demonstrates to his pupil a "beautiful clinical case," while maintaining a humorous aloofness from the suffering of the patient. Olschki (v. *infra*, Appendix) would emphasize the aloofness of Virgil with regard both to Piero and Dante; these last two form a pair (a pair of politicians), according to Olschki, and there takes place between them a "spiritual drama" from which Virgil disassociates himself. I should object that it is rather Virgil and Dante who form a pair—a pair of poets: it is thus that Piero sees them (*E se di voi alcun nel mondo riede, Conforti la memoria mia* . . . [And if one of you returns to the world, comfort my memory . . .]). There is no evidence whatsoever that Virgil feels no interest in his pupil—or that he feels no sympathy for Piero: he shows evident concern for the rehabilitation of Piero's reputation, which Dante shall undertake (thus whatever entente exists between Piero and Dante has been encouraged by Virgil!). In the end, then, there is no strict arrangement of two against one: Virgil, while more intimately connected with his pupil, feels for Piero, and at the same time, would further the association of Piero and Dante. Cf. the slightly divergent triangle of poets in the Brunetto Latini episode where Virgil effaces himself lovingly, but never loses sight of his pupil.

[4] It is quite true that ancient literature offers examples of creatures that are just as *unequivocally* hybrid as are Dante's plant-men—viz. the Centaurs, half men and half beasts. But the blend of animal and human is in itself less repugnant than that of plant and human: indeed the ancients, who did not reject hybridism *in se,* could represent the Centaurs as essentially noble beings (even Dante, who in canto XI, has them, with their "bestial" form, symbolize the sin of bestiality, must speak respectfully of *il gran Chirone, il quale nudrì Achille* [The great Chiron who raised Achilles]). The undoubted loathsomeness of those bird-women, the Harpies, is hardly a case in point: the horror with which these were regarded by the Greeks was due, not to the fact itself of their hybridism, but to the blend of the beautiful (*virginei facies*) with the hideous which they offered. To Dante, on the other hand, they probably represented perversions, *qua* blends: he does not insist on the disturbing beauty of their faces, replacing *virginei* by *umani:* to him the main significance of these creatures lay precisely in their blend of the animal and the *human.*

And this must needs be so, since to the medieval Christian poet the concept of hybridism is, in itself, repellent. The Christian system does not recognize "evolution of species": the species are neatly delimited according to a hierarchic order which purports to know the fixed and once-for-ever established *dignitates, proprietates* and *virtutes* of man, animal, plant, and mineral. Hybrid creation is outside of the natural plan of God; and, at the hands of Dante, it becomes, according to the law of the *contrappasso,* a symbol of sin and punishment—of punishment for the "anti-natural" sin of suicide by which the God-willed connection between body and soul has been broken. This plant-man, then, is no picture of a happy solidarity between natural man and animated nature but, on the contrary, of a tragic captivity of the soul (*anima incarcerata*) in a minor form of nature; by the creation (after the death of the body) of this monster which combines the human and the non-human, the poet succeeds in demonstrating the gulf that exists in nature between the human and the non-human. Thus the whole spirit of the Dantean metamorphosis is opposed to that of Ovid: the pagan poet with his pantheistic love for nature (of which man is a part), who could discover a nymph in every fountain, a dryad in every tree, was able to see in metamorphosis only the principle of the eternal change of forms in nature—animating this by the fiction of past human passion and grief, describing the whole "con copia e grazia tra boccaccesca e ariostea [with a fullness and grace somewhere between that of Boccaccio and that of Ariosto]" (D'Ovidio). It could be said that in Ovid the (gradual) transformation of a human into a vegetal being seems to take place almost *naturally;* but with Dante the link between nature and man has been broken by a tragic-minded Christianity; where Ovid offers to our view the richness of organic nature, Dante shows the inorganic, the hybrid, the perverted, the sinful, the damned. A metamorphosis at the hands of Dante must be, not graceful, in the way of Boccaccio and Ariosto, but tragic—in the way of Dante.

But while an Ovidian metamorphosis is presented as "natural," it is perhaps less "real" than that of Dante. Ovid is dealing with legendary lore which he retells *as if* he believed; his fabulations play in a remote past and they have the patina of a legend. But the two subjects of Dante's metamorphosis, Pier delle Vigne and the anonymous suicide, were near-contemporaries of the poet: they appear in his poem as belonging to the eternally present and as illustrating the judgment of God that is universally true—"de te fabula narratur." And the fate of these two in the other world is presented by Dante not as legend but as reality[5]: the real

---

[5] There is a great gulf between the belief of a Dante in the objective reality of expiation (even though the nature of the manifold punishments be shaped by his imagination) and the almost whimsical attitude of a Hawthorne, who writes romantic novels of expiation. The representations of this novelist (who was acquainted with the punishment-by-*contrappasso* of both Bunyan and Dante) are tempered with an "as if," or an "as it were": he raises questions that invite new possibilities of interpretation, he in-

judgment that God has in store for the soul of the sinner *in statu ani-marum post mortem* [In the state of the souls after death]; it is described in terms more graphic and more convincing than those of the ancient tales. De Sanctis has emphasized the directness of Dante's narration: he eschews the elegant impressionism of Virgilian devices which serve to anticipate, and thus to soften, the impact of events (*Mihi frigidus*

---

troduces suggestions meant to anticipate the "smile" of the sophisticated modern reader. There is not with him the firmness of design that characterizes the work of Dante; whereas the medieval poet affirms unhesitatingly always the *one* inevitable consequence of a sin, Hawthorne seems willfully to attenuate the very correspondence he has established between sin and punishment, offering this as something fortuitous, as something which might have been otherwise: he is an heir to the tradition of deep-rooted belief, but he makes of this a folkloristic quicksand. The two following passages from "The Scarlet Letter" are highly illustrative of this modern vagueness:

It [the Scarlet Letter] had been intended, there could be no doubt, as an ornamental article of dress; but how it was to be worn, or what rank, honor, and dignity, in by-past times, were signified by it, was a riddle which (so evanescent are the fashions of the world in these particulars) I saw little hope of solving. And yet it strangely interested me. My eyes fastened themselves upon the old scarlet letter, and would not be turned aside. Certainly, there was some deep meaning in it, most worthy of interpretation, and which, as it were, streamed forth from the mystic symbol, subtly communicating itself to my sensibilities, but evading the analysis of my mind.

While thus perplexed—and cogitating, among other hypotheses, whether the letter might not have been one of those decorations which the white men used to contrive, in order to take the eyes of Indians,—I happened to place it on my breast. It seemed to me,—the reader may smile, but must not doubt my word,—it seemed to me, then, that I experienced a sensation not altogether physical, yet almost so, as of burning heat; and as if the letter were not of red cloth, but red-hot iron, I shuddered, and involuntarily let it fall upon the floor.

So Roger Chillingworth—a deformed old figure, with a face that haunted men's memories longer than they liked—took leave of Hester Prynne, and went stooping away along the earth. He gathered here and there an herb, or grubbed up a root, and put it into the basket on his arm. His gray beard almost touched the ground as he crept onward. Hester gazed after him a little while, looking with a half fantastic curiosity to see whether the tender grass of early spring would not be blighted beneath him, and show the wavering track of his footsteps, sere and brown, across its cheerful verdure. She wondered what sort of herbs they were, which the old man was so sedulous to gather. Would not the earth, quickened to an evil purpose by the sympathy of his eye, greet him with poisonous shrubs, of species hitherto unknown, that would start up under his fingers? Or might it suffice him, that every wholesome growth should be converted into something deleterious and malignant at his touch? Did the sun, which shone so brightly everywhere else, really fall upon him? Or was there, as it rather seemed, a circle of ominous shadow moving along with his deformity, whichever way he turned himself? And whither was he now going? Would he not suddenly sink into the earth, leaving a barren and blasted spot, where, in due course of time, would be seen deadly nightshade, dogwood, henbane, and whatever else of vegetable wickedness the climate could produce, all flourishing with hideous luxuriance? Or would he spread bat's wings and flee away, looking so much the uglier the higher he rose towards heaven?

horror membra quatit/Eloquar an sileam? [My limbs tremble with icy horror/Shall I speak or remain silent?]); instead the details as sensed by Dante are put squarely before the reader in a manner "che il naturale messo avanti renda irresistibile l'impressione del fantastico [that the presentation of the natural render irresistible the impression of the fantastic]." The whole paradox of the *Divine Comedy* rests in the procedure of describing as real, and of conceiving as describable with the same precision that might be applied to an object of the outer world, that which, to our secularized imagination today, would seem to be the product of a gratuitous play of phantasy. Indeed, it is when the events are the most "fantastic" that they are presented most realistically: the fate of the plant-man Piero *must* be believed by us because it is accepted so completely by the victim himself: we see how he has adapted himself to his new estate when, in proclaiming his loyalty to his chief, he swears, not as men do, by their heads, but as plant-men (apparently) must do—*per le nove radici d'esto legno* [by the new roots of this tree].[6]

And not less must we believe that the events that transpire were accepted as real by Dante the pilgrim: Dante the author has filled this canto with details that afford *sense-data* to this character who is the chief witness, details which offer, in particular, an appeal to the eye and the ear. When Dante first comes upon the scene he is told by Virgil to watch out for strange apparitions (*riguarda ben, sì vedrai . . .*); Dante's gaze is at first disappointed, for he sees (*vedea*) nothing but rows of plants, but, in compensation his ears are assailed by the sound of voices lamenting (*sentia . . . trarre guai*), that seem to come from unseen sources; it is this conflict between the visual and the auditory that accounts for Dante's initial confusion. But in the manifestations of the plant-man, Dante is privileged both to hear and to see: as he tears off a leaf, the stump moans and then becomes black with blood (*gridò . . . bruno* [cried out . . . dark]). And in the single phrase *usciva inseme parole e sangue* [words and blood came out together] the two sense-data are fused together: there gushes forth a stream of "speech-endowed blood," of "bleeding screams" —a hideous revelation of the hybrid, which we must accept as a unit-manifestation, because of the singular verb *usciva*.[7]

And now we have arrived at the point where we may consider the nature of the *"speech"* (I am using this term to mean, not "language," but "the production of language") of the suicides. No commentator, so far as I know, has attempted to analyze this process—though Dante himself

---

[6] Thus I must reject the translation of *nove* by "strange": that Piero could so simply "take over" and modify in accordance with his new status, the traditional manner of making oath, seems to me evidence that he has ceased to find his condition strange. *Nove* is best translated "new"; thus we are reminded of the genesis of his vegetal body which is the product, not of gradual evolution from the human, but of a "new" birth. Cf. the expression *forme novelle* used of the souls in *Purg.* xxv, 88.

[7] Here we have to do with a kind of hendiadys, as in *farò come colui che piange e dice* [I will act as one who weeps and speaks] in the Francesca episode, or *Parlar e lagrimar vedrai insieme* [You will see me speak and weep together] (*Inf.* xxxiii, 9).

has taken pains to give us an elaborate hint of it; compare the famous simile:

> Come d'un stizzo verde, che arso sia
> da l'un de' capi, che da l'altro geme,
> e cigola per vento che va via;
> sì de la scheggia rotta usciva inseme
> parole e sangue . . .

[As from a green branch that is burning at one end and drips and sputters from the other with escaping vapor, so from that broken stick words and blood came out together . . .]

Casini, who notes the effectiveness of such details as the "ensemble" of drops of sap and sound of wind, comments on the graphic quality of this description and cites Venturi who praises its verisimilitude ("verità d'imagine e perspicuità di forma [imagistic truth and perspicuity of form]"). But to consider this simile mainly as a device for enlivening description (an attitude that is a survival of rhetorical aesthetics) is to overlook the explanation which it contains for us of the "origin of language" as this is produced in the plant-men.[8] Obviously the ensemble of sap and windy sound which Casini admired is meant to offer a parallel with the ensemble of blood and words that issues from the plants: in both the visual and the acoustic are distinguished and fused by the poet. We have to do with a poetic equation: blood = sap, words = wind, thus the language of the plant-men is mere *flatus vocis*, wind-begotten speech. This is borne out clearly in the lines that introduce the last words of Piero, as he prepares to make answer to a question of Dante's:

> Allor soffiò il tronco forte,[9] e poi
> *si convertì quel vento in cotal voce.*

[The branch then blew hard and the breath then changed to a voice.]

[8] This fact is overlooked by all the commentators I have read on this passage: De Sanctis interprets the simile to mean that Dante does not hear the words spoken by the plant (!); that his soul is concentrated in his eye. This is surely not true: Dante is ear as well as eye. Torraca's contribution is to point out parallel similes in Provençal poetry, in which the "weeping" of a fire-log is compared to the weeping of a poet-lover; he overlooks the fact that this particular simile is meant to throw light on weeping that is precisely *non*-human.—He may compare the "dehumanized" weeping of the pope who *piangeva con la zanca* [was weeping with his shanks] in *Inf.* xix, 45.

[9] D'Ovidio comments on this passage, but only to question the significance of *forte:* why did it blow so *hard?* He answers, correctly enough, that because of the lapse of time since the tearing off of the twig had first given issue to speech, a greater effort was needed for the plant to draw breath enough to last out his words. But D'Ovidio might better have emphasized *soffio* than *forte*—as well as the entire line *si convertì quel vento in cotal voce* which describes the transformation of wind into voice or words (both meanings are possible with *voce*).

But apart from delimiting the windy nature of the speech of hybrid beings, the simile serves to assign it to a rank according to a hierarchy of values. The fact that Dante chose to describe a hissing, guttering fire-log by way of characterizing the genesis of speech in his *uomini-piante* shows that he conceived this as representing a purely physical process: the issue of blood and cries is on the same low "material" level as is the issue of sap and hissing sound from a fire-log. Indeed, the fact that we have to do with speech of a non-human order, with speech that is a matter of bodily discharges, was already suggested by the terrible line *usciva inseme parole e sangue;* and that this is speech which is conditioned by physical factors alone is revealed by the incident in which Dante tears off the twig from the plant, thereby providing the channel through which the stream of blood and words could pour forth: only by such a physical gesture could the plant be enabled to "speak"—only by being torn and wounded.

This truth is hammered into our ears again in the latter part of the canto, devoted to the second (anonymous) suicide:

> e menommi al cespuglio che piangea,
> per le rotture sanguinenti, invano.

[And he led me to the bush that was weeping in vain from its bleeding rents.]

—again blood and words are coupled, again there is a reference to the tearing of a channel (*per le rotture*) through which the two-fold utterance of suffering finds an outlet.[10] A few lines later, after this plant has begun to speak, Virgil refers to its condition in words that echo all the concepts just treated:

> . . . "Chi fosti che *per tante punte*
> Soffi con sangue doloroso sermo?"

[. . . "Who were you, that through so many wounds breathe with blood this mournful speech?"]

But the most vivid reference to the terrible conditions upon which speech may be released in the plants is to be found in the lines describing the function of the Harpies:

> l'Arpìe, pascendo poi de le sue foglie,
> fanno dolore, e al dolor finestra.

[Then the harpies, feeding on its leaves, at once cause pain and an outlet for pain.]

---

[10] In this case the mutilation is caused not by Dante but by Giacomo da Sant' Andrea, the spendthrift who hides behind the bush into which the suicide has been transformed; that he chose this particular hiding place may perhaps be explained by the fact that in life Giacomo, after squandering his fortune, had attempted to commit suicide.

What Dante did once and inadvertently to a particular bush the Harpies do systematically, in aevum, to the whole group of plant-men; by feeding on the leaves of the bushes they open wounds and provide an outlet for the grief that they have caused: eternally there must come forth *inseme parol e sangue.*[11]

And with this reference to the Harpies we may note that the problem concerning the "genesis of speech," so important to this particular canto, becomes one with the arch-problem of the whole edifice of the *Inferno:* that of the *contrappasso.* That Dante has transformed the loathsome harbinger-birds of Virgil into instruments of moral punishment is obvious and has been generally recognized (De Sanctis, D'Ovidio, Torraca, Vossler); it also seems clear to me that the eternal laceration wrought by the Harpies upon the suicides, is meant to be the punitive counterpart of their own act of self-laceration:[12] one may note that the words with which the second suicide refers to the mutilation visited upon his plant body (*lo strazio disonesto/c'ha le mie fronde sì da me* DISGIUNTE [the dishonest violence which has disjoined my branches from me]) echoes the *disvelta* that is to be found in Piero's description of his act of suicide: *Quando si parte l'anima feroce/dal corpo ond'ella stessa s'è* DISVELTA [when the fierce soul has departed from the body of which it has divested itself].

[11] It must have been noted that, in our attempt to describe the process by which language is achieved for the plant-men, we have drawn from passages which deal with the fate of Piero, of the anonymous suicide, and of the group as a whole. For, though the suicides are individually doomed (*Ciascuno al prun de l'ombra sua molesta* [each on the bush of its harmful shade]), they share a common fate—and each identifies himself with the whole: consider the plural used by Piero, *Uomini fummo,* and the line *come l'altre* (!) *verrem per nostre spoglie* [like the others we will come for our bodies]. The story, thrice told, is yet the same story, made terribly explicit: "this is the doom of Piero, this is the doom of any suicide, this is the doom of all." And Dante wants us not only to comprehend his dread truth; he would have us hear the *sounds* of this doom made manifest: the cries uttered by two blood-tinged voices, first that of Piero, finally that of the anonymous suicide, emerge from a chorus to which the whole multitude of plant-voices contribute: *tante voci uscisser tra quei bronchi;* this is the first sound we hear, and it reverberates throughout the canto. But, lest our ears grow dull, through constant exposure to the unholy din, Dante allows this chorus to be broken for a moment as the spendthrifts, pursued by hounds (again the *contrappasso:* they are torn and destroyed by ravening beasts because in life they greedily destroyed what should have remained whole), burst upon the center of the stage: for a moment human screams dominate all others, rising above the chorus of the plant-voices. By this sudden introduction of the normal (framed by the two episodes of individual plant-men) the abnormal is made more frightful.

[12] Torraca suggests another variety of *contrappasso:* he would explain the onslaughts of the Harpies as due to the fact that in their life on earth the suicides "had not endured the onslaughts of affliction." Thus to him the great sin of these creatures would lie not so much in the anti-natural act of suicide itself as in their lack of fortitude; somewhat similar is the attitude of Vossler, who states that the suicides were punished because they had not found in life "das lösende Wort."

(Of course, this before-mentioned bodily mutilation was executed not by the Harpies but by Giacomo, who, like Dante with Piero, became unwittingly an accomplice of the Harpies.) But the function of the Harpies was not alone that of renewing everlastingly the wounds of the suicides, as De Sanctis and D'Ovidio note, but, as Dante himself specifically states, "to cause grief and, by the same token, to provide an outlet for it" (*al dolor finestra*): to make the suicides suffer, at the same time allowing them the cruel consolation of expressing their suffering through the medium of their own ghastly brand of speech.[13] Thus Dante, in drawing the logical consequences of the law of *contrappasso,* has created a semi-human plant-like speech for his hybrid plant-souls (just as the devils and Nembrotte are endowed with a speech of their own: *del cul fatto trombetta,* Inf. XXI, 139; XXXI, 67, *Rafel mai amech zabi almi*).

And all this lies implicitly contained in that simple phrase, that conventional arrangement of subject + predicate: *il suo tronco gridò!*[14]

Now let us turn to the *"language"* or style of the canto. It is obvious that in discussing this second problem it would not be proper to limit ourselves to the language of the suicides: though Dante has devised a peculiar method of speech for these hybrid beings, he could not do otherwise than to represent their actual words as belonging to normal, human language, on the same level as that of the other characters—or of the author himself. One distinctive feature of the style of this canto consists

---

[13] This is a consolation doubly cruel in that the expression of their suffering seems only to renew their grief: the tyranny of the need for self-expression by language, the self-mutilating sadistic power of speech which while seeming to give consolation only aggravates the wound—this has never been more powerfully symbolized, nay more graphically been depicted, than in this macabre episode.

[14] Later on we find the much more matter-of-fact verb *dire* used in the same connection: *Noi eravamo ancora al tronco attesi,/credendo c'altro ne volesse dire.* [We were still intent upon the tree, thinking that it wished to say more].

Such bold sentences, which mold a subject and a predicate not "naturally" belonging together in a sentence which makes this coupling appear as natural, revives the original polar current which exists in any sentence with the two members: subject-predicate. According to H. Ammann, *Die Sprache* II, 103, a verbal sentence depicts a "Zu-Wort-Kommen" of a living process: an observation is made by showing us something living ("ein Lebendiges"), the subject, as displaying its natural activity ("Lebensvorgang") in the predicate; in any sentence there is an "Urrythmus" of tension and relaxation which betrays itself in the musical shadings with which the sentence is pronounced:

$$<\quad>\qquad<\quad>\qquad\qquad<\quad>$$

the roses flourish, the brook rustles. In the case of *il suo tronco gridò (dice),* the mold of the sentence makes appear as natural a highly paradoxical statement; in the same manner, the oath *per este nove radici* . . . molds a counter-natural attitude into the frame of a traditional oath. Both cases reflect the hybridism of plant-speech.

in the use, to an extent unparalleled elsewhere in the *Inferno,* of onomatopoetic terms: consider, for example, the following list of harsh-
sounding, consonant-ridden words which (often occurring in the rhyme)
appear scattered throughout the canto for the purpose of evoking the
concepts "trunk, bush" and "cripple, mutilate, dismember":

nodosi	fronde sparte	rosta	aspri sterpi	bronchi
tronchi	'nvolti	sterchi con tosco	schiante	scerpi
sterpi	monchi	tronco	scheggia rotta	nocchi
disvelta	stizzo	cespuglio	strazio	triste cesto

As we pass in review this bristling array of words we have almost the
impression of being faced with a new language that recalls little of the
melody and fluidity of the Italian tongue; these words have much of
the quality that is to be found in Provençal, with its tendency toward
monosyllabism and its clusters of consonants. Compare, for example:[15]

> Al prim pres dels breus jorns braus
> Quand brand'als brueils l'aura brava,
> E ill branc e ill brondel son nut,
> Pel brun tems secs qu'el desnuda . . .
>
> Guillems Fabres nos fai *en brau lengage*
> Manz braus broncs bren bravan de brava guia
> E rocs e brocs que met en son cantage.

[At the first approach of the brief harsh day, when the harsh wind shakes the
wood and the branch and bough are made bare by the arid dark weather
which strips them . . .
  Guillems Fabres composes for us in harsh language many harsh knots . . .
in a clever way . . . and roads and thorns that he puts into his song.—Trans.
uncertain, see Levy, *cit.*—Ed.]

In the passage just above there is an interesting allusion to the "brau
lengage": this must refer to the deliberate device on the part of Provençal
poets to exploit the effect of harsh strength to which their word-material
so easily lent itself. And it is only probable that Dante's procedure, as
illustrated in the list above, harks back to this tradition, representing an

---

[15] V. Diez, *Poesie der Troubadours,* p. 88; Levy, *Suppl.-Wb.* s.v. *benc.* Cf. also
Scheludko, *Arch. rom.* XV, 159.

Italian "softening" of the *brau lengage*.[16] But it must be observed that, at the hands of Dante, the use of this device is attended with greater refinement and artistic economy; it is only seldom, for instance, that he offers an accumulation of onomatopoetic words within a line (as he does in *stecchi con tosco . . . ch'ode le bestie e le frasche stormire* [poisonous thorns . . . who hears the beasts and the crashing of the branches]): for the most part such elements are scattered, so that the canto is throughout pervaded with sound symbolism. Moreover, while the Provençal poets were apt to resort to this procedure to excess, delighting in sound effects for their own sake,[17] Dante was careful to limit it to cases where it was suitable to the context, where it would serve best to give a graphic representation of the ideas of moral crippling and laceration: the visual and the aural pictures of moral disease are consonant in their disharmony. In this way Dante was illustrating the medieval (and ultimately ancient) ideas concerning the correspondence between meaning and sound (cf. his opinion, expressed in the *Vita Nuova,* about the "amorous" sound of the word *amore*).

The consistent procedure just noted of expressing disharmonious conceptions by means of harsh-sounding words has been passed over by commentators; all, however, have remarked the abundance of rhetorical artifices to be found in this canto. The use of such devices as antithesis, alliteration, repetition of words and word-stems, puns and etymologies,[18] belongs to a long rhetorical tradition, and, according to Schiaffini ("Tra-

---

[16] The same *brau lengage* is alluded to in such lines as *Così nel mio parlar voglio esser aspro* [so I wish to be harsh in my speech] of the *Madonna Pietra* poem (*Rime* 103) and the first line of *Inf.* xxii: *S'io avessi le rime aspre e chiocce* [If I had harsh and clucking verses]. These echo the "harsh rhymes" of the *sirventes*-technique of the troubadours which, "strictly conventional and oratorical as they are" (Borgese, *Speculum* xiii, 190), were adapted by Dante to his poetry of wrath.

[17] A more "sincere" stylistic device of the Provençal poets is to be met with in their *descorts:* poems made deliberately discordant by means of a medley of metrics and languages, in order to correspond to the "out of tune-ness" of the soul of the poet. This parallelism of form and content which may seem naïvely pedantic to us today is to be explained by the high appreciation which the Middle Ages felt for the symbolic act: it may be applied to anything, whether great or small: symbolism, as used by man, is a consequence of the symbolism everywhere so manifest to human eyes, which God has put into his creation.

[18] It was a favorite procedure of the times to offer punning etymological interpretations of names. In this canto there is no pun that may compare, for example, with the *de Vinea . . . vinea* "vine-yard" found in the writings of a correspondent of Piero's (v. Schiaffini, p. 100), and yet the *ambo le chiavi* [both of the keys], uttered by Dante's Piero, reflects the same tendency to play on names: obviously this contains an historical allusion to the other Peter, guardian of the keys. Indeed, exactly the same allusion is to be found in the writing of the same punning correspondent: *imperii claviger, claudit et nemo aperit, aperit et nemo claudit* [Keeper of the keys of the empire, who closes so that none shall open, who opens so that none shall close] (Schiaffini, l. c.). D'Ovidio points to this line as a source of *ambo le chiavi*—but without mentioning the allusion involved in both cases. Cf. the underlying pun *Orsini—orsacchi* in *Inf.* xix, 71.

dizione e poesia"), the combination of these with the overloaded harshness of sounds was itself a regular procedure of medieval writers (in the passages just cited from the poetry of Provençal troubadours we may note that the "harsh words" have been coupled with semi-etymological alliterations).

But it is possible to trace the rhetorical devices used by Dante to a more specific source: the majority of them occur in the language of the first suicide Piero, and Novati has proved that they are simply echoes of the elegances of style with which the historical personage Pier delle Vigne was wont to embellish his prose writings. Thus it would appear that Dante's choice of these rhetorical artifices was due to a desire on his part for historical characterization; Auerbach has pointed out a consistent tendency in Dante to make the souls in the other world recognizable by having them retain certain distinctive traits of character and physical appearance; here, then, we should have to do with a "linguistic" portrayal, corresponding to the general dogmatic procedure of preserving in the Beyond the earthly features of the various characters. Novati's proof is convincing and his discovery is important in that it offers an objective explanation for the presence of the devices in question; after him, no commentator could resort to such a subjective interpretation as that earlier advanced by De Sanctis, to whom the rhetorical passages in the speech of the suicide Piero were an indication of his (momentary) lack of sincere feeling!

Unfortunately, however, the commentators who have followed Novati have seized upon the "fact" of historical correspondence in order to stress a supposed piece of ironical and malicious caricature offered by Dante. It is remarkable how quick are professors of philology to gloat over any seeming expression of malice, if this is coupled with verbal skill. The most outspoken member of this guild is Vossler:

> Diese grosstiligen oder heroischen Bürokraten, die wir Deutschen besser kennen als jedes andere Volk, können tigerhaft und auch sich selbst gegenüber unmenschlich werden. Stürtzt oder entlässt man sie, so töten sie sich oder verfallen der Lächerlichkeit. *Auch in ihrer privaten Ausdrucksweise erkennt man den amtlichen Stil.* . . . Schwer und hoffnungslos gekränkt, verschliesst er [Piero] sich und verholzt im buchstäblichen Sinn des Wortes. . . . Ihre [der 'trotzigen und eitlen Gewaltmenschen'] Seele, die nicht gedeihlich wachsen und leiden konnte, verknöchert zum Dorngestrüpp. . . .

> [These heroic bureaucrats in the grand style, which we Germans know better than other nations, can become tiger-like and inhuman even with respect to themselves. According to whether one attempts to ruin them or leave them alone, they kill themselves or sink into absurdity. Even in private life one can recognize the official style. . . . Greviously and hopelessly stricken, (Piero) becomes locked within himself and literally grows wooden. . . . The souls (of the "sulky and empty men of authority") which cannot flourish or endure ossify and become underbrush. . . .]

It is not difficult to see how Vossler has been induced by a purely German phobia and by the existence of a purely German word-association ("ein verknöcherter Bürokrat") to superimpose a fantastic analogy of his own upon the parallelism willed by Dante. Having learned from Novati that the language of Dante's Piero is substantially that of the historical Piero, and that this represented the "chancelry" or "bureaucratic" style of the times, he proceeds to identify the Capuan *dittatore* with the bureaucrats whom he has known and despised in Germany; he even goes so far as to suggest that, since in life Piero was an "ossified bureaucrat" it is only fitting that he must become a crippled thornbush in the Beyond. Moreover he assumes that Piero was one of those whose style, in spite of themselves, betrays the bureaucrat even in daily life—a victim, as it were, of a stylistic *tic!* And we are asked to believe that it is such a trivial and comical creature that Dante has made the chief figure of this canto; Vossler's implications about the private nature of Piero (is the Beyond anything like "private life"?) are entirely without foundation, as is also his assumption that the style of his writings was not noble and elegant, but poor fustian, and matter for derision. We are surely warranted in rejecting the "caricature-theory" (as does D'Ovidio: "In questi vezzi di stile Dante non mise un' intenzione quasi di caricatura. [With this stylistic manner, Dante did not intend caricature.]").

Moreover, I believe that the desire to achieve a historical characterization was not the sole, or even the prime, artistic motive behind the use of these rhetorical devices. At Dante's hand these become filled with a larger significance; they offer a sort of linguistic, or onomatopoetic rendition of the ideas of torture, schism, estrangement, which dominate the canto (much as the harsh-sounding words served to suggest the ideas of "crippled" and "trunk"). Compare, for example, the involved and twisted lines below, which bear in themselves the stamp of self-torture and self-estrangement, and ultimately of infructuous paradoxy:

> L'animo mio, per disdegnoso gusto,
> credendo col morir fuggir disdegno,
> ingiusto fece me contra me giusto.

[My mind, in a disdainful mood, thinking that it could by dying flee disdain, made my just self unjust against me.]

After this hopeless entanglement in a verbal thicket, the lines become simple and candid (in the limpid tone of Racine's *Le jour n'est pas plus pur que le fond de mon cœur*), evoking a clearing: one emerges into the bright open sunshine:

> vi giuro che già mai non ruppi fede
> al mio signor, che fu d'onor sì degno.

[I swear to you that I never broke faith with my Lord, who was so worthy of honor.]

There is here a correspondence between involved sentence and involved feeling, between simple sentence and candid feeling—a shifting of the shape of the sentences according to the shape of mood. In the line *Ingiusto fece me contra me giusto* [made my just self unjust against me] I hear sounding above the intricacies of préciosité, the note *contra*, symbol of the counter-natural: the repetitions of word-stems (*ingiusto—giusto; me contra me*) suggest the outrage wrought by one half of the human soul against the other; here we may note, to a certain extent, a parallelism with the *"moi dédoublé"* as this is suggested in the most effective line of the second suicide: "io fei *giubbetto* A ME *delle* MIE *case* [of my own house I made myself a gibbet]." Torture and destruction again form the motif in the lines of Piero that describe the flames of the passion of envy, steadily mounting until all is consumed and honor reduced to strife:

> infiammò contra me li animi tutti;
> e li 'nfiammati infiammar[19] sì Augusto,
> che i lieti onor tornaro in tristi lutti.

[inflamed all minds against me and the inflamed did so inflame Augustus that the happy honors turned into sorrowful mourning.]

Again, in the powerfully charged sentence describing the two-fold activity of the Harpies, we have to do, not only with repetition but with zeugma: *Fanno dolore e al dolor finestra.* The very compression of this line is symbolical of a grief which, although given continual utterance, must endlessly repeat itself nor ever find release.[20] Finally we may consider the pattern, old as epic poetry, "*a* but not *b*," which occurs three times in as many lines at the beginning of the canto:

> Non frondi verdi, ma di color fosco;
> non rami schietti, ma nodosi e 'nvolti;
> non pomi v' eran, ma stecchi con tosco.

[Not green boughs, but of a dark color; not straight branches, but gnarled and twisted; no fruits were there, but poisonous thorns.]

---

[19] This particular repetition, the repetition of a finite verb in the form of a past participle, is a device with a long past in Latin (and especially late Latin) poetry and prose writing, cf. Stolz-Schmalz-Leumann-Hofmann, *Lat. Gr.* p. 831: *Mars hanc videt visamque cupit politurque cupita* (Ovid); *Croesum cepit captumque . . . donavit* (Orosius).

[20] Compare a similar procedure in the famous line *Galeotto fu il libro, e chi lo scrisse*, where the subject *Galeotto* represents first the title of a book, then a human agent. Again one feels, in such a zeugmatic condensation, an expression of painful, fateful coercion. Cf. also *Inf.* XIX, 72 *che su l'avere e qui me misi in borsa*.

D'Ovidio comments on the effect produced by the repetition of the device: he sees therein a deliberate monotony of syntax which "imitates that sort of calm that great stupefaction is wont to produce." But he says nothing about the device itself. To me this negative pattern, with its insistent note of schism, suggests the στέρησις or *privatio* by which, in ancient as in medieval philosophy, the evil is clearly defined as something characterized by the absence of good; Dante would make us see that this forest is a "wicked" forest.

It must have been observed that the passages above represent not only the language of Piero, but also of the second suicide and of Dante himself. This would clearly invalidate the premise of those who see in the author's use of these rhetorical devices only a program of historical characterization —unless, forsooth, we are to believe that Dante has blundered as an artist and, forgetting his original purpose, has proceeded blindly out of what modern psychologists would call automatism.[21] But it is difficult to imagine such a lapsus on the part of the conscious artist that Dante was; I should say that Dante has not forgotten but rather transcended his original purpose: granted that this may have been the starting point and may explain the fact that his attention was called to the stylistic features of the civil servant Piero, still, once his poetic imagination had seized upon the devices that characterized this style, they could adapt themselves to a larger design, to play their part in the evocation of that atmosphere of disharmony which pervades the whole canto.[22] From this point of view, the more practical question of historical identification sinks into insignificance; it is right that the second suicide, a crippled being in the image of Piero, should share the crippled style of Piero; or that the pilgrim Dante, so sensitive to the disharmonious atmosphere surrounding the plant-souls, should record his reactions in phrases evocative of this disharmony.

This he does, with most startling effect, in the line to which Grandgent gives especial emphasis and which has proved such a stumbling-block to commentators of the "historical characterization" school: *Cred'io ch'ei credette ch'io credesse.* . . . In my opinion this line is the most felicitous possible "psychological characterization," serving to suggest vividly Dante's state of mind at this stage of the narration: i.e. the disruption of his mental communication with his master, as a consequence of the *smarrimento* [bewilderment] indicated in the previous line, when Dante's

---

[21] This would indeed seem to be the attitude of Grandgent, if we may judge by his phrase, ". . . either purposely or unconsciously"; we are asked to believe that Dante, filled with reminiscences of the chancelry style of writing, allowed the speech habits characteristic of the *dittatore* to encroach upon his own.

[22] One may recall in this connection the scene in Canto xv where Dante, in his intimate conversation with Brunetto Latini, turns to a new and more profound use certain of the rules of *bienséance* once propounded by Brunetto himself (for quotations v. the Torraca ed. of Dante, ad xv, 43; v. also 121-123).

attention is diverted in various directions (advised by Virgil to "look" out for things unheard of, he is able only to recognize sounds); the verse *cred'io* . . . is the "onomatopoetic" rendering of his mental state of estrangement and confusion. Valid in itself, this tortuous mode of expression is also effective in an anticipatory function: before the curtain rises on the main protagonists, before the awful implications of their fate are unfolded before us, the note is sharply struck which shall pervade the whole canto.[23]

The rhetorical device illustrated by this significant line is simply that of repetition; indeed this is involved in all the passages discussed above—though often in combination with other devices. That, in nearly every case, the effect achieved is fundamentally the same is due of course to a deliberate artistic intention; the mere repetition of words, no more than any other stylistic device, is not anything formulable in the abstract, but must always be felt and tested against the background of the particular psychic climate. In this canto Dante is mainly interested in evoking the one conception of moral disharmony, whereas, in the Francesca episode, for example, in the line *Amor che a nullo amato amar perdona* [Love, which will excuse no loved one from loving in return], he uses the compelling forcefulness of word-repetition in order to offer a verbal equivalent of the coercion toward reciprocation that is inherent in real love. In *caddi come corpo morto cade* [I fell as a dead body falls], this same device serves to reinforce the impression of an inertia imposed by physical laws; in Malherbe's *Rose, elle a vécu ce que vivent les roses* [Rose, she has lived as roses live] it is a symbol of a serene surrendering to the laws of Nature; in the Latin sentence which inspired Racine: *Titus reginam Berenicem ab urbe dimisit invitus invitam* [Titus, against his will, sent Queen Berenice from the city, against her will] it suggests the united impulses of the lovers which were dominated by their act of renunciation. The motto of stylistics should be (not *tot capita tot sententiae* but) "so many sentences, so many meanings": if style must express a psychic content, it can do this only by adapting the given devices to the particular situation: repetition in itself is multivalent; its specific nuance is brought out in the specific situation through a kind of collaboration between the situation and the devices offered by language—through an "adhesion" of language to the psychic content.

In all the passages discussed, Dante has used a stylistic pattern that was familiar in a manner specifically adapted to a particular situation or

---

[23] This same procedure may also be noted in Dante's use of onomatopoeia, as when Virgil, at the beginning of the canto, is made to use the epithet *monchi* (significantly occurring in the rhyme with *tronchi* and *bronchi*) in order to state the simple idea, "your suppositions of the moment will prove to be wrong": *Li pensier c'hai si faran tutti monchi* (here, "mutilated" is used of ideas!; in both cases, then, we are offered a shibboleth of mental aberration).

character: the rhetorical device is never used for its own sake, "in order to use the well-known rhetorical device of . . . ," as philologists like to reason; Dante recreates the given stylistic patterns by restoring their original strength. The *Amor che a nullo amato amar perdona* of the Francesca episode, followed by two other lines with an anaphoric *amor,* inserts itself easily into a well-known medieval pattern used by all preachers and orators (cf. *Per me si va,* several times repeated, inscribed on the gate of Hell; v. Hatzfeld on "Anaphoric Hymnal Style"); it is nevertheless an eternal expression of the nature of love—so much so that the modern reader (even the medievalist when he happens to be "just" a reader) does not even sense the presence of an old pattern. Striking examples of that "originality *à partir du connu*" characteristic of the real genius, who rereads the palimpsest of language!

Appendix: The Anonymous Suicide in Inferno XIII

Ever since De Sanctis led the way in his appreciative study of the "*personaggi eroici*" who throng the cantos of the *Inferno,* the commentators, stirred by a delight in the strong personalities of "Renaissance" proportions (which the *Inferno* was better able to satisfy than the other two *cantiche*), have, in dealing with this episode, tended too much to concentrate their gaze on the figure of the man Piero; De Sanctis entitles his essay on this canto "Piero delle Vigne," D'Ovidio "Il canto di Piero delle Vigne," Olschki ex professo deals only with the problem "Dante and Peter de Vinea." By raising him into such high relief one has obscured the fact that Dante intended him to be subordinated to the "law of the circle"; for he is presented, not only as an individual with a story of his own, but as the spokesman of a group with which he shares a common fate (as he himself avows), and as the interpreter of a universal judgment— which, we may suppose, had no little importance for Dante (cf. note 11). Moreover, by the process of isolating this figure for purposes of analysis, one destroys the artistic unity of the canto itself [24] which, like any great work of art, must be judged from the point of view of its ensemble effect. One must surely question the temerity of Croce's procedure, whereby Dante's work is split into the two parts: "lyrical poetry" (in which are presented the "powerful individualities") and "theological novel."

A particular result of this general attitude, when applied to Canto XIII, is the glorification of Piero at the expense of the second and anonymous suicide. Those who bother to mention him consider him

---

[24] —or, better, of the "episode": the episode of the plant-men is really brought to an end only in the opening lines of canto XIV, where Dante complies with the request of the second suicide to gather together the leaves torn from his body: *raünai le fronde sparte.*

worthy of only a few cursory remarks, and these are usually derogatory: D'Ovidio (who prophesies that this will continue to be "the canto of Piero") decries the "tragicità patibolare e grossolana" of the *"mot de la fin"* (*io fei giubbetto a me de le mie case*) in which the anonymous suicide refers to an "impiccagione a domicilio"; Vossler echoes the Italian critic, declaring this figure to be a man of no "feiner Gemütsart." Such judgments are in my opinion erroneous; they are perhaps to be explained by the fact that the second suicide, overshadowed by the first, has not been considered sufficiently striking to warrant a more careful examination. To my mind he is exceedingly important: not as an individual (for it cannot be denied that, as a "personality," Piero is far more arresting), but as essential to the structure and the ultimate significance of the episode itself.

From the point of view of structure one may note two types of parallelism which indicate that the two figures must be considered together; we have already called attention to parallelisms of style, and to the examples cited above others may be added: *"tristo* cesto"—"la farà *triste";* "al cespuglio che piangea . . . *invano"*—"que' cittadin . . . avrebber fatto lavorare *indarno."* ["sad tuft"—"will make it sad"; "the thicket which wept . . . in vain"—"those citizens would have worked in vain"]. The second parallelism concerns the "two gestures": it may be remembered that Dante, held spellbound by the awful revelations of the plant-souls, finds no words with which to address them (he speaks only to Virgil, who talks for him to the suicides); the only overt tokens of his association with the suicides are given when at the beginning of the episode he tears off the leaf from the plant-man Piero, and at the end, gathers up, in an Antigone-like movement, the fallen branches (torn off by Giacomo da Sant' Andrea) around the dismembered plant-body of the second suicide. If we had only the stylistic parallels, we might be justified in interpreting them as indicating that the episode of the anonymous suicide (though still essential artistically) is merely an echo, a faint reminder of the first and more elaborate episode dealing with Piero; but in the case of the two complementary gestures it is unquestionable that the second of them strikes a note of climax and finality: Dante atones for his unwitting act of opening wounds by this deliberate and compassionate act of restoration; the episode is finally rounded out by this gesture, which would set at rest the troubled condition which the other gesture had called forth.

The incident of the second suicide, then, is highly essential to the structure of the poem; it is no less true that this figure is itself important to the *theme* of the canto, which (it must never be forgotten) concerns the workings of divine justice. And this figure is important precisely because of its lack of "individuality": Piero is indeed a great individual (in size he is a *gran pruno,* whereas the other is represented as so small that Virgil must bend over to speak to him), but, by the same token, this Renaissance-like figure is *only* an individual. The second suicide, on the other hand, has a greater rôle: he is all the Florentines who have slain themselves; he is Florence herself, who is steadily committing suicide by giving herself up to intestine wars: though the Baptist has succeeded Mars as patron saint of Florence, still the former *sempre con l'arte sua la farà triste* [will always make it sad with his art]. It is with the tragedy of his native city that the anonymous suicide is concerned—not, like Piero, with his personal fate, his personal reputation (*Conforti la memoria mia*). And if we think of him as the representative of Florence, his last line in the canto appears as a sublimely terrible evocation of the self-destruction of a city: *Io fei giubbetto a me de le mie case.*[25] Little wonder that Dante is moved by *la carità del natio loco* [love of my native city] (XIV, 1); and as he gathers up tenderly the dismembered and scattered leaves, he is paying devotion to his native city.

If we compare the relationship between Dante and the (anonymous) Florentine on the one hand, and Dante and the Capuan Piero on the other, a certain parallelism becomes apparent: in each case we have to do with a gesture and a mood. But in the scene with Piero both these manifestations are of lesser significance: indeed the gesture of breaking off the twig was directed, not toward Piero himself but toward what to Dante was still only a bush; thus it could reflect nothing of his attitude toward the suicide. His attitude is of course reflected in the word *pietà:* in *tanta pietà m'accora* he tells us that he is moved to pity by the sad story of Piero. But surely in Dante's as in Corneille's scale of values, the feeling of pity for the sufferings of an individual must be less noble than the more comprehensive emotion of patriotic devotion. Thus, by weighing the significance of these parallel manifestations (which offer the only *direct* evidence on which we may rely), one arrives at the conclusion that, of the two suicides it is with the anonymous figure, despised and rejected by critics, that Dante would identify himself—not with the "powerful individuality," Piero.[26]

[25] The implications of the word *case* were overlooked by D'Ovidio, who sees in this line only the trivial theme of an "impiccagione a domicilio." But in the age of the medieval walled-town, *case* inevitably must have suggested a "house among houses"; the use of this word places the anonymous suicide against the background of his city Florence.

D'Ovidio also points to the vulgarity of the word *giubbetto*. That this was in French a popular, indeed a vulgar, term is stated by Arpad Steiner (*MLN* 1942) who quotes the thirteenth-century William of Auvergne to the effect that it belonged to the "argot des malfaiteurs." But the very "vulgarity" of this word succeeds in suggesting most graphically the depth of degradation to which the House of Florence had sunk. A vulgar term is not necessarily anti-poetic: did not Dante, in moments of high poetic exaltation, resort to such terms as *puttana, bordello,* in his poetry of wrath? (And, significantly enough, does not his elegant *dittatore* Piero precisely refrain from using *puttana* of Envy and use *meretrice?*) Cf. also Torraca on *drappo, Inf.* XV, 112.

[26] Cf. a similar diptych (the councilman of Lucca—Ciampolo Navarrese) in Cantos XXI-XXII.

It is quite another conclusion which Olschki has reached and which he presents in the article entitled "Dante and Peter de Vinea" (*Romanic Review* xxxi, 105-111). By omitting all reference to the anonymous suicide, by weighing only the evidence, direct and indirect, contained in the first episode and interpreting this in the light of biographical data, he has succeeded in making a case for the close identification of Dante and Piero: the *pietà* which Dante represents himself as experiencing is to Olschki an indication that the poet has identified his own fate with that of the civil servant Piero, and this sympathetic association explains the fact that Piero is presented as innocent of the crimes with which he had been charged and of which he had been found guilty—according to the only documents which survive today. The fact that Piero is allowed to vindicate himself is obviously proof that Dante was himself convinced of the other's innocence, and it would seem only reasonable to assume that Dante was possessed of other evidence than that which has come down to us. But, according to Olschki, the poet was led to present Piero as an innocent victim of *invidia* and calumny for no other reason than that he, Dante, once a high official like Piero, had suffered such a fate: to Olschki the self-justifying portrait of Piero is evidence that Dante the man has identified himself with the historical character of Piero:

> . . . his [Dante's] sentiment for Peter de Vinea as a fellow-sufferer is confirmed by the similarity of the actual happenings. Both of them . . . were sentenced for malversation in public office and on like charges. Conscious of his own innocence, and convinced that it was easy, and customary, to have a political opponent convicted of malpractice in office in order to dispose of him, Dante transferred his own experience to the chancellor and regarded him as the defenseless victim, like himself, of envious malignity. Thus he rescued the chancellor, whom he revered as highest official of the Empire, as poet and rhetorician, from the ignominy that clouded his posthumous repute. The feeling of companionship in life-experience induced him, again, to pass a self-willed judgment, which might also clear his own self of the suspicions cast upon him by his fellow men. These personal motives gave rise to his conviction, and to the legend, that Peter de Vinea was, blameless, thrown into misery. . . .
>
> The world-judge adjudicates not according to the public opinion of his day, but according to his own conscience and his political experiences.

What we are really asked to believe, then, is that Dante's favorable judgment of Piero is the result, not of inquiry and weighing of evidence, but of sheer supposition—a judgment motivated largely by his own grievance against an unjust society: he cleared Piero in order to clear himself. I cannot keep from feeling that such an interpretation must cast discredit on the integrity of Dante's reasoning; nor can I understand the practical psychology underlying such a manoeuvre on Dante's part: if his judgment were based on sympathetic intuition alone, if there were at hand in his day no reliable objective evidence of **Piero's** innocence, how could he expect to convince his readers of this innocence? And, unless they were so convinced, Dante could hope to gain little success in clearing his own name, by drawing a parallel between himself and a character so questionable. Moreover, even assuming that he had a fair chance of rehabilitating the reputation of Piero, still this could serve Dante's own aim of self-rehabilitation *only* if a parallel between the two men were clearly established in the poem—and this Dante fails to do. He has not always failed to do this: in the episodes devoted to Brunetto Latini, for example, it is expressly indicated that Dante is identifying his own experience with that of his teacher (since Brunetto prophesies the ingratitude of Florence toward Dante); how is one to explain a lack of any such indication in this case, when, if we accept Olschki's interpretation, so much hangs upon the clear establishment of a personal parallel?

In the absence of such an establishment, Olschki is forced to depend upon such hints as Piero's denunciation of *invidia* (from which Dante too had suffered) and the reference to Dante's *pietà* toward Piero (a feeling "which comes over him whenever [and only when] he has before his eyes victims of passions or misfortunes like his own"). If this last statement ("and only when") were true it could only mean that Dante was incapable of distinguishing between pity and self-pity; fortunately, however, it may be easily disproved by a glance at the dictionary of Blanc, s.v. *pietà*, where we are referred to such lines, for example, as *lamenti . . . / che di pietà ferrati avean gli strali;/ond'io li orecchi con le man copersi* [lamentations . . . whose arrows were tipped with pity, wherefore I covered my ears with my hands] (xxix, 44) which describe Dante as pierced by the shafts of pity as he listens to the lamentations of the falsifiers in torment; is Dante here identifying himself as a falsifier? (Cf. also, in xx, 28, the *"pietà"* expressed for sooth-sayers, and the rebuke of Virgil: *Qui vive la pietà quand' è ben morta* [here pity lives when it is truly dead].) And as for the evidence supposedly offered by the reference to *invidia* in the following passage:

> La meretrice [*invidia*] che mai da l'ospizio
> di Cesare non torse li occhi putti,
> morte comune, *de le corti vizio . . .*

[the harlot (envy) who never took her whorish eyes from Caesar's house, mankind's undoing, vice of the court . . .]

it seems to me that Olschki is reversing the emphasis intended by Dante, when he says:

> The events leading to his condemnation had the same source at the Imperial Court as in Republican Florence, because the "invidia" that decided

the poet's fate was *not merely the vice peculiar to princely courts, but the universal undoing of mankind:* "Morte comune, de le corti vizio."

Surely the passage as a whole presents *invidia* as characteristic of the court *in particular;* the last line, while conceding this to be a general evil *(morte comune),* labels it, nonetheless, "the court vice" (we should translate then: "not merely the . . . undoing of mankind, but [especially] the court vice"). Piero is here concerned with describing the situation at the court of Sicily, where *invidia* played such a destructive rôle; if Dante had meant that this description was at the same time and in the same degree applicable to democratic Florence, there is no reason why Piero should not have proceeded to draw such an analogy.

"In Exitu Israel de Aegypto"

by Charles S. Singleton

The opening scene of the *Comedy* is the scene of a conversion: from a dark wood of sin a man faces toward the light at the summit of a mountain, and strives to advance toward that light. The light comes from "the planet that leads men aright by every path," and later, as the goal at the summit, will be seen as *sol iustitiae,* and ultimately revealed as the Sun that lights the blessed in Heaven. On any reading, that light is God's light.

The act of turning away from sin and of turning toward such a light is *conversio,* as Dante and the theology of his time understood that term.[1] This, moreover, is not the only instance of conversion in the journey to God, as Dante has chosen to represent that journey. It is but the first of three conversions. Or, since this first, on the prologue scene of the poem, proves unsuccessful, and then, in a "repeat performance," *is* successful, perhaps we should count it twice, so that we have *one* plus *three* conversions in the whole course of the journey.

Certainly the "unsuccessful conversion" of the prologue scene must be viewed as distinct from the other three lying beyond it, if for no other reason than that it takes place on the scene of this life, whereas the others come along the way of a journey through the life after death, which begins with Canto III Inferno.

Now, in the prologue conversion, as we may call it, in spite of a desperate struggle to advance toward the light at the summit, the man who moves alone on that scene falls back toward the darkness and would be lost there again, did Virgil not come to lead him the "long way" around. On the slope three beasts appear to block his way and cause him to lose what he had gained, and to "ruin" to the low place again, where the sun is silent. Conversion, the turning to the light, has failed—at least for the time being. The "corto andare" up the mountain may not be taken, and Virgil does not come to lead up, toward the light, but down, into the darkness of Hell.

"'In Exitu Israel de Aegypto,'" by Charles S. Singleton. From *78th Annual Report of the Dante Society of America* (1960). Reprinted by permission of the Dante Society of America, Inc.

[1] On this point, and for ample references in support, see my *Dante Studies 2: Journey to Beatrice,* Harvard University Press, 1958, pp. 39-56.

Conversion, in this sense, will be seen to happen again, when the wayfarer emerges from the darkness of Hell to see the stars once more. Here now the outline of a mountain is again visible in the dawning light, and this time the wayfarer climbs the short way up the slope. Virgil guides now, even though, curiously enough, Virgil does not know the way. However, "the sun that is rising now will show the way" [2]—and we catch in that verse the distinct echo of the other, in the prologue canto, that speaks of the planet that guides "dritto per ogni calle."

The opening scene of the *Purgatory* bears a most striking resemblance to the prologue scene, as few readers will fail to see. There a sense of "return" is very strong indeed,—and little wonder: this scene matches the prologue in so many essential features that the whole prologue action seems somehow to happen again—but with the all-important difference noted: the conversion is unsuccessful in the first instance, and succeeds in the second.

We know now what Dante's basic method of allegory is in the *Comedy*.[3] It is allegory by evocation. Intermittently, along the line of a journey beyond, a double vision is summoned up, as journey *there* brings journey *here* to mind, journey *here*, that is, as represented in the prologue scene. The prologue lays the very groundwork of the allegory in this sense, planting the possibility of it and making that possibility objective within the poem, because part of the poem's structure. Hence nothing is more basic to the whole edifice than the prologue action. Along the line of the journey beyond will come signals to correspondences, to resemblances, to points of contact with that prologue scene, even as in one of the most impressive moments of this when the scene at the beginning of the *Purgatory* brings to mind the opening scene of the poem.

It would seem that we have been somewhat blind to Dante's method in allegory, but not to that alone. We have even failed to see what the master pattern is by which the poet gave airy shape to his prologue scene. Curiously enough, our blindness has persisted in the face of the clearest pointers to what that pattern is, both within the poem and without. Perhaps it was only that we had first to understand the prologue action as a *conversion* before we might glimpse the matrix into which that action is cast. Once we did understand that this was conversion, however, we ought at least to have recalled a certain paragraph in the *Letter to Can Grande* where Dante is concerned to point out that the departure of the children of Israel in the time of Moses signifies, in the moral sense, the "conversion of the soul from the grief and misery of sin to the state of grace." That Exodus is the established and familiar "figure" of conversion, we could not be told more plainly. If the historical event of the Exodus

---

[2] *Purg.* I, 107-8.

[3] For a full treatment of the matter, see my *Dante Studies 1: Elements of Structure*, Harvard University Press, 1957, pp. 1-17; 84-89. Also the whole analysis of the allegory of the journey, in the volume cited above.

can point beyond itself, signifying conversion, may not a conversion, any conversion, point back to the historical event of Exodus? This is all we needed to wonder in order to see precisely what guided the poet's hand as he drew the prologue picture. Yet of course, until we could view that as the picture of conversion, it would not occur to us to ask the question.

Exodus is the master pattern of the prologue action, the underlying image that dictates both the essential features of the scene of the action, as well as the outline of the action itself. To be sure, there is nothing here that we need construe as a departure from Egypt, as we watch this man leave the dark wood behind. No Moses guides here, neither are we told of fat lands that lie beyond any river Jordan. We know of no promised land here, unless the light at the summit of a mountain may stand for that. But, if we will sharpen our eyes a little, here on this scene there is *water*, dangerous waters, from which a man manages to escape and come to shore—to a shore which is a *desert* shore and the beginning, apparently, of a "great desert." [4] There the beasts appear before him. Perhaps it is then that we begin to remember what came upon the children of Israel when they had crossed the Red Sea and entered upon the way of the desert: the temptations, the impediments, the backslidings. A flight, a crossing of dangerous waters, a desert place where "beasts" beset the way: these are the simple features through which we may begin to glimpse the fact that somehow "Exodus" is happening here, in figure.

In fact, it is the first simile of the poem which first introduces us clearly into the whole figure of Exodus:

> E come quei che con lena affannata,
> uscito fuor del pelago a la riva,
> si volge a l'acqua perigliosa e guata,
>
> così l'animo mio ch'ancor fuggiva,
> si volse a retro a rimirar lo passo
> che non lasciò già mai persona viva.

[and as one who struggles forth from the deep to the shore and, panting, turns to gaze back upon the perilous waters, so my mind, still fleeing, turned to look upon that pass which never left anyone alive.—Translations throughout are by the author.]

The simile, in its first term, puts water, perilous waters, upon the scene, as well as the figure of a man who struggles forth from those waters (surely the figure of a swimmer), panting from his exertions as he stands upon the shore to look back upon that *pelago* where he had almost perished; all of which is matched, in the second part of the simile, by the man (or his *soul*, this being a moral landscape) who, fleeing in fear, now turns to look

---

[4] *Inf.*, I, 64: "Quando vidi costui nel gran diserto."

back upon a *passo* "that never left anyone alive," *passo* corresponding to *pelago* of the first part. How do we picture such a body of water? No doubt, as an *ocean deep,* first of all, since *pelago* implies as much. However, *passo* can well suggest a *passing through* or a *crossing over,* and thus bring the feature of a *shore* or *shores* into the picture, however distant those shores may be. Later, Ulysses speaks of his long ocean voyage as an *alto passo,* while later that same voyage is termed a *varco.*[5] Similarly, the boat that ferries souls over to the shore of Purgatory, holding to much the same route as the ancient hero took, is said to cross "between shores so distant." [6] It would seem that we should think of the *passo* of the first simile so, that is, think of *shores* as we picture it, so that this man, as he comes from the water, may be viewed as crossing over, from the one shore, which is not seen, to the other, which is.

The simple features are there: the dangerous water, a flight which is a "crossing over," then a desert shore which is the beginning of a "gran diserto," a mountain rising from the desert, then the beasts. How many times we have watched the rapid little action upon that stage, so starkly simple in its few properties, and yet have failed to see how "Exodus" is happening there—until one day in our reading we may come upon a certain chapter in St. Gregory's *Moralia,* and then suddenly we see the master pattern that guided the poet's hand as he staged *conversio:*

At ne conversus quisque jam sanctum se esse credat, et quem moeroris pugna superare non valuit, ipsa postmodum securitas sternat, dispensante Deo, permittitur ut post conversionem suam tentationum stimulis fatigetur. Iam quidem per conversionem Rubrum mare transitum est; sed adhuc in eremo vitae praesentis ante faciem hostes occurrunt. Iam peccata praeterita velut extinctos Aegyptios post terga relinquimus; sed adhuc nocentia vitia, quasi alii hostes obviant, ut ad terram promissionis pergentibus coeptum iter intercludant. Iam priores culpae, velut insequentes adversarii, sola divina virtute prostratae sunt, sed tentationum stimuli, quasi hostes alii contra faciem veniunt, qui et cum nostro labore superentur.[7]

But lest a man [conversus quisque] should believe himself holy immediately on his conversion, and security should overthrow him, whom the contest with pain could not overpower, he is permitted, in the dispensation of God, after his conversion, to be wearied with the assaults of temptations. The Red Sea was already crossed by his conversion, but enemies still oppose him to the face while in the wilderness of this present life. We leave already our past sins behind us, as the Egyptians dead on the shore. But destructive vices still assail us, as fresh enemies, to obstruct the way on which we have entered to

[5] *Inf.* XXV, 132: "Poi ch'entrati eravam nell'alto passo"; *Par.* XXVII, 82-83: "sì ch'io vedea di là da Gade il varco folle d'Ulisse."

[6] *Purg.* II, 32-33.

[7] *Sancti Gregorii Magni Moralium Lib. XXIV, In Caput XXXIII B. Job* in *Patrol. lat.,* vol. 76, col. 301.

the land of promise. Our former offences, as enemies who were pursuing us, already had been laid low by the power of God alone. But the assaults of temptations meet us to our face, like fresh enemies, to be overcome with our own endeavors also.[8]

What, in the oblique ways of poetry, the poet could only suggest, Gregory tells us openly. The interesting point to note is how, as he writes of conversion, he passes into the figure of the Exodus: "Iam Rubrum mare transitum est. . . ." One does not suspect, up to that point, that thought of any Red Sea is anywhere present in this disquisition on conversion and what can follow upon conversion. Yet when the phrase "Red Sea is crossed" comes in, and the whole event of the Exodus is called to mind, we feel at once the natural relevance of the figure. Somehow the departure of the children of Israel from Egypt can be seen in every conversion, not merely because in every conversion an "Egypt," or a worldly life of sin, is left behind, as *conversus quisque* flees in fear from it, but because the entire resemblance continues most impressively in what happens *after* conversion, after the Red Sea is crossed: for, lo!, the sinful inclinations, the "obnoxia vitia" which the *conversus* had thought to have put behind him are suddenly there before his face, impeding the way of his advance, even as the "temptations" came upon the Israelites in the way of the desert. "Exodus" happens again, even in this respect— indeed *especially* in this respect, as Gregory would have it, for that is his point.

Little wonder that as we read Gregory on conversion, the prologue scene of the *Comedy* flashes upon our mind. Were it chronologically possible, we might even take Gregory to be writing a gloss on the first canto of the *Inferno*. But the reverse of this, that the poet took from Gregory, is not at all probable. Dante most certainly did not have to read the *Moralia* to get the notion that *conversio* might be conceived on the pattern of Exodus. Exodus is simply *the* figure of conversion, as he knew well enough to tell Can Grande.

Looking back upon the prologue scene of the poem through such reminders, we realize that the first simile of the first canto would not be what it is or where it is, indeed would not be at all, if the underlying and controlling pattern of Exodus were not there, requiring it. That model, or mold, demands that on this scene of conversion there be water, a *passo* somehow like one that did not leave "the Egyptians" alive, at least. Here there must be a crossing of that water, in fearful flight, here there may even be a moment of turning to look back upon the dread peril left behind (and this Gregory also remembered to get into his picture). Then there will be a turning, a facing toward the promises, and an advance

[8] The translation is taken from *The Morals on the Book of Job by Gregory the Great* (done by "members of the English Church"), Oxford, 1850 (in 3 vols.), vol. 3, Part I, pp. 68-69, but is a little retouched.

across a "desert shore," which is also a "great desert," when lo! the temptations: in Gregory's phrasing the "obnoxia vitia" come with a phrase *sed
adhuc*, in Dante's they come with an *ed ecco*. It is almost as if the *vitia*,
or the beasts, were *expected*. As, of course, they are. We might know they
would come, for does the Exodus not happen over and over again in every
conversion? Then how could the temptations fail to come in the desert
way?

The unmistakable confirmation of the fact that the Exodus figure is
the controlling image and matrix of the prologue scene of the *Comedy*
comes at the beginning of the *Purgatory*, thirty-three cantos later, where
the wayfarer "returns" to a similar scene. Again as he comes forth from
an infernal valley and a "silvestra via" to see the stars, it is the hour of
dawn. Again he finds himself upon a desert shore, again stands looking
out over waters that are clearly labeled dangerous. This time, to be sure,
he does not come across those waters, but he does come from a *passo* which
might be said "never to have left anyone alive." He himself does not cross
over the dangerous waters lying off shore, but as he stands there to watch,
a boat comes over that *pelago*, piloted by an angel. There are more than
a hundred souls in the boat, and, as it approaches, they are heard to sing
a song of the Exodus as they come. With that touch there may be no mistake about it: not only is an "Exodus" happening here, at the beginning
of the *Purgatory*, but precisely because that is what is happening, the
prologue action seems also to be happening again, as in figure or metaphor. Yet a difference visible in the very resemblance is at once most
striking; here now it is not a swimmer who struggles to shore, but a boat
that comes over the water and lands with the greatest of ease, piloted by
an angel who is the minister of the Lord and who "scorns all human
means." Indeed, if we may now speak of two "Exoduses," one in the
prologue and one here at the beginning of the *Purgatory*, at once we see
that this latter Exodus is more like the real event. It was by a miracle
that the Lord brought His chosen people across the Red Sea to the
desert shore beyond, and clearly a boat piloted by an angel corresponds
better to that than does the figure of a man struggling to cross over "by
human means." Moreover, as these souls join company with Virgil and
Dante here on the "desert shore" and all are seen as "pilgrims" [9] who
seek the way to "the promises" what happens is also more like what
happened to the Israelites. "Temptations," corresponding to the beasts
on the prologue scene, do come here, even as in the real event of the
Exodus. Casella sings a song of love and, lo! these new "pilgrims" forget
the promises, forget that they are pilgrims, and gather around the singer
"as if nothing else touched their minds." Yet their backsliding is allowed
to last but a moment. Old Cato rushes upon the scene to make them
mindful of their journey and to send them upon their way up the moun-

[9] *Purg.* II, 61-63.

tain slope. Again we are much closer to the historical Exodus, and again the great point of difference between what happens in this second "Exodus," and what happens in the first, is brought home to us.

Much further along in the *Purgatory* come verses that are as a kind of invitation to look back upon the two Exoduses and to take the sure measure of this difference between them. On the first terrace of Purgatory proper, a special version of the Lord's Prayer is recited in which each of the familiar verses becomes a whole terzina. Thus, in place of "panem nostrum supersubstantialem da nobis hodie" we hear:

> Dà oggi a noi la cotidiana manna
> sanza la qual per questo aspro diserto
> a retro va chi più di gir s'affanna.[10]

[Give us this day the daily manna without which, in this harsh wilderness, he who toils most to advance goes back.]

Here is precisely the focus upon the two Exoduses that we need in order to take the measure of the difference between them. "Manna" may easily stand for all the divine assistance given to the Israelites when they had crossed the Red Sea and set out upon the desert way, "manna" is grace, of course; and "manna given" or "manna not given," in the way of the desert, is the whole point of difference. In the prologue "Exodus" no manna falls, and the more the wayfarer struggles to cope with the beasts there, the more he falls back. In the second "Exodus," in Purgatory, "temptations" do indeed come as before, but the guiding and protecting hand of the Lord is always there to help the pilgrim on his way, and this time the ascent of the mountain proves possible. Where in the first attempt he had fallen back, the wayfarer now climbs "the short way up." In the focus of double vision, in which one Exodus calls the other to mind, such a difference could not be more apparent to any reader who sees the matter in these terms. But will the reader see it? The poet seems to have wondered.

At certain points along the line of the journey, as every reader will recall, the poet speaks out in direct address to his readers, urging them to sharpen their eyes and to look at the truth visible beneath the veil. That truth is a moral truth, as we might guess, visible only in the double vision of allegory. We have seen that such double vision can rest upon the vision of a double "Exodus." Could it be that the truth the reader is invited to see beneath the veil, the moral truth, is a matter of the difference between these "Exoduses"? Why is "manna" not given in the one? Why is "manna" given in the other? The poet will prompt his Christian reader to put the question to himself and, at points where that

---

[10] *Purg.* XI, 13-15.

difference is most striking, to sharpen his eyes and see the answer as it is realized in the action of his poem.

If this journey to God begins in the figure of an Exodus, and then leaves that figure, to return to it after a long descent through Hell, the reason for this is clearly a matter worthy of attention. What we have here, in simplest statement, is a first attempt to climb that fails, then a long descent that returns the wayfarer to the second attempt that succeeds. Can this configuration of event in the journey beyond be pointing to the truth that it is necessary for *us* to descend that we may ascend (this being, in the moral allegory, *our* journey)?

Such an injunction is familiar enough in Christian doctrine, if we know that the descent is a descent to humility; yet the reason for this, the necessity of it in these terms, may not be quite so familiar. Happily, the poet allows that very question to come, along the way of the *Paradiso,* and has Beatrice answer it; and we shall do well to bring her words to bear upon a point of doctrine that has simply dictated the entire main outline of the journey as a descent through Hell, all the way to the girding on of the rush of humility on the desert shore of Purgatory Mountain.

In the seventh Canto of *Paradiso* the question arises why God chose the way of our Redemption that He did choose, sending His Son to take on our flesh and to die upon the Cross. As Beatrice proceeds to resolve Dante's *dubbio* in the matter, we recognize the familiar point of doctrine. We are reminded that the sin of our first parents was essentially one of pride, a disobedience, a willful aspiration to be *sicut dii,* even as the serpent had promised them they would be upon eating the forbidden fruit. Nor must we forget that we all sinned when Adam sinned.

Now, by such sinful aspiration to ascend and be "as God," man was left powerless to make due atonement, for the enormity of that sin, and its very nature, made it impossible for him to *descend,* as far as he had aspired to *ascend* in his disobedience:

> Non potea l'uomo ne' termini suoi
> mai sodisfar, per non potere ir giuso
> con umiltate obediendo poi,
>
> quanto disobediendo intese ir suso;
> e questa è la cagion per che l'uom fue
> da poter sodisfar per sè dischiuso.[11]

[Man could never make satisfaction within his own limits, being unable, by subsequent obedience, to descend so low in humility as, in his disobedience,

---

[11] *Par.* VII, 97-102.

he had aspired to ascend; and that is why it was impossible for man to make satisfaction by himself.]

Now, since man of himself (*ne' termini suoi*) was unable to make due atonement, God in His mercy chose to do this for him, by sending His Son to descend to the humility of the flesh:

> e tutti li altri modi erano scarsi
> a la giustizia, se'l Figliuol di Dio
> non fosse umiliato ad incarnarsi.[12]

[and all means were short of justice except for the Son of God to humble Himself, becoming flesh.]

Here Beatrice speaks only of the "humility" of the Incarnation, but means to suggest what every Christian reader will know, the even greater "humilities" suffered in obedience to the Father: death upon the Cross, the descent to the tomb, the descent to Hell. Indeed, even as the verses spoken here by Beatrice clearly imply, the whole divine act of the atonement must be viewed as a descent to humility on the part of God, that very descent which man was powerless to make "ne' termini suoi," after his willful ascent in pride. Man could not descend *low* enough, yet a descent so low was necessary if a just atonement was to be made. It was Christ who descended low enough to effect that atonement. By His descent to humility He atoned for man's ascent in pride, thus opening the way for man himself to ascend. Our Redemption through Christ rests, therefore, upon a fundamental pattern of *descent-ascent,* and the texts that might be adduced to witness that basic point of doctrine are indeed legion, and are easily garnered from Scripture and from the tradition. One of the many to be found in the works of St. Augustine alone may here be chosen to represent them all:

> But our Life came down to this earth and took away our death, slew death with the abundance of His own life; and He thundered, calling to us to return to Him into that secret place from which He came forth to us—coming first into the Virgin's womb, where humanity was wedded to Him, our mortal flesh, though not always to be mortal; . . . For he did not delay, but rushed on, calling to us by His death, life, descent, and ascension to return to Him. And He withdrew from our eyes, that we might return to our own heart and find Him. For He went away and behold He is still here. He would not be with us long, yet He did not leave us. He went back to that place which He had never left, for the world was made by Him. And He was in the world, and He came into this world to save sinners. Unto Him my soul confesses and He hears it, for it has sinned against Him. O ye sons

---

[12] *Par.* VII, 118-120.

of men, how long shall ye be so slow of heart? Even now when Life has come down to you, will you not ascend and live? But to what high place shall you climb, since you are in a high place and have *set your mouth against the heavens?* First descend that you may ascend, ascend to God. For in mounting up against God you fell. . . .[13]

The conceptual *necessity* of the entire descent through Inferno is plainly visible in such a passage. By His descent to humility Christ opened the way for man to rise to salvation. It was Christ Himself who showed us how to descend, and then, by His Resurrection and Ascension, how we may ascend. "Descend that you may ascend"; such is the injunction upon every Christian, for we all bear the burden of Adam's sin; the proof of which is that when we turn toward God and strive to ascend to Him, we have not the strength to do so. Indeed we discover that, if we struggle to ascend by our own powers (*ne' termini nostri*), we simply fall back into the darkness the more we strive.[14] The burden of Adam's sin is too much with us. But it was Christ who showed us the way: we have first to descend in order to ascend.

The very timing of the journey through Hell points to the familiar doctrine of Christ's descent and of "imitatio Christi." The wayfarer, that *conversus quisque* who cannot climb the mountain, begins his descent into Hell on the evening of Good Friday, and on Easter Sunday morning, just before dawn, comes forth from the "tomb" of Hell[15] to find himself upon a desert shore once more. And everywhere, in the opening verses of the *Purgatory*, are the signals of Resurrection. All is newness of life.

The entire pattern of meaning here, as it is seen to extend through no less than a third of the poem, is so emphatically underlined in these several ways that we can hardly have failed to glimpse it in our reading of the poem. One can only wonder, though, why not a single modern commentary of the poem finds time to mention it. We may wonder—but we really know the answer. The simple fact is that by now we have gone almost as far as we could possibly go in our trend to play down or exclude from attention the deeper Christian meanings of this great poem; and such a trend is an old one by now. It began very soon after Dante, in a revolution we have sometimes called a Renaissance.

The man who returns *through descent* to the desert shore, there to gird on a rush, returns to attempt once more to cross the "great desert" and ascend the mountain. It would seem to be this girdle of rush that makes all the difference now. This time the advance to the promises will prove successful. The descent to humility has been a return to "Exodus."

---

[13] *Confessions* IV, xii, translated by F. J. Sheed, New York, 1943, p. 73.

[14] For a most persuasive analysis of this point, as borne out by the famous enigma of the *pie' fermo* (*Inf.* I, 30), see John Freccero, "Dante's Firm Foot" in *Harvard Theological Review*, LIII (1959), pp. 245-281.

[15] *Inf.* XXXIV, 128.

Indeed the mere fact that rushes grow upon this desert shore should in itself have served as the clearest kind of signal of such a return, at least for any reader who knows that *Sea of Rushes* is the Red Sea's other name! [16]

Exodus-conversion, then the descent-ascent pattern of our Redemption through Christ, then a return to the first figure: such is the essential outline of the journey up to the point of the girding on of the rush. But if there is an understandable connection between the Exodus and "our conversion," as Dante writing to Can Grande said there was, may there not also be a necessary connection between that same Old Testament event and "our Redemption through Christ," i.e., the very figure of descent-ascent? But again it is Dante himself who gives the answer in that same *Letter:*

> nam si ad litteram solam inspiciamus, significatur
> nobis exitus filiorum Israel de Egypto, tempore
> Moysis; si ad allegoriam, nobis significatur nostra
> redemptio facta per Christum; si ad moralem sensum,
> significatur nobis conversio. . . .[17]

[Now if we attend to the letter alone, the departure of the children of Israel from Egypt in the time of Moses is presented to us; if the allegory, our redemption wrought by Christ; if the moral sense, the conversion of the soul. . . .]

Gradually we learn again to read Dante's great poem in its deeper Christian meanings, to see it as the great "imitation" it is. The poet chose his model well. That model was nothing less than God's way of writing. The poet's way will imitate that Divine polysemous way, whereby an event such as Exodus can signify both our Redemption through Christ and the conversion of the soul. The two significations have their common root in Exodus because Exodus is their *figura.*

When the souls, who in their "crossing over" sing of Exodus, come up to Virgil and Dante on the desert shore, asking about the "way to the mountain," something happens for the first time in the poem: a merging of two dimensions of its structure, of "journey" and of "state of souls after death." This is brought about through the notion of "pilgrim" (and therefore of "pilgrimage") made explicit for the first time here in Virgil's reply:

---

[16] Or, "Sea of Reeds": *Yam Suf* in the Hebrew; for which see almost any encyclopedia, s. v. I must admit, however, that I have been unable to establish the fact that Dante, or the Christian Middle Ages, knew of this *other* name for the Red Sea.

[17] *Epistola ad Canem Grandem* 20-25.

E Virgilio rispuose: "Voi credete
forse che siamo esperti d'esto loco;
ma noi siam peregrin come voi siete." [18]

[And Virgil answered: "Perhaps you think that we are familiar with this place; but we are pilgrims even as you are."]

Such a merging of the two dimensions could never have happened in Hell, of course. There souls may not be seen as "pilgrims," eternally *fixed* in their places as they are. Nor may souls in Paradise be thought of as being "in via," for they have reached the *patria*. But Purgatory, as Dante chose to picture that realm of the Afterlife, can lend itself especially to the metaphor of pilgrimage. Souls there can indeed be seen as pilgrims, and so join the company of the wayfarer who is constantly realizing that metaphor. Thus, later, Statius will fall in with Virgil and Dante, and move forward with them toward "the promises." The whole of Purgatory, in hope and aspiration if not in fact, is a place where a forward movement toward a "promised land" takes place, and always with a sense that such a movement is group movement: entire groups of souls become pilgrims, along with Dante and Virgil there.

It is within the confines of the particular area which we have come to call the *Ante-Purgatory* that such a sense of forward movement is most pervasive—and little wonder, since this is precisely the area of Purgatory where Exodus is the controlling master image, where Exodus (in figure) happens again, and where the prologue event is repeated, with the great difference noted. Here in Ante-Purgatory, even though the "temptations" do come,[19] there is a positive advance toward the promises. We recalled Casella's song of love as the first of those "temptations." That was at the beginning of this "pilgrimage." Now we may look to the last "temptation," at the end of the pilgrimage through Ante-Purgatory, and see an even stronger outcropping of the Exodus figure, where "our old Adversary," the serpent, comes to the souls that are gathered in the valley of the princes.

As evening falls, the many souls who sit together upon the beautiful and fragrant greensward there are heard to sing a song most appropriate to the hour, the *Salve Regina*. We had first seen them as "princes," but now if we can call to mind (as we are surely expected to do) the words of the antiphon they sing, we can sense that a change of figure takes place, for that song is nothing less than a prayer addressed to Mary by "the exiled sons of Eve" who abide yet "in this vale of tears." [20]

---

[18] *Purg.* II, 61-63.

[19] There are other motifs through the Ante-Purgatory (a strain of "homesickness," a theme of "backward glances") which also bear out the Exodus figure in ways which may not be examined here.

[20] The first stanza of the *Salve Regina*, as Dante knew it, went as follows:

Then, moments later in the deepening dusk, these souls sing yet another song, the *Te lucis ante*. Again the reader is expected to recall the words of that prayer, or at least those which come at the end of its second stanza: "hostemque nostrum comprime." [21] This second song now is a prayer addressed to the Creator, imploring His protection through the night, asking Him especially "to drive back our Enemy."

Now, it is just at this point that all the souls, who are gathered here to sing such prayers, are viewed as a single group, as an "essercito":

> Io vidi quello essercito gentile
> tacito poscia riguardare in sue,
> quasi aspettando, palido e umile.[22]

[Then I saw that noble host grow silent, pale and humble, gazing upwards as though expectant.]

All are as one "army" now, and the adjectives can be in the singular (the adjective that makes the rhyme will not escape our special notice!). Already their song has explained why all are pale as they look up to Heaven. That pallor comes from the fear of "our Enemy" who is expected to come in the night; and they look toward Heaven, of course, because their prayer is for help from on high, from Mary, as their first song had it, or from the Lord, as now, that the Enemy who will come at night be driven back. The whole attitude and posture is one of humility, even as the adjective in the emphatic rhyme position is declaring. These souls trust in the Lord, and wait upon His protection here.

The implored protection is given: two angels descend "from Mary's bosom," taking up their posts, like guards or sentinels, on either side of this "army" of souls. If we pause to take in the scene as a whole, will it

---

> Salve Regina misericordiae:
> Vita, dulcedo, et spes nostra, salve.
> Ad te clamamus exsules, filii Hevae,
> Ad te suspiramus, gementes et flentes,
> In hac lachrymarus valle.

[21] The first two stanzas of the hymn, as Dante knew it:

> Te lucis ante terminum
> Rerum Creator poscimus
> Ut solita clementia
> Sis praesul ad custodiam.
>
> Procul recedant somnia
> Et noctium phantasmata,
> Hostemque nostrum comprime
> Ne polluantur corpora.

[22] *Purg.* VIII, 22-24.

not remind us of some scene of Exodus? Why not a certain scene of encampment before Mount Sinai?

Mense tertio egressionis Israel de terra Aegypti, in die haec venerunt in solitudinem Sinai. Nam profecti de Raphidim, et pervenientes usque in desertum Sinai, castrametati sunt in eodem loco; ibique Israel fixit tentoria e regione montis.[23]

[The King James Version reads as follows: "In the third month, when the children of Israel were gone forth out of the land of Egypt, the same day came they into the wilderness of Sinai. For they were departed from Rephidim and were come to the desert of Sinai, and had pitched in the wilderness; and there Israel camped before the mount."]

The connection of the one scene with the other could seem merely one reader's arbitrary association, were it not for the whole context of "Exodus" through Ante-Purgatory, of which this scene is but a part, and of which the theme of "temptation in the desert" is also a part; and were it not that inside the gate of Purgatory proper we meet with a quite special backward glance over this whole episode, the coming of "our Enemy." Again they are verses that come in the Pater Noster recited on the first terrace. This time, in place of the familiar "ne nos inducas in tentationem," we hear the paraphrase:

> Nostra virtù che di leggier s'adona,
>   non spermentar con l'antico avversaro,
>   ma libera da lui che sì la sprona.

[Our strength, which is so easily daunted, test not with the old adversary, but deliver us from him, who spurs it so.]

Then, significantly enough, the souls add a special qualification to this ending of their prayer:

> Quest'ultima preghiera, signor caro,
>   già non si fa per noi, chè non bisogna,
>   ma per color che dietro a noi restaro.[24]

[This last prayer, dear Lord, we make not for ourselves, for there is no need, but for those that remain behind us.]

We know that the phrase "those who remained behind" is rich in ambiguity. We, the living, are intended, as the next terzina makes clear. But so are those who have remained behind, outside the gate, in Ante-

[23] *Exod.* XIX, 1-2.
[24] *Purg.* XI, 19-24.

Purgatory, intended by those words also. There could be no clearer declaration that the whole of Ante-Purgatory is a place where temptations
can still beset the way, even as we had seen in the coming of the "antico
avversaro" there, the serpent, perhaps the same that "gave Eve the bitter
food." [25]

We are helped further to see that Exodus is still the controlling figure
here, near the end of the Ante-Purgatory, by what the wayfarer himself
looks up to see at this point—and by this we are reminded of what he
had seen in the sky that morning, when his "pilgrimage" began. There,
at the outset, as dawn came on, Dante had taken notice of four especially
beautiful stars near the pole of this southern hemisphere.[26] Now, as he
stands with the "essercito" of souls in the little valley (and is thus one
with them) he looks up once more to see three stars where the four had
been, and is told that the three have *replaced* the four.[27] Now, given the
context here, and the certain presence of the Exodus figure as noted, how
shall we fail to recall that the Lord was with the army of the Israelites as
it moved across the desert, a pillar of cloud by day and a pillar of fire by
night? These groups of stars do appear to preside, one over the day, one
over the night.[28]

In fine, in the "way of the desert" as it reaches through the vestibule
area of Purgatory, "manna" *is* given. The guiding and protecting hand
of the Lord is here to drive back the Adversary who comes. Not so on the
prologue scene. The beasts were not driven back. To be sure, there was
a certain relay of grace in Heaven, from Mary to Lucia, from Lucia to
Beatrice, from Beatice to Virgil, and help did come with Virgil; but it
was nothing to match the descent of two angels from Mary's bosom. Here
now, where the "pilgrims" look up to the Lord and wait upon Him, pale
and humble, help descends *directly* from Mary.

Such is the context in which the poet chooses to address his reader directly—indeed the poet does this at just the moment when the term "essercito" leads us into an "Exodus" scene and recalls the other "Exodus"
of the prologue:

> Aguzza qui, lettor, ben li occhi al vero,
>   chè 'l velo è ora ben tanto sottile,
>   certo che 'l trapassar dentro è leggero.
>
> Io vidi quello essercito gentile
>   tacito poscia riguardare in sue
>   quasi aspettando, palido e umile;

[25] *Purg.* VIII, 99.
[26] *Purg.* I, 22-24.
[27] *Purg.* VIII, 91-93.
[28] On the meanings of the two groups of stars in the allegorical journey, quite apart
from their being a part of the Exodus figure, see *Dante Studies 1 (cit.)*, pp. 141 ff.

e vidi uscir dell'alto e scender giue
due angeli con due spade affocate,
tronche e private delle punte sue.

Verdi come fogliette pur mo nate
erano in veste. . . .[29]

[Reader, sharpen your eyes well to the truth here, for now the veil is indeed
so thin that to pass beneath is surely easy. Then I saw that noble host grow
silent, pale and humble, gazing upwards as though expectant: and I saw two
angels appear on high and descend, holding two flaming swords that were
broken off and deprived of their points. Their raiment was green as fresh new
leaves. . . ."]

Green is the color of hope, and the hope of those who have humility,
who wait upon the Lord for protection, is not in vain. "Manna" descends, angels come, and as long as His angels are watching over us, and
three stars shine down upon us, the dangers which beset our way cannot
be such as to require sharp-pointed swords to drive them back, for swords
can be as token swords where He guides. So much of the "truth" we are
surely expected to see, if we sharpen our eyes. But the poet's whole
method in moral allegory extends beyond any such limited context. That
allegory depends on the evocation of double vision, and double vision is
always possible if the prologue scene of the poem can be recalled, not
only for the *resemblance* it may have with this journey beyond, but for
the *difference* visible now *within* the resemblance. *Trapassar dentro,* in
this poet's address to the reader, will mean a *trapassar indietro,* all the
way back to a prologue scene at the beginning.

Still further confirmation of the fact that the meaning here holds to
the contextual image of Exodus is to be noted as the scene of the poem
passes from that of an "encampment," on the lower slope of a mountain,
to the episode of the wayfarer's first dream in Purgatory, when night
comes and he falls asleep beside Sordello and Virgil and the "essercito
gentile." [30] The dream comes in the hour just before the dawn, and proves
to be prophetic—as it might be expected to be, coming at such a time.
In the dream the wayfarer sees an eagle circling above him, its golden
wings outspread, ready to swoop down; and it seems to the dreamer that
he is where Ganymede was when he abandoned his companions and was
caught up to the "consistory of the gods." Then the eagle does descend,
terrible as lightning. It carries the dreamer "up to the fire," which "imagined" fire seems to burn him, so that he awakens.
As Dante wakes up to look about him, he is frightened to see that he

[29] *Purg.* VIII, 19-29.
[30] *Purg.* IX, 1 ff.

is now no longer where he was when he fell asleep, and that it is broad day now. Virgil comforts him by explaining what had happened, telling how just before dawn (hence, in the hour of the dream) Lucia had come to him in the vale where he sat beside the sleeping Dante, asking to be allowed to take up the sleeping man and to "make his way easier"; then she had carried him up the long steep slope of the mountain, all the way (or almost) to the gate of Purgatory proper.

The prophetic nature of the dream is now evident enough. The dream was actually realized while it was taking place as a dream. The eagle, in the realization, is Lucia, and the fire that had seemed to burn the dreamer was Purgatory proper, the gate of which is now within sight, a little further up the slope.

As the reassured wayfarer climbs toward that gate, the poet speaks out in yet another address to his reader:

> . . . e come sanza cura
> vide me 'l duca mio, su per lo balzo
> si mosse, ed io di retro inver l'altura.
>
> Lettor, tu vedi ben com'io innalzo
> la mia matera, e però con più arte
> non ti maravigliar s'io la rincalzo.[31]

[and when my Leader saw me relieved of worry, he set out along the cliff toward the height, and I followed. Reader, you see well how I am uplifting my theme, therefore do not wonder that I bolster it with greater art.]

It is always important to have the precise context of these addresses to the reader before us. Here it is one of climbing the mountain, climbing now to the very gate of Purgatory, which gate is described in the verses immediately following the above. In the address itself, what the reader is told he can see so well now is how the poet is uplifting his "matera" here.

Given the nature of this poem, the poet's "matera" can be nothing if not the *record* of his journey beyond, which he as poet is setting down, with all the art at his command. Thus, to urge the reader to see how the poet's "matera" is being uplifted with more "arte," is to invite him to look at what "matera" (the record), and "arte," are now setting before his eyes, namely, the last lap of a successful climb up the mountain to the very gateway to "the promises"—for such is indeed the area of Purgatory proper, as seen from within. This gate is the portal to the "true city," as we realize most clearly when a soul on one of the terraces is asked much the usual question by Dante: "Are there any Italians here among you?" and replies, speaking for all its companions:

[31] *Purg.* IX, 67-72.

"O frate mio, ciascuna è cittadina
d'una vera città; ma tu vuo' dire
che vivesse in Italia peregrina." [32]

["O brother, each is a citizen of a true city; but you mean one that lived in
Italy a pilgrim."]

However, it is not merely this last lap of a successful climb that the
address to the reader would have him consider. To see "how the *matera*
is raised" is to look back over the whole account of the journey so far
(else we may not see how this is any "last lap").

But Lucia! Is it not significant that it is Lucia, and not another, who
comes here? Is her very re-appearance here not like an address to the
reader, prompting him (as that other address had done) to look back, all
the way back to the prologue, to hold the event of a successful climb *here*
against that of an unsuccessful climb *there*, and to remark that very *difference*? The coming of Lucia here is a recall to the prologue event that
can be compared to another given along the line of the descent through
Hell: the reference to the girdle of rope with which the wayfarer had
once thought to take the *lonza* with the painted hide.[33] By the mere
mention of the *lonza* the reader is returned to the prologue scene—for
where else has he met with mention of any such beast, or the attempt to
"take it," that is, to cope with it? So now with Lucia's coming. We shall
not fail to remember how hers was the middle role in the relay of grace
that ended with Virgil's coming to the rescue in the "gran diserto." By
Lucia's coming the reader is returned to the prologue (which means a
return to the Exodus figure) and invited to consider the difference between *then* and *now*, "Exodus" then and "Exodus" now. *Then* no Lucia
descended *directly* to make this man's way easier on the mountain slope;
now Lucia herself descends and carries him the long way up. Neither did
help descend *then* from Mary, certainly not *directly*, as it has but now
done in the descent of two angels "from Mary's bosom."

Thus, first from Mary, then from Lucia, help comes here, *de sursum
descendens*. What if the next one who came to help this man on the
mountain slope were a Beatrice? And what if she came to Virgil there?
But so it is! [34] —only that will be part of another dream, and will lie
beyond the pattern of Exodus. Nonetheless, even there, recall to the prologue will continue to operate.

[32] *Purg.* XIII, 94-96.
[33] *Inf.* XVI, 106. On the "corda" here and the method in allegory, see *Dante Studies I*
(*cit.*), pp. 4-5.
[34] *Purg.* XIX, 26-32. Beatrice is not named here. It is a "donna santa e presta" who
comes, saying: "O Virgilio, o Virgilio." I submit that we are to understand that she is
Beatrice, however, and precisely by reason of the repeated sequence: Mary, Lucia,
Beatrice.

Twice the reader is addressed directly by the poet when the context, in general and in particular, is evocative of Exodus. The first such address comes when help is seen to descend from Mary to the "encampment" of the *essercito,* where the serpent is wont to come. The second comes when we pass to the dream of the eagle's descent, realized by Lucia's "making the way easier." But that this second episode of the dream is also imbedded in the context of Exodus we have yet to see.

Actually, the allusion to Ganymede does its own proper work, serving very well to give us a scene on a mountainside comparable to the scene here in Purgatory, and to bring in an eagle that will detach one figure from the rest, Ganymede from his companions, as Dante from the *essercito* of souls. But the point to bear in mind is that this scene of "encampment" before the mountain is above all reminiscent of Exodus. But can this eagle in the dream be itself any part of an Exodus figure? To see the answer we have only to read a little farther in the passage already remembered from Exodus:

> Mense tertio egressionis Israel de terra Aegypti, in die hac venerunt in solitudinem Sinai. Nam profecti de Raphidim, et pervenientes usque in desertum Sinai, castrametati sunt in eodem loco; ibique Israel fixit tentoria e regione montis. Moyses autem ascendit ad Deum, vocavitque eum Dominus de monte, et ait: Haec dices domui Jacob, et annuntiabis filiis Israel: Vos ipsi vidistis, quae fecerim Aegyptiis, quomodo portaverim vos super alas aquilarum, et assumpserim mihi.[35]

> [In the third month, when the children of Israel were gone forth out of the land of Egypt, the same day came they into the wilderness of Sinai. For they were departed from Rephidim, and were come to the desert of Sinai, and had pitched in the wilderness; and there Israel camped before the mount. And Moses went up unto God, and the Lord called unto him out of the mountain, saying, thus shalt thou say to the house of Jacob, and tell the children of Israel; Ye have seen what I did unto the Egyptians, and how I bare you on eagles' wings, and brought you unto myself.]

Nor is this all. We must also remember that later, in *Deuteronomy* (and therefore near the *end* of Exodus, even as in the poem at this point we are nearing the end of the Exodus figure of Ante-Purgatory) the eagle enters again where again there is mention of the help the Lord gave to Israel in the desert. Indeed here we feel we have come even closer to the particular detail of Dante's dream and the context of Exodus in which it is rooted (as unnecessary italics can suggest):

> Invenit eum in terra diserta, in loco horroris, in vastae solitudinis; circumduxit eum et docuit, et custodivit quasi pupillam oculi sui. Sicut aquila pro-

[35] *Exod.* XIX, 1-4.

vocans ad volandum pullos suos, et *super eos volitans, expandit alas suas* et
assumpsit eum. . . .[36]

[He found him in a desert land, and in the waste howling wilderness; he led
him about, he instructed him, he kept him as the apple of his eye. As an
eagle stirreth up her nest, fluttereth over her young, spreadeth abroad her
wings, taketh them, beareth them on her wings. . . .]

Lucia is "grace" *de sursum descendens,* and in the dream the eagle is
"grace." In the dream the eagle descends, in the fact Lucia comes. Such
is the "manna" given to the man who strives to climb the mountain
again, because that man now wears the girdle of humility, having learned
in the journey through Hell to put off the other girdle of self-reliance.
A girdle is plainly a symbol of strength, strength of one kind or another,
be the girdle a *corda* or a *giunco.* The man in the prologue action had
worn the first kind, the girdle of his own powers, because by God's dispensation (even as St. Gregory instructed us) he was there left to discover
how weak those powers are. Now the same man climbs the "desert" slope
again where the "temptations" can still come (as the coming of a serpent
proves all too clearly), but now he is girt with the rush of humility, now
he waits upon the Lord, even as the souls in this place who look up so
pale and humble.

As we get the whole of the moral truth before us, in terms of the difference a girdle of rush can make, we may also recall other familiar verses,
this time from *Isaiah,* where again we hear mention of eagle's wings:

Deficient pueri et laborabunt, et juvenes in infirmitate cadent; qui autem
sperant in Domino mutabunt fortitudinem, assument pennas sicut aquilae,
current et non laborabunt, ambulabunt et non deficient.[37]

[Even the youths shall faint and be weary, and the young men shall utterly
fall: But they that wait upon the Lord shall renew their strength; they shall
mount up with wings as eagles; they shall run and not be weary; and they
shall walk, and not faint.]

From where an eagle (or Lucia) had set him down, the gate of the
"true city," the entrance to "the promises," can be seen, and this man
climbs the last lap of his "Exodus" now, with no difficulty at all. This
time he faints not, neither does he fall back.

Aguzza qui, lettor, ben li occhi al vero.

---

[36] *Deuter.* XXXII, 10-11.
[37] *Isaiah* XL, 30-31.

Dante's *DXV*

by R. E. Kaske

In the thirty-second canto of Dante's *Purgatorio*, we are shown an allegorical survey of the fortunes of the Church Militant in the time following Christ's ascension. The triumphal car of the heavenly procession (the Church) has been left by the Griffon (Christ) bound firmly to the great tree (11. 49-60). After the ascension of the Griffon (1. 89), the car is assailed by a series of allegorical enemies representing major vicissitudes in the history of the Church (11. 112-35): an eagle, a she-fox, a gift of feathers left in the car by the eagle on a second visit, and finally a dragon. The result of these assaults is to turn the once triumphal chariot into a broken, feathered, seven-headed monster (11. 136-47); and the end of the canto finds it possessed by a "wanton whore" obviously recalling the "great whore" of the Apocalypse, along with a ferocious giant introduced as her lover (11. 148-60). It is with reference to these final outrages that Beatrice, in the following canto, delivers her prophecy concerning "a Five Hundred, Ten, and Five" (or a *D, X,* and *V*), which has made an honest reputation as one of the most perverse cruxes in literary history:

34   Know that the vessel which the serpent broke
       Was, and is not; but let him whose guilt it is, believe
       That the vengeance of God does not fear sops.

37   Not for all time without heir will be
       The eagle who left the feathers in the car,
       Through which it turned monster, and afterwards prey;

"Dante's *DXV*," by R. E. Kaske. An abridgement of the first two parts of "Dante's 'DXV' and 'Veltro,'" *Traditio*, XVII (Fordham Univ. Press, 1961), 185-254 (referred to hereafter as *Trad.*). The original articles include, along with a somewhat more detailed form of the present argument, a related interpretation of the "Greyhound" prophecy in *Inf.* I, 101-11 (pp. 227-52), and can be consulted for fuller documentation, as well as illustrations, throughout. A few small additions and corrections are, however, included in the present version in or at footnotes 1, 10, 13, 17, 30, 31, and 35. All translations are by the author. Abridged by permission of the editors of *Traditio* and the Fordham University Press.

40   For with certainty I see—and therefore tell it—stars,
        Secure from every let and every hindrance,
        Already near, ready to give a time

43   In which a Five Hundred, Ten, and Five,
        Sent from God, will kill the thief
        With that giant who sins with her.

A fresh attempt on this formidable puzzle, by one who cannot even profess to be a Dantist, may seem peculiarly open to what a contemporary scholar has called "the mild raillery that attends those who persist in offering solutions of problems apparently worked to death." Yet a survey of the massive bibliography surrounding the *DXV* produces the strong impression that none of the explanations proposed so far has won for itself any real core of acceptance. If this one-sentence summary of six hundred years' scholarship is accurate, it suggests that a fruitful approach is less likely to emerge from comparative re-assessments of the existing theories, than from an exploration of some of the all-but-forgotten corners of medieval Christian tradition, in search of an interpretation that will fit the figure and its context more precisely.

The basis for so strange an allusion can be found, I believe, in a well-established medieval allegorization of a monogram which appears consistently in the liturgical books of Dante's time. Then as now, the Canon of the Mass was immediately preceded by a short series of prayers called the Preface, beginning with the words *Vere dignum et iustum est:* "It is truly meet and just, right and availing unto salvation, that we at all times and in all places give thanks to Thee, O holy Lord, Father almighty, everlasting God. . . ." In missals and sacramentaries from the ninth century through at least the early part of the fourteenth, this liturgical formula commonly begins with some form of the monogram ⊕ composed of the initial letters of the opening words *Vere dignum,* joined and embellished by the cross which results from an added horizontal stroke at their center.[1] Though properly representing the two words *Vere dignum,* the monogram is often substituted for various larger segments of the opening formula, down to *eterne Deus* ("everlasting God"); on the other hand, it sometimes stands only for *Vere* plus the initial *d* of *dignum,* or for the word *Vere* alone, or even for the single letter *V.* From the ninth century on, but particularly during the twelfth and the

---

[1] The development of this monogram is sketched by Adalbert Ebner, *Quellen und Forschungen zur Geschichte und Kunstgeschichte des Missale Romanum im Mittelalter: Iter Italicum* (Freiburg i.B., 1896), pp. 432-43. Seventeen examples of it are reproduced in *Trad.* at p. 188. For further references, see *Trad.*, appendix, pp. 252-4; an interesting addition to the list appears in the Walters Art Gallery's *Illuminated Books of the Middle Ages and Renaissance* (Baltimore, 1949), pl. XII-a. The sacramentary, by contrast with the missal, contained only those parts of the Mass recited by the celebrant, but included also the prayers used by the bishop or priest at other services.

thirteenth, this picturesque but familiar character is a favorite subject
for illumination (*Trad.*, figs. 2 ff.).

Among twelfth and thirteenth century liturgists, the monogram is
conventionally interpreted as a symbol of the mysterious union of natures
in Christ—the *V* signifying His human nature, the *D* His divine. This
explanation, apparently invented in the twelfth century by John Beleth,
is repeated near the end of that century by Sicard of Cremona, and in
the latter part of the thirteenth by the great liturgist William Durandus.
I quote the version that turns up finally in the *Mammotrectus,* a popular
compendium written by an Italian Franciscan, John Marchesini of
Reggio, not far from the year 1300:

> When *Vere dignum et iustum est* is spoken, note that the letter *V* is written
> by way of intimating the two substances in Christ. [This letter] is open on
> one side, and on the opposite side is connected or joined—by which features
> it designates the humanity of Christ, which has its origin on His mother's
> side and is coupled to His divinity. But the letter *D,* which is closed on all
> sides by a circular round, designates the divinity of Christ, which is neither
> opened by a beginning nor closed or terminated by an end. So also, the
> point at which the letters are joined in the sign of a cross is the holy Cross,
> through which things human are united to things divine.[2]

At least one highly embellished example of the monogram itself, found
in a Salzburg missal from the last half of the twelfth century, bears on
its outer frame four Leonine verses expressing the same interpretation.[3]

So far, then, this monogram offers us the two end-letters of Dante's
DXV in reverse order, along with a potentially interesting allegorization
of them; but no central *X*. Various strong suggestions of an *X* do exist
within the monogram, however, particularly in the vicinity of the juncture between the *V* and the *D*. Most simply, the central cross itself
becomes a clear *X* when the figure is turned slightly in either direction.
Again, the vertical center-line of the monogram, with its curving forks at
the top and bottom, bears an inevitable and consistent resemblance to
medieval forms of *X* in which the point of juncture appears vertically
elongated;[4] and this structural likeness is sometimes greatly heightened

---

[2] *Mammotrectus super Bibliam,* II, 13, "De canone" (Venice, 1486). Beleth, *Rationale
divinorum officiorum,* ch. 44 (J.-P. Migne, *Patrologia latina* 202, col. 53); Sicard,
Mitrale, III, 6 (*PL* 213, col. 122); and Durandus, *Rationale divinorum officiorum,* IV, 33
(Lyon, 1540), fol. 52ᵛ—who adds that the monogram is placed at the beginning of the
Preface because in the Preface ". . . things human are joined with things divine in a
heralding of the Savior."

[3] Georg Swarzenski, *Die Salzburger Malerei von der ersten Anfängen bis zur Blütezeit
des romanischen Stils* (Denkmäler der süddeutschen Malerei des frühen Mittelalters,
II; Leipzig, 1913), tab. 112, fig. 382; and Textband, pp. 106, 162.

[4] For examples of this type of *x,* see the specimens from thirteenth century northern
Italian MSS reproduced by Hermann Delitsch, *Geschichte der abendländischen Schreib-
schriftformen* (Leipzig, 1928), p. 129, abb. 38 b-c; and *Trad.,* p. 190, n. 10, and fig. 1.

by features of individual design (*Trad.*, fig. 2). Occasionally, the horizontal arm of the cross is modified into some semblance of an ornamental X. Decorative branches, tendrils, or foliage within the open spaces of the V and the D frequently take the form of a single large X—sometimes luxuriantly curved, and with its point of juncture often apparently hidden behind that of the central cross. Smaller but more distinct decorative X's are particularly common at the top and/or bottom forks of the vertical center-line; they are also found at the center of the cross, and sometimes on its horizontal or vertical arms.[5] I do not mean to insist, of course, that these decorative devices were necessarily intended as alphabetical X's by the men who drew them; my argument is that the poetic imagination of Dante, alive as it must have been to possible significances of design, would surely have had little difficulty in finding visual suggestions of an X at or near the center of the *Vere dignum* monogram, particularly in highly ornamented examples.

Besides such visual suggestions, the central part of the monogram contains two possible kinds of figurative "X." One is the central cross, which, as we have seen, is explained by medieval liturgists as the Cross of Christ; the inevitable connection between the Cross and an X is expressed, for example, by Isidore of Seville, who speaks of "the letter X, which both signifies the Cross in a figurative sense, and designates the number ten." [6] A second and more important figurative "X" is the pictorial representation of Christ Himself at the center of the monogram (*Trad.*, figs. 14-17), which becomes especially popular in the twelfth and thirteenth centuries; one hardly needs to be reminded of the standard medieval designation of Christ by the Greek letters *chi, rho, sigma* (reproduced in Latin as *Xp̄s*), or of the further abbreviation to a Greek *chi*, naturally associated with Latin X. This picture of Christ in the monogram is always strongly Apocalyptic—is, in fact, the conventional figure of Christ in glory, familiar in illustrations of the Apocalypse and in portrayals of the Last Judgment generally. Besides appearing within the monogram itself, the picture becomes in a larger way the distinctive iconographical feature of the Preface in medieval missals and sacramentaries—sometimes accompanying the monogram independently, sometimes replacing it altogether, and sometimes partly absorbing it. In some examples, the image of Christ has grown to a full-length portrait within the monogram, replacing the central cross (*Trad.*, fig. 16). In others, the monogram itself has been reduced to a mandorla (an elliptical frame with pointed ends) like that which conventionally frames the picture of Christ in glory, either separately or as a part of larger Apocalyptic scenes;

---

[5] For examples of these various kinds of decorative detail, see *Trad.*, figs. 3 ff., p. 190, and the accompanying notes.

[6] *Etymologiae*, I, iii, 11, ed. W. M. Lindsay (Oxford, 1911); see also I, iv, 14. A similar association is made by the thirteenth century Joachist Peter John Olivi (quoted in *Trad.*, p. 191, n. 16).

in at least one such instance, however, the figure as a whole still stands for both the word *Vere* and the initial *d* of *dignum,* as shown by the text "-ignum et iustum est" immediately following it (*Trad.,* fig. 17). The monogram and the Apocalyptic figure of Christ have here become one.

I propose, then, that in Dante's *DXV* we are to recognize a symmetrical reversal of this monogrammatic "VXD"; that the *D* and the *V* represent Christ's divine and human natures respectively, just as in the medieval allegorization of the monogram; and that the central *X* represents the person Christ as the meeting-point of these two natures—paralleling the significance of the cross at the center of the monogram, "through which things human are united to things divine." This interpretation of the *X* receives incidental support from the common association of the letter *X* with the name "Christ" (mentioned above), as well as from the corresponding position occupied by the Apocalyptic picture of the person Christ between the *V* and the *D* of the monogram. By a rather striking coincidence, the *V* and *D* correspond also to the initial letters of the Italian words *Vomo* (*Uomo,* "man") and *Dio* ("God"). If all this is so, the event prophesied by Beatrice must surely be a future coming of Christ, the *Deus-homo* or "God-man"—whether to be thought of as the traditional "second coming," or in terms of some less orthodox eschatology. Such an interpretation is in turn strongly supported by the Apocalyptic character of the picture in the monogram, particularly in view of the Apocalyptic imagery of the preceding canto; and possibly also by the traditional prominence of the Cross (signified by the cross within the monogram) at Christ's final coming, following a standard exegesis of the "sign of the Son of man in the heavens" of Matt. 24:30.

For Dante's reversal of the *D* and the *V* there are several plausible explanations, probably more or less complementary. If, as I suspect, the full meaning of Dante's symbol embraces also the numerical values of the three letters as digits of a single larger number, the order *D-X-V* would in fact be the only one possible. This reversal does, however, contribute to the theological coherence of the figure as well, by making the *D* of Christ's divine nature precede the *V* of His human nature instead of vice versa. A subtler significance is perhaps created by the position of the *Vere dignum* monogram at the beginning of the Preface of the Mass, in connection with "a heralding of the Savior" (note 2 above)—looking forward to a real re-enactment of the sacrifice on the Cross, the completion of Christ's historical first coming. If in these terms we can allow ourselves to conceive of the monogrammatic "VXD" as an anticipation of the first coming, with the precedence of *V* signifying the greater outward prominence of Christ's humanity, Dante's reversal of the letters to *DXV* may be seen as a dramatic "heralding" of the divinity which will shine forth at Christ's final coming.[7] In any

---

[7] This difference in the prominence of Christ's two natures at His first and second advents is a commonplace; see *Trad.,* p. 193, n. 24.

case, this symmetrical reversal of the three letters seems much more in accord with Dante's usual practice than do the various other rearrangements sometimes proposed—most notably, the transparently simple and imaginatively rather unrewarding change from *DXV* to *DVX*, or "Dux" ("leader").

But if this really is Dante's intended significance, why has he chosen to introduce an already enigmatic figure by way of the further numerical conundrum "a Five Hundred, Ten, and Five"? A superficial though not altogether irrelevant answer might be that Beatrice's prophecy is expressly called a "great enigma" (XXXIII, 50); for a more precise explanation, we must turn at this point to a somewhat anticipatory discussion of Dante's giant, who has been introduced along with the whore as a usurper of the car and is to be killed with her by the *DXV*. According to a common medieval exegesis of Gen. 6:2–4, the giants of the Old Testament were double-natured, born of a union between the sons of God and the daughters of men. So pervasive is this idea, that by analogy with it Ps. 18:6 (Vulgate), "He has exulted as a giant to run his course," is from the time of Ambrose consistently interpreted as a prophetic reference to the fusion of the divine and human natures in Christ.[8] With these familiar correspondences in mind, it would seem reasonable to see in Dante's giant a double-natured antithesis of Christ the *Deus-homo*—Himself represented not only in a future coming by the double-natured *DXV*, but also in His first coming by the double-natured Griffon in Cantos XXIX-XXXII. One might also expect, however, to find some sort of connection between this giant and the imagery of the Apocalypse, surrounded as he is in the poem by Apocalyptic figures like the whore, the dragon, the monster-car with seven heads and ten horns, and finally the *DXV* Himself. Though there is no giant in the text of the Apocalypse, one does appear with a good deal of consistency in medieval commentary on the famous Apoc. 13:17-8: "And [the beast shall bring it about] that none may buy or sell except him that has the character or name of the beast, or the number of his name. Here is wisdom. He that has understanding, let him count the number of the beast; for it is the number of a man, and the number of him is six hundred sixty-six." Among the many ingenious interpretations of this number 666, one of the most popular is that which explains it as the sum of the numerical values represented by the letters of the Greek word *teitán*, "giant"—which, through an explicit parallel with the double-natured giant Christ, is in turn made to signify the Antichrist. In the words of a thirteenth century exposition traditionally attached to the name of Albertus Magnus:

---

[8] For the Old Testament giants, see particularly Augustin Calmet, *De gigantibus*, in J.-P. Migne, *Scripturae Sacrae cursus completus* (Paris, 1837-45), VII, 764-77; for Christ as a giant, my article "*Gigas* the Giant in *Piers Plowman*," *Journal of English and Germanic Philology*, LVI (1957), 177-85.

According to Bede, this name is *Teytan,* which is translated "giant"; for the Antichrist, just as if he surpassed all in power, will usurp this name, declaring himself to be that One of Whom the psalmist says, "He has exulted as a giant." The number of this name, moreover, is six hundred sixty-six, which can be understood thus: *T* represents three hundred, *E* five, *I* ten, *T* three hundred, *A* one, *N* fifty—which added up, make six hundred sixty-six. . . . [Antichrist] has called himself . . . the giant of double substance, that is, divine and human.[9]

My conclusion is that Dante's giant represents primarily the Antichrist, expressed in the Apocalypse through the number 666, the "number of the beast"; that his antithesis in the *Purgatorio* is Christ, expressed through the number 515, the "number" of the *DXV* or *Deus-homo;* and that Dante's numerical introduction of the *DXV* is, accordingly, a device for pointing up His antithetical relationship to this numerically begotten Antichrist. In addition, just as Dante's 515 reflects the *Vere dignum* monogram, so the 666 of Apoc. 13:18 is often explained by commentators as a reflection of the familiar monogram formed from the Greek letters *chi* and *rho*—a traditional symbol of Christ, which will be unjustly appropriated by the Antichrist (*Trad.,* p. 195 and n. 29). It seems just possible also that the partial parallel between 666 and 515 may have been heightened for Dante by some knowledge of an early version of Apoc. 13:18 in which 666 is replaced by the number 616; a brief treatise *On the monogram of Christ,* ascribed to Jerome, contains an elaborate exegesis of this Apocalyptic 616, relating it to the word *teitán,* the Antichrist, a monogram associated with him, and the vice of pride.[10] And finally, this whole pattern of antitheses can perhaps be supplemented by a detailed correspondence between the numbers 666 (or 616) and 515, based on the intricate numerical analyses developed in commentaries on Apoc. 13:18.[11]

So far, this interpretation of Dante's *DXV* seems to me stronger in three fundamental ways than any of those offered previously: first, in its reliance on a traditional symbol of some potential profundity, whose currency within Dante's own time can be specifically and extensively documented; second, in the orderly precision with which the component parts of the *Vere dignum* monogram can be fitted to those of the DXV,

[9] Ed. A. Borgnet, *B. Alberti Magni . . . opera omnia* (Paris, 1899), XXXVIII, 675-6. For further references, in commentary on Apoc. 13:17-8 as well as in other eschatological writings, see *Trad.,* pp. 194-5, nn. 27-8.

[10] *De monogramma Christi,* ed. G. Morin, *Sancti Hieronymi presbyteri Tractatus sive Homiliae in Psalmos quattuordecim* (Anecdota Maredsolana, III, 3; Maredsous, 1903), pp. 194-8 (also in *PL,* Suppl. Vol. 2, cols. 287-91). Besides a disparaging reference to Irenaeus, *Contra haer.,* V, 30 (*PG* 7, cols. 1203-4), the number 616 appears also in a popular pseudo-Augustinian cycle of homilies on the Apocalypse, ed. Morin, *Sancti Caesarii episcopi Arelatensis opera omnia* (Maredsous, 1942), II, 247 (*PL* 35, col. 2444).

[11] Omitted here; see *Trad.,* pp. 196-8.

with respect to both pattern and meaning; and third, in the distinct relationship that this interpretation establishes between the *DXV* and another figure in the immediate context, which in turn provides an intelligible reason for Dante's numerical introduction of the *DXV*.[12] What remains is to demonstrate an accord between this proposed meaning of the *DXV* and other crucial passages of the *Divine Comedy,* in Cantos XXXII and XXXIII as well as in the poem at large. Though space forbids a complete presentation of the evidence here,[13] let us survey some of its more important details, beginning with the series of Apocalyptic images that culminate in Beatrice's prophecy of the *DXV*.

In *Purg.* XXXII, 148 ff., the whore and the corrupted car on which she sits—clearly reflecting the "whore sitting on a beast" of Apoc. 17:3 ff.—seem designed as a complex symbol of the Church in the time of the Antichrist, here developed through a partial unification of two previously distinct symbols for the Church: the "lovely lady" of *Inf.* XIX, 57 ff., and the triumphal car of the heavenly procession. The "lovely lady" I take to be a meaningful fusion of the "bride" in Canticles and the "woman clothed with the sun" in Apoc. 12, both traditional figures of the Church; her transformation into the Apocalyptic whore is supported not only by the context in *Inf.* XIX (ll. 56-7, 106-11), but also by the popular eschatological theme of the Church as the seduced and corrupted "bride of Christ," and a remark of Ubertino da Casale that the Church "in her first age is the woman clothed with the sun; and in the end of her fifth age (so far as pertains to the wicked), she is to be judged as Babylon and the whore."[14] The whore in *Purg.* XXXII-XXXIII seems to approximate Peter John Olivi's complex idea of the "carnal Church"—roughly, the multitude of the wicked within the Church (*Trad.,* pp. 203-4)—and to signify the corrupted Church insofar as its members have become estranged from *good,* the final cause of the human will. The car, damaged and overgrown though apparently not basically transmuted, seems to signify the corrupted Church insofar as it has become crippled and disguised in its role as the vessel of *truth,* the final cause of the human intellect. It is in accord with this distinction that the *DXV* will destroy the whore but not, presumably, the car.

[12] The question of the *a priori* likelihood of such an interpretation, as well as the possibility that the eschatological reference derived from the monogram may be applied ultimately to a temporal savior, is discussed in *Trad.,* pp. 199-202. A somewhat neglected interpretation of Cantos XXXII-XXXIII, which coincides with my own at several points, is that of Enrico Proto, *L'Apocalissi nella Divina Commedia* (Naples, 1905).

[13] See *Trad.,* pp. 202-27; with reference to p. 205, n. 56, I take this opportunity to add that the reading *altitudinem* in Quidort's *De Antichristo* is in each instance supported by MS Venice, Bibl. Marciana III.177 (2176), fol. 36ᵛ, from which the edition of 1516 presumably was printed.

[14] *Arbor vite crucifixe Iesu,* V, 8 (Venice, 1485; reproduced, Turin, 1961). fol. 229ʳ and p. 461 respectively; references throughout are to both issues.

Dante's giant in *Purg.*, XXXII, 151 ff., already suggested as a figure of the Antichrist, corresponds in several further particulars to the anthropomorphic Antichrist familiar in medieval eschatology. Our first view of him, sitting upon the car of the corrupted Church, allegorizes the prediction of 2 Thess. 2:4 that the Antichrist "opposes, and is lifted up above all that is called God, or that is worshipped, so that he sits in the temple of God, showing himself as if he were God." Some pertinent explanations of the verse are summarized in 1300 in a *Treatise on the Antichrist* by John Quidort of Paris:

> There have been others who have maintained that he will sit in the Church of God as if he were God, that is, the vicar of God. If, however, one says more properly not *in templo Dei* but *in templum Dei* (for so it is in the Greek), and accordingly says, "he will sit *in templum Dei,*" [the meaning is that he will sit] as though he and his followers *were* the temple of God, declaring that the rest of the faithful are therefore outside the Church. . . . Augustine likewise mentions these explanations [*City of God*, XX, 19], though they can also be satisfactorily expounded [so as to mean] that he will sit *in templum Dei*, that is, over the temple of God and the Church.[15]

The giant's dalliance with the whore (1. 153) reflects another traditional interest of the Antichrist, based on Dan. 11:37, ". . . and he will have desire of women"; its allegorical significance, according to the thirteenth century *Book on the Antichrist* by William of St. Amour, is that he will desire the souls of men "so that he may make them commit fornication with him against the Lord, seeking the adoration of a god from those who are pliant and unstable after the manner of women."[16] Dante's initial picture of the whore and the giant, then (11. 148-53), is a composite of traditional images, juxtaposing the "sitting" of the whore in Apoc. 17:3 (and 18:7) with the "sitting" of the Antichrist in 2 Thess. 2:4; debasing the once-triumphal car into a point of coalescence for the figures of the beast on which the whore sits and the Church on which the Antichrist sits; and combining the traditional lustfulness of the whore and of the Antichrist into a terrible parody of the Church as the bride of Christ— a significance obviously pointed by the familiar pictorial representation of Christ and the Church as seated lovers.[17] The concept of the Antichrist

---

[15] *Tractatus de Antichristo et eius temporibus*, ed. with *Expositio magni prophete Ioachim in librum Beati Cirilli* . . . (Venice, Lazarus de Soardis, 1516), fol. 45ᵛ. See also Thomas Malvenda, O.P., *De Antichristo*, VII, 7 (Rome, 1604), pp. 356-8; the "Index de Antichristo," *PL* 220, cols. 272-3; and *Trad.*, p. 206, n. 57.

[16] *Liber de Antichristo et ejus ministris*, III, 12, ed. E. Martène and U. Durand, *Veterum scriptorum . . . amplissima collectio* (Paris, 1733), IX, 1407 (mistakenly ascribed to Nicolas Oresme). See also *Trad.*, pp. 206-7, nn. 58-9.

[17] Besides the references in *Trad.*, p. 207, nn. 60-1, see Hans Wentzel, "Unbekannte Christus-Johannes-Gruppen," *Zeitschrift für Kunstwissenschaft*, XIII (1959), 171, figs. 11-2.

as lover of the whore is itself closely approximated by William of St. Amour, who explains the boast of the whore in Apoc. 18:7, *"I sit as a queen, and I am no widow,* having as her mate Antichrist and the devil. . . ."[18]

Within this context, the "avid and vagrant eye" of the whore (l. 154; also 150) may carry an allegorical suggestion of spiritual instability, sharpened by the verbal correspondence between *l'occhio . . . vagante* and medieval interpretations of the *viros . . . vagos* ("vagrant men") assembled by Abimelech in Judges 9:4, as followers of the Antichrist.[19] The significance of the whore's casting her eye on Dante himself (l. 155) seems to depend primarily on Jer. 3:1-3:

> It is commonly said: If a man shall put away his wife, and she, going from him, shall marry another man, shall he return to her any more? will not that woman be polluted and defiled? You, however, have committed fornication with many lovers. Nevertheless return to Me (says the Lord), and I will receive you. Lift up your eyes in a straight gaze *(or on high),* and see where you have not prostrated yourself. . . . In you the forehead of a woman has become that of a whore. . . .

A famous thirteenth century Joachistic commentary on Jeremias, traditionally attributed to Joachim of Flora himself, interprets these verses in a way that bears directly on the situation in our final passage of *Purg.* XXXII. The two men are Christ and the Antichrist; the woman is the corrupted Church, who is now admonished:

> *Lift up,* from the mirror of dignity, *your eyes,* fastened upon the dregs of cupidity, *in a straight gaze,* of just contemplation, *and see,* blinded by the darkness of error [but now] illumined by the faith of heavenly learning, *where now* [sic] *you have prostrated yourself:* the place of your prostitution and the act of your iniquity. The place is the world, situated in wickedness; this in which the Church is "prostrated" is earthly cupidity. . . .[20]

At the beginning of the *Inferno* (I, 16-8), the character Dante has "lifted up his eyes"; at the present moment in the *Purgatorio,* he represents the perfected human nature to which that act has ultimately led, climactically described in the closing lines of Vergil's farewell (*Purg.* XXVII, 140-2). The whore—signifying not only the corrupted and

---

[18] *De Ant.,* IV, 10, col. 1434.

[19] Isidore, *Quaest. in lib. Iudic.,* VI (*PL* 83, cols. 387-8), repeated by the *Glossa ordinaria* (*PL* 113, col. 528) and William of St. Amour, *De Ant.,* II, 11 (col. 1363), and III, 7 (col. 1383). For the spiritual state presumably allegorized by the eyes of the whore, see Augustine, *De lib. arb.,* I, 77-8; and for references generally, *Trad.,* pp. 207-8, nn. 62-5.

[20] *Abbatis Ioachim diuina prorsus Ieremiam prophetam interpretatio* . . . (Cologne, 1577), pp. 59-60.

deformed Church, but also its individual members, corrupted and deformed to varying degrees—recognizes in Dante the fulfillment of the command "Lift up your eyes" and the potential perfection of her own nature, which at one volitional level she has no choice but to desire; [21] her casting her eye on Dante is an initial motion toward reform, paralleling Dante's first raising his eyes to the summit (*Inf.* I, 16), but ending in a return into "the wood" (*Purg.* XXXII, 158) that recalls inevitably the "dark wood" from which Dante has escaped in the opening lines of the poem.

Dante's own role in the allegory, then, is that of the elect who in the final time will remain free from domination by the Antichrist; and this role seems supported by an analogy between Dante as beholder and recorder of the Apocalyptic drama within the *Purgatorio,* and John the Evangelist as beholder and recorder of the Apocalypse—an aspect much emphasized in medieval illustration of the Apocalypse, and pertinently glossed by William of St. Amour: "Now the damnation of the whore is shown to John, personifying the elect of that time. . . ." [22] This whole interpretation, in turn, seems to clarify the giant's kissing the whore before her attention to Dante (1. 153), beating her after it (11. 155-6), and finally dragging the car itself out of Dante's sight (11. 157-60), as an allegorizing of the eschatological commonplace that the Antichrist will win the wicked through gifts and blandishment, the "good" through persecution and torture, and the elect—if possible—through simulated miracles. [23] The first two means I take to be signified by the giant's kissing and beating the whore, respectively; the third temptation, here represented as a concealment of the Church itself (11. 159-60), is inflicted on Dante—who, as the truly elect, withstands it.

This pattern of eschatological imagery is resumed in Beatrice's prophecy of the *DXV.* Her announcement that the altered car "was, and is not" (XXXIII, 35) obviously echoes Apoc. 17:8, in which the beast on whom the whore rides "was, and is not." Traditional commentary on the verse interprets these words as an allusion to the brevity of the Antichrist's reign and the quickness of his downfall, taking them to mean in effect, "is, and shall not be"; and Olivi, in a passage closely dependent on

---

[21] Ps.-Albertus Magnus, *Compendium theologicae veritatis,* III, 1, *ed. cit.* (of Albertus), XXXIV, 90: ". . . just as man naturally seeks what is good, so he naturally abhors what is evil, and flees." See also *Trad.,* p. 209, nn. 67-8.

[22] *De Ant.,* IV, 7, col. 1423. For John in illustrations of the Apocalypse (above), see for example L. Delisle and P. Meyer, *L'Apocalypse en français au XIII⁰ siècle* (SATF; Paris, 1900), appendix, especially pl. 8 top; and for references generally, *Trad.,* p. 210, nn. 69-73.

[23] *De Ant.,* III, 7, col. 1386. The word *trassel* ("drew it") in line 158 also points up the eschatological allusion of the passage, related etymologically as it is to the forms of Latin *traho* and *attraho* ("draw," "draw to") used in eschatological works with almost formulaic regularity to describe the Antichrist's drawing the Church into his power; see *Trad.,* pp. 210-1, n. 74.

Joachim of Flora, applies the expression in a similar way to the combined whore-and-beast which for him signifies the "carnal Church." [24] Beatrice's allusion, then, ostensibly a sardonic comment on the present corruption of the car, seems to hint also at its future purification through the promised extinction of the whore. In the following line (36), her reference to "the vengeance of God" is paralleled not only by the Scriptural prophecy that Christ will appear "giving vengeance to those who know not God" (2 Thess. 1:8), but also in medieval eschatology at large. Her further remark that this vengeance "will not fear sops"—apparently alluding most immediately to the sop by which a murderer could at one time escape justice in Florence—may carry an additional suggestion heightening its implicit theme of confusion between human and divine justice; according to Peter Lombard, for example, the Antichrist himself will interpret Ps. 10(1):14, "Thou seest, since Thou considerest labor and grief, that Thou mayest deliver them into Thy hands," as an assurance that God will withhold His vengeance through fear.[25]

Beatrice's next lines (37-9) include a reference to the eagle of Canto XXXII, clearly representing the temporal power of Rome:

> Not for all time without heir will be
> The eagle who left the feathers in the car,
> Through which it turned monster and afterwards prey. . . .

So far as I am aware, the prevailing tendency is to explain this "heir" as someone who will inherit the eagle itself—that is, as a future temporal ruler. Surely, however, the subject under discussion at this point is not the eagle, but the car. It is the car that has been the subject of the preceding tercet (ll. 34-6); and here too it has been alluded to paraphrastically, in terms of the action performed on it by one of its allegorical assailants. Our present reference to the eagle leads directly back to the result of the gift upon the car (l. 39)—a curiously incidental inclusion, if lines 37-8 allude primarily to the rulerless empire. And finally, the whore and the giant to be killed by the *DXV* (the direct prophecy of Whose advent begins with this tercet) are the usurpers not of the eagle but of the car. The whole immediate context, then, indicates that the "heir" is someone who is to succeed the eagle—now temporarily "heirless"—in possession of the car. The resulting concept of the Church as onetime "possession" of Rome parallels an indictment familiar in thirteenth century Joachistic writings. If all this is so, it is difficult not to see in this tercet an allusion to the common eschatological belief that the final time will include the extinction of the Roman Empire; the

[24] Olivi on Apoc. 17:8, ed. Felice Tocco, *Lectura Dantis: Il canto XXXII del Purgatorio* (Florence, 1902), pp. 44-5 (quoted in *Trad.*, p. 211).

[25] *PL* 191, col. 143 (quoted in *Trad.*, p. 212).

usurpation of its power, and of the Church itself, by the Antichrist; and the ultimate return of Christ to reclaim His Church. That such traditions could be applied to the political situation in the early fourteenth century, and by sophisticated minds, is demonstrated in a *quodlibet* of 1310 by Nicolas of Lyra, who at one point replies to an argument based on Jerome's statement that the coming of the Antichrist will be preceded by the fall of the Roman Empire: "But that observation of Jerome seems to work no less well for the opposing side, because the Roman Empire is now disappearing, as it seems, and does not survive except in name; for the Romans neither rule nor elect, and neither has [the emperor] any authority in Rome nor the Romans in the empire." [26]

The prophecy of the *DXV* is immediately introduced by Beatrice's reference to the stars

> Secure from every let and every hindrance,
> Already near, ready to give a time. . . . (11. 41-2)

Whatever the allusion here, it is evidently the same as that inspired earlier in the *Purgatorio* by Dante's recollection of the "ancient she-wolf":

> O heaven, through whose wheeling it would seem believed
>   That our conditions here below are changed,
>   When will he come through whom she shall depart? (XX, 13-5)

At first glance, this insistence on the role of the heavens may seem less compatible with a final advent of Christ than with the emergence of a temporal leader subject to the powers of nature and fortune. In neither passage, however, is the awaited arrival explicitly attributed to the power of the heavens. In Canto XXXIII, the stars are to give a "time in which" the *DXV* will appear. In Canto XX, the reference could easily be to the consummation of the celestial movement; and in any case, the expression I have rendered as "it would seem believed" (*par che si creda;* 1. 13) seems a curiously tentative introduction for so generally acknowledged a fact as the influence of the heavens. Now in 1297, Arnold of Villanova composed the work known to us in a later revision as the *Treatise Concerning the Time of the Coming of the Antichrist,* in which he defends the possibility of predicting this event by astronomical computation, offering the year 1366 as the product of his own inquiry. The resulting controversy—including the inevitably related disputes about the second coming of Christ and the end of the world—seems to have flourished

---

[26] *Utrum possimus scire an Antichristus sit natus vel non natus adhuc,* MS Vat. lat. 982, fol. 87ʳ. Jerome on Dan. 7 (*PL* 25, cols. 531-3). For documentation supporting this entire paragraph, see *Trad.,* pp. 213-4 and nn. 83-7.

with particular vigor during the next fifteen years, involving among others John Quidort, Peter of Auvergne, Nicolas of Lyra, Guido Terrena, and Henry of Harclay, one article of whose skeptical *quaestio* on the subject is entitled, "Whether the Advent of Christ can be Known through Astronomy." A prominent aspect of the problem is the implicit contradiction between the astronomical theory that the world will endure through one complete annual revolution of the heaven of fixed stars, or 36,000 years; and the common eschatological belief that it will end in the seventh millennium from its creation—by medieval reckoning, already well underway in the fourteenth century.[27] Such a controversy must, at the very least, have established a topical connection between astronomical speculation and Christ's second coming, and so would provide a likely enough explanation for Dante's two astronomical references. The noncommittal "it would seem believed" (XX, 13) would then become understandable as an allusion not to the acknowledged significance of the heavenly movements in general, but to their disputed significance in this particular respect. This interpretation, in turn, suggests a possible parallel between "through whose wheeling" (*per cui girar;* XX, 13) and "through whom" (*per cui;* XX, 15), based on a traditional figurative association of Christ's first and second comings with the revolution of the heavens (*Trad.,* p. 216 n. 94).

The killing of the giant by the *DXV* (XXXIII, 44-5) corresponds precisely, of course, to the eschatological commonplace of the killing of the Antichrist by Christ, derived primarily from 2 Thess. 2:8: "And then shall be revealed that iniquitous one, whom the Lord Jesus shall kill with the spirit of His mouth; and He shall destroy him with the brightness of His coming. . . ." [28] Various similarities can be found between this fall of the Antichrist and that of the whore in Apoc. 18, like the fact that each is emphasized by commentators as a death both physical and spiritual (*Trad.,* p. 217, n. 98). Their simultaneous death in the *Purgatorio* is paralleled in an argument by William of St. Amour (following closely his description of the Antichrist as mate of the whore, quoted above) that the rejoining of the wicked in 1 Thess. 5:3 will occur before rather than after the death of the Antichrist, while they are still "sitting as a queen [Apoc. 18:7]—especially since that iniquitous one is to perish together with his whole body of followers [allegorically, that is, the whore]

---

[27] See for example Arnold, ed. Heinrich Finke, *Aus den Tagen Bonifaz VIII* (Vorreformationsgeschichtliche Forschungen, II; Münster i.W., 1902), pp. cxxix-clix and 210 ff.; Franz Pelster, "Die Quaestio Heinrichs von Harclay über die zweite Ankunft Christi und die Erwartung des baldigan Weltendes zu Anfang des XIV. Jahrhunderts," *Archivio italiano per la storia della pietà,* I (1951), 25-82; B. Hirsch-Reich, "Heinrichs von Harclay Polemik gegen die Berechnung der zweiten Ankunft Christi," *Recherches de théologie ancienne et médiévale,* XX (1953), 144-9; and *Trad.,* pp. 214-7 and nn. 88-95.

[28] See Malvenda, *De Antichristo,* X, 13-5, pp. 502-6; the "Index de Antichristo," *PL* 220, col. 277; and *Trad.,* p. 217, n. 96.

by the brightness of the Lord's coming . . . nor would the final persecution of the iniquitous one end with his death, if wicked survivors
were to remain after him. . . ." [29] Beatrice's description of the *DXV* as
"sent from God" (*messo di Dio;* 1. 44) is generally familiar from the New
Testament, where it is approximated more than fifty times. The oper-
ation of this "sending" (*missio*) among the Persons of the Trinity is
analyzed at length by medieval theologians, who, in defining the "sending" of the Son by the Father, distinguish between continual "invisible"
sendings and the unique "visible" sending brought about through the
Incarnation.[30] In an exegesis of Apoc. 10:7—"But in the days of the
voice of the seventh angel, when he shall begin to sound the trumpet,
the mystery of God shall be consummated . . ."—William of St. Amour
relates what appears to be this concept of "visible sending" to the second
coming, in a way that produces a close verbal parallel to Dante's *messo
di Dio* along with a meaningful play on the word *angelus* ("angel" or
"messenger") and a reference to the killing of the Antichrist in 2 Thess.
2:8:

> Will not the beginning of the trumpet of this seventh angel—that is, of
> Christ the Lord, because He, sent by the Father (*a Patre missus*), is by pre-
> rogative, as it were, called the Prince of angels, and the "Angel" of great
> counsel, and the Seventh, to Whom each trumpet of the other angels leads
> up, and He is a byword for perfection just as is the number seven—[will not
> this beginning] be brought to completion when He shall kill the man of
> iniquity with the spirit of His mouth? [31]

Beatrice's prophecy is immediately followed by her further mysterious
comment,

> And perhaps my recital, obscure
>   As Themis and the Sphinx, persuades you less
>   Because in their fashion it clouds the mind;
>
> But soon the facts will be the Naiades
>   That will solve this great enigma
>   Without damage of flocks or of corn. . . . (11. 46-51)

A distinctive error in the medieval text of Ovid's *Metamorphoses* puts
it beyond doubt that these references to Themis, the Sphinx, and the

---

[29] *De Ant.,* IV, 10, col. 1434.

[30] See for example Peter Lombard, *Sententiae,* I, xv, 9-12 (*PL* 192, cols. 561-2); the
commentaries on *Sent.,* I, xvi, 2, by Albertus (A, art. 1), *ed. cit.,* XXV, 441-5, Bonaven-
tura (q. 3), *Opera omnia* (Quaracchi, 1882), I, 283-4, and Aquinas (q. 1, art. 1-4); and
Summa theol., I, 43, 1-5.

[31] *De Ant.,* IV, 12, col. 1440; the reading *perfectus erit* (unfortunately preserved in
Trad., p. 219, first line) clearly should be *perfectum erit.*

Naiades are derived primarily from the allusions in a brief passage
(*Met.*, VII, 759-62) introducing the story of Laelaps, the hunting-dog
of Cephalus (11. 763-93): how, after the death of the Sphinx, a second
monster was sent to afflict Thebes; how this monster was pursued by
Laelaps; and how both animals were turned into marble statues. In
the *Ovide moralisé* (written not far from the possible dates of the
Purgatorio, and in any case traditional in much of its content), the
monster is interpreted as the beast of the Apocalypse, evidently with a
suggestion of his usual significance as the Antichrist; the transformation
of the two animals is attributed to Jupiter and allegorized as the final
intervention of God, Who, when He sees the affliction of His people,
"will send them good help" (VII, 3672).[32] This story of Laelaps can be
related also to the "Greyhound" of *Inf.* I (*Trad.*, pp. 230-1); here, let us
notice simply that this allegorization of it may indicate a further eschatological note in Beatrice's prophecy.

If this labored analysis has been essentially sound, it implies that
Dante's eschatological allusion in Cantos XXXII and XXXIII is more
firmly grounded in the meaning of the Apocalypse and its surrounding
tradition, and is also more consistent and purposeful, than has sometimes
been supposed; and that an interpretation of the *DXV* as Christ in a
future advent is therefore less unlikely than we have been led to believe.
These conclusions, in turn, open further possibilities for eschatological
interpretation within the two cantos. For example, it seems probable
that the successive attacks on the car in Canto XXXII, together with
Beatrice's prophecy in Canto XXXIII, allegorize the last six of the
"seven ages of the Church," developed particularly in commentary on
the "seven seals" of Apoc. 6-8—with, perhaps, the eagle signifying the
second age (that of the persecutions); the fox, the third (that of the early
heresies); the dragon, the fourth (that of the hypocrites or "false broth-
ers" within the Church); the further corruption of the car in XXXII,
136-47, the fifth (an age variously defined by different commentators); the
usurpation by the whore and the giant, the sixth (the time of the Antichrist); and the future arrival of the *DXV*, the seventh (the time of peace
after the death of the Antichrist). Again, there is reason for suspecting
that Dante's sleep in XXXII, 61-9, implicitly compared to the experience
of the three Apostles at the Transfiguration (11. 73-82), may signify a
spiritual "coming" of Christ into the hearts of the faithful, here placed
appropriately between the allegorical figures of His first coming (the
Griffon) and of His final coming (the *DXV*). And in Canto XXXIII, 10-2,
Beatrice's repetition of Christ's "A little while and ye shall not see

---

[32] The entire passage is VII, 3645-78, ed. C. De Boer *et al.* (Verhandelingen der
Koninklijke Akademie van Wetenschappen te Amsterdam afdeeling Letterkunde, N.R.
XXX, 3; 1931), III, 101-2. De Boer, I, 10-1, places the date of the *Ovide* between 1291
and 1328, most probably between 1316 and 1328. For interpretations of the same general kind by Dante himself, see *Conv.* II, i, 3; and IV, xxviii, 13-9.

Me . . ." (John 16:16) carries overtones of the final coming which may reveal added complexities in the analogy between Christ and Beatrice pointed out by Professor Singleton. With these suggestions,[33] I turn from *Purg.* XXXII-XXXIII to certain more distant parts of the poem.

In *Purg.* XII, a passage of thirty-nine lines (25-63) describes the examples of pride that Dante and Vergil find sculptured in the stone over which they walk. The first four tercets of this passage (11. 25-36) begin with the word *Vedea* ("I saw"), the second four (11. 37-48) with the exclamation *O*, and the third four (11. 49-60) with the word *Mostrava* ("It showed"); the final tercet (11. 61-3) repeats the three as the initial words of its three lines. There can be little doubt that these repetitions are an acrostic, spelling out the word *VOM*—that is, *Uom'*, or *Uomo* ("man"). In lines 25-60, the examples of pride are arranged as a series of pairs, each consisting of a Classical figure paralleled by a Biblical but pre-Christian figure; the concluding tercet presents the fate of Troy. It seems clear, then, that the passage occupied by this acrostic must in some way be concerned with mankind fallen but not yet redeemed, still subject to the undiminished effects of the pride implicit in the disobedience of the Fall; and that it is "man" in this sense who is alluded to in the *Uomo* of the acrostic.[34] If this is true, the removal of the *P* of pride from Dante's forehead by the angel later in the canto (11. 97 ff.) is a small inevitable analogy of the Redemption, which relieved man of at least the worst effects of the pride underlying Original Sin. Now the whole account of these sculptures and their effect on Dante (11. 16-75) has been a somber and unrelieved meditation on the ravages of pride; as such, it contrasts unmistakably with the joy and renewal of spirit that attends the arrival of the angel and Dante's subsequent purification (11. 77 ff.). The new note is first struck in Vergil's announcement of the angel, beginning "Lift up your head . . ." (11. 77-84)—which, in terms of the analogy I have just proposed, would be a "heralding of the Savior," a looking forward to a "Redemption." If we examine this speech for signs of a possible acrostic, we find that its two complete tercets begin respectively with *Vedi* ("See"; 1. 79) and *Di* ("With"; 1. 82), whose initial *V* and *D* correspond to the two components of the *Vere dignum* monogram. In addition, *Vedi* repeats the word *Vedea* which in the first four tercets of the acrostic and in line 61 furnishes the initial of *Vom'* (*Uomo*); while *Di*, if it is subjected to a process analogous with *Vom'* > *Uomo*, becomes *Di'* > *Dio* ("God"). The pattern is intensified by the obvious strong alliteration of *v* and *d* in the speech, particularly the *venir verso . . . vedi . . . dal . . . del . . . dì* of lines 80-1. I take the *VD* of these two tercets,

---

[33] They are treated more fully in *Trad.*, pp. 220-4. Charles S. Singleton (above), *Commedia: Elements of Structure* (Dante Studies, I; Cambridge, Mass., 1957), pp. 45-60.

[34] See the clear statement by Ercole Rivalta, ed., *La Divina Commedia: Purgatorio* (Florence, 1946), p. 471 (quoted in *Trad.*, p. 225).

then, as an extension of the acrostic *VOM,* signifying a coming "Atonement" through its allusion to the *Vere dignum* monogram in the Preface of the Mass, and meaningfully attached to a speech that bears a natural analogy to a heralding of the Redemption. This whole development is supported also by the correspondence between Vergil's "Lift up your head. . ." (1. 77) and Luke 21:28, ". . . lift up your heads, for your redemption approaches"; by the common designation of Christ as *angelus,* in its original sense of "messenger"; by Vergil's reference to approaching noon (11. 80-1), itself a familiar figure of Christ, the Crucifixion, or the Redemption; and perhaps by the choice of Vergil himself as speaker of the "prophecy." [35] The relation of lines 79-84 to the *DXV* is, I suppose, obvious.

Outside of Beatrice's prophecy itself, however, probably the clearest single piece of evidence for an eschatological interpretation of the *DXV* is her well-known exclamation, late in the *Paradiso,* concerning the heavenly city:

> Behold our seats so filled
> That few people more are awaited here. (XXX, 131-2)

So far as I can see, these lines must imply a comparatively small number of people who have yet to undergo death, and so also a comparatively short period of future earthly time. Any reasonable possibility of explaining them instead as a comment on the proportion of Christian mankind who attain salvation, seems eliminated by the cause-and-effect relationship between the first line and the second, as well as by the overall proportions of the *Divine Comedy;* and to suggest that Dante's "few people" may refer to a number small only according to some unexpressed criterion, and by other standards perhaps rather large, would surely be to ignore all considerations of emphasis as it is normally conceived to exist in the written word. In addition, the very currency of such eschatological prophecy in early fourteenth century Italy makes it difficult to imagine how Dante could have erred into so clear a statement of so patently eschatological a concept in the process of trying to say something else. Within the fictional world of the *Comedy,* at any rate, this brief passage stands not only as a clear announcement of the impending end of time, but also—unless we are willing to take refuge in the facile assumption that "Dante was inconsistent"—as a contradiction of any other plausible significance for the coming of the *DXV.*

Finally, if this whole lengthy defense has carried conviction, Beatrice's prophecy of the *DXV* falls symmetrically into place as the climactic

---

[35] The first two of these points are not in *Trad.;* for the figure of "noon" or the "sixth hour," see p. 226, n. 118.

"revelation" in the *Purgatorio,* corresponding to the vision of Lucifer at the end of the *Inferno* and to that of the Trinity at the end of the *Paradiso.* As part of such a pattern, the prophecy of the *DXV* seems in every way more credible than the pageant of the Church or the appearance of Beatrice in *Purg.* XXIX ff., which are sometimes proposed. Like the two visions, it occupies the final canto of its canticle; like Lucifer and the Trinity themselves, the *DXV* is represented as "triune"—God, man, and the Person in Whom the two are joined. It is in keeping with the finality of heaven and hell that the "trinity" of the *Inferno* is beheld as a static vision of completed and unchanging evil, and the Trinity of the *Paradiso* as a static vision of perfect and unchangeable good; the *DXV,* by contrast, is not beheld, but is announced in a prophecy to be fulfilled in time. The reason, I would suggest, lies in the nature of Purgatory itself: a place of no final state, but of progressive repair for past evil and of hope for future beatitude. In traditional eschatology, it is the advent of the *DXV* (whether in precise chronological terms, or simply as the dominant symbol of the final days) that will set the boundary between time and eternity, abolish all change along with Purgatory itself, and divide mankind forever between the timeless kingdoms of "triune" evil and Triune Good. Seen in this light, Beatrice's prophecy becomes the announcement of an ever-approaching final harmony and a message of hope to those righteous who still inhabit a world of change—on the ledges of Purgatory, or on earth as part of the struggling and bedeviled Church Militant.

Civitas

by Alessandro Passerin d'Entrèves

. . . To suppose that Dante's political doctrine is summed up in the dream of the universal Empire, to describe his ideal merely as that of *il ghibellin fuggiasco*,[1] are errors of perspective of which we must try and rid ourselves if we want to determine the full range of his outlook on politics. Dante was and remained to the end—as every reader of the *Comedy* knows—a proud Florentine, a son of the greatest and proudest of medieval Italian cities. Born and bred in the bosom of a flourishing city-state ("nel quale nato e nutrito fui in fino al colmo de la vita mia" are his words in the first book of *Convivio*), Dante is first and foremost a citizen of Florence, and Florence is the root of his knowledge of and interest in politics. It is the name of Florence that we read inscribed on the front page of the poem: "Incipit Comedia Dantis Alagherii Florentini natione non moribus"; the allegiance is there, notwithstanding the judgment. In the highest glory of Paradise, when he is nearing the goal of his journey and the fulfillment of his quest, it is still Florence that Dante has in his heart of hearts: the only place on earth where he could ever have proclaimed, in the words of another great poet: "hier bin ich Mensch, hier darf ich's sein."

> Se mai continga che 'l poema sacro
> al quale ha posto mano e cielo e terra,
> sì che m'ha fatto per più anni macro,
>
> vinca la crudeltà che fuor mi serra
> del bello ovile ov'io dormi' agnello,
> nimico ai lupi che li danno guerra;
>
> con altra voce omai, con altro vello
> ritornerò poeta; ed in sul fonte
> del mio battesmo prenderò 'l cappello. . . .
> *(Par.* xxv. 1-9.)

[1] Foscolo, *I Sepolcri,* l. 174.

> If it ever come to pass that the sacred poem to which both heaven and earth have set their hand, so that it has made me lean for many years, should overcome the cruelty that bars me from the fair sheepfold where I slept as a lamb, an enemy to the wolves that make war on it, with another voice now and other fleece I shall return a poet and at the font of my baptism take the laurel crown. . . .

Clearly, no study of Dante's political thought can be complete if it does not take into account the influence exerted on it by his experience of the city-state. The trouble is that there remain very few documents of Dante's speculative approach to politics in his years of apprenticeship. In those years he did not speculate, but lived and acted. How much more would we like to know about the "Guelfism" of Dante—a subject which is often mentioned but little explored! Reminiscences of his youth are frequent enough in Dante's work, both prose and poetry. They are too well known for me to recall them here. But what is significant and must be underlined in this connection is the fact that Dante never renounced his Guelf antecedents. He actually prided himself on them. Not only Bruni's words, but the episode of Farinata bear witness to this. In later days he would discharge his wrath equally upon Guelfs and Ghibellines. But he certainly never became an "imperialist" without qualification. The core of his political philosophy remained essentially *civic*. Cosmopolitanism was forced upon him by the bitter lesson of exile. It was never anything more to him than an aspiration, a cloak to conceal his scars.

> But we, to whom the world is our native country, just as the sea is to the fish, though we drank of Arno before our teeth appeared and though we love Florence so dearly that for the love we bore her we are wrongfully suffering exile—we rest the shoulders of our judgment on reason rather than on feeling. (*De Vulg. Eloq.* 1. vi.)

If we want to know what Dante's real feelings were we have only to read the next sentence: "As regards our own pleasure or sensuous comfort there exists no more agreeable place in the world than Florence."

If then the municipal spirit pervades the whole of Dante's work, with only some few exceptions, it is no paradox that the idea of the city should provide the basic assumption of his reflections on politics. The word *città* is a keyword in the *Comedy*. There is not only the opposition between the City of the Damned and the Heavenly City. The word is used to denote the fundamental and "typical" form of human association. Retracing the growth and development of man, Marco Lombardo, in the sixteenth Canto of *Purgatorio*, indicates the setting up of *la vera città* as the primary imperative, even though of the true city men discern only the tower. In the eighth Canto of *Paradiso*, Carlo Martello asks Dante the direct question: " 'Or dì; sarebbe il peggio / per l'uomo in terra, se non fosse cive?' "; and the answer comes back without a shadow of hesitation:

" 'sì' rispuos' io; 'e qui ragion non cheggio.' " " 'Now tell me, would it be
worse for man on earth if he were not a citizen?' 'Yes,' I replied, 'and
here I ask no proof.' " The great Cantos of Cacciaguida are a celebration
of city life and of citizenship: it is Florence again, though the Florence
of old, *dulcis memoria.* It is well to read these Cantos with the invectives
of *Inferno,* xvi, of *Purgatorio,* vi and xxiii, in mind, to realize that Cacciaguida's description is not only an idealization, but a lesson.

"Fiorenza dentro da la cerchia antica . . . si stava in pace, sobria e
pudica." The pattern of the "good city" gradually unfolds before our
eyes: one could almost take it for a complete political program. The
good city is limited in size: Florence was happy within the precincts of
her old walls; would God that she had not expanded, and that she had
preserved the "purity" of her population. The good city is moderate in
wealth: Florence of old was *sobria;* the sudden riches ("la gente nova e i
subiti guadagni") were the cause of her degeneration. The good city is
based on sound morals: *pudica,* like the virtuous women of old, so different from *le sfacciate donne fiorentine* of the present. Above all, the good
city is based on concord and on the absence of internal strife: so was
Florence before the rift between Guelf and Ghibelline, when the lily had
not yet beeen stained with the blood of factions. Surely the good city is
the only place for a man to live: fortunate the old Florentine who could
be a good citizen as well as a good Christian!

> A così riposato, a così bello
>   viver di cittadini, a così fida
>   cittadinanza, a così dolce ostello,
>
> Maria mi diè, chiamata in alte grida;
>   e ne l'antico vostro Batisteo
>   insieme fui cristiano e Cacciaguida.
>   (*Par.* xv, 130-5.)

To a citizen's life so peaceful and so fair, to a community so loyal, to so
sweet a dwelling-place, Mary gave me when called on with loud cries, and in
your ancient Baptistery I became at once Christian and Cacciaguida.

But what is the real meaning of all this: is it anything more than a
nostalgic reminiscence of the past? Can the dreams of a disillusioned man
be called a political program? They could certainly not, unless we were
able to substantiate the poetry of the *Commedia* with more positive evidence.

It was not only allegiance to Florence and municipal patriotism that
led Dante under Carlo Martello's cross-examination to stress so unhesitatingly the value of citizenship. It was a solid conviction which kept
ripening in him all through the years. How tempting it is to trace the

possible sources of that conviction back to Dante's youth! Dr. Nicolai
Rubinstein has recently explored "The Beginnings of Political Thought
in Florence." [2] He has provided decisive evidence of the existence in the
city itself of a fairly well-defined "political ideology" which certainly
formed the background of Dante's earliest reflections on the subject. In
the absence of all other sources that ideology must be sought in the awak-
ening of historical interest in the past and the formation of a body of
beliefs about the origins and vicissitudes of the city, such as are set forth
in the *Chronica de Origine Civitatis* (end of the twelfth, beginning of
the thirteenth century) and in Sanzanome's *Gesta Florentinorum,* written
shortly after 1230. In these first attempts to relate the history of Florence,
two motifs are particularly significant: the place given to the antagonism
between Florence and Fiesole and the importance attributed to the
Roman descent of the Florentines. The earliest manifestation of political
ideas in Florence would thus appear to be one of growing "nationalism"
—perhaps the Italian *campanilismo* is a still better word. Dr. Rubinstein
has traced these ideas all through the thirteenth century, and his conclusions are one of the most illuminating contributions I know to the
study of the Florentine element in Dante's political thought. Actually
Dante himself gives us more than one hint of what ideas were current
among the Florentines about the ancient nobility of their city and of
their stock. In the same Canto of Cacciaguida from which I have already
quoted at length, he portrays the Florentine mothers telling their children
the fabulous stories "de' Troiani, di Fiesole e di Roma." Thus, from
the very cradle, were young citizens brought up in a spirit of intense civic
loyalty and pride. It is this spirit that breathes in Cacciaguida's words.

Yet, in the gradual formation of Dante's thought, it is possible also to
detect the influence of less parochial elements. If Brunetto Latini was
Dante's first teacher—and we know from Giovanni Villani how much he
contributed to *digrossare* the Florentines and to teach them to guide and
to rule their republic *secondo politica*—it is from him that the young
poet may perhaps have learnt the first definition of the city as "uno
raunamento di gente fatto per vivere a ragione." [3] And it is very probably in the philosophical studies which he began after the death of
Beatrice that Dante must have discovered—in the *scuole de li religiosi*
and in the *disputazioni de li filosofanti* to which he refers in *Convivio,*
II. xii—that notion of the positive value of the State which was to form
the keystone of his political doctrine. One point, at any rate, can be made
with almost absolute certainty: viz. that Dante's views on the ultimate
basis of the State and on the nature of politics are derived from the
Thomist, and indeed from the Aristotelian teaching, and remained faith-

[2] In *Journal of the Warburg and Courtauld Institutes,* vol. v, 1942.
[3] *La "Rettorica" italiana di Brunetto Latini,* ed. Maggini, 1915, p. 33.

ful to it down to the end. The *qui ragion non cheggio* of *Paradiso*, viii. 17, finds its explanation in *Convivio*, IV. iv, and in *Monarchia*, I. iii, the two basic passages in the whole of Dante's theory of politics. To be a citizen is not only good, it is necessary: for man is by nature a political animal—*compagnevole animale*. It follows that man can find the "good life" only in the State, and that the State is the end, and as it were the crown, of the true nature of man.

Thus Dante's experience of the Florentine background could be supplemented with the teaching of the most up-to-date political philosophy of his day: for that philosophy was comparatively new and was just beginning to be diffused through the lecture-rooms of medieval Europe. It was a philosophy of optimism, in harmony with the new optimism of the age; a philosophy admirably suited to enhance the confidence of men whose experience of the State had such strange similarities to that of the ancient Greeks, and one that was ever after to leave a lasting mark upon the political consciousness of the West. Did Dante derive his notion of the State directly from Aristotle's *Politics* or indirectly through the channel of Aquinas? The question is irrelevant to our purpose. What is infinitely more important is to notice that Dante, like St. Thomas, has no use for the older and traditional view of the "conventional" origin of the State, *poena et remedium peccati*. The establishment of law and order among men, with the setting up of authority, is not the outcome of dire necessity or of mere lust for power. It springs from the very root of human nature, whose end is *bene sufficienterque vivere*, the attainment of that "vita felice, a la quale nullo per sè è sufficiente a venire sanza l'aiutorio d'alcuno [happy life, to which no man is self-sufficient enough to come without another's help]."

This conviction Dante sets forth as a self-evident truth in his answer to Carlo Martello; but it must have been formed by the Poet at a very early stage of his reflections on politics, and this can be shown from two among the most interesting autobiographical passages in his later works, where in fact he is at pains to correct his earlier views on the subject. In the *Monarchia*, where the emphasis is no longer on the city but on the Empire, Dante tells us of a time when he had "marveled that the Roman people had been raised to supremacy on the terrestrial globe, with none to resist. For it was my thought," he adds, "as I looked upon the surface only, that they had gained it by no right but merely by the force of arms"—"nullo iure sed armorum tantummodo violentia" (*Mon.* II. i. 2). In the *Convivio* the same notion is also referred to as purporting that "la romana potenzia non per ragione nè per decreto di convento universale fu acquistata, ma per forza, che a la ragione pare esser contraria." ". . . the Roman power was acquired not by reason nor by decree of universal consent, but by force, which seems to be the contrary of reason." (*Conv.* IV. iv. 8)

This reference to the notion that force, not reason, is the ultimate foundation of power is of capital importance in several different ways. It is interesting first of all as a reference to the old Christian doctrine of the sinful origin of political authority, the doctrine echoed in the famous invective of Gregory VII against Henry IV: this doctrine can only improperly be called "Augustinian" or "medieval" (for it is not the only answer which St. Augustine or the Middle Ages gave to the problem), but it certainly played a considerable part in medieval political thought. It is further, and foremost—with its contrast of the *de facto* against the *de iure* existence of the Roman Empire—a direct reference to one of the favorite arguments of "anti-imperial" writers both in Dante's day and earlier: an argument which he himself, as a Guelf, may have accepted willingly in his youth. But it would also appear from the context both of the *Convivio* and of the *Monarchia* that in those references Dante had in mind an earlier stage of his reflection on politics, when he was not yet aware that the rational justification of the particular State could equally well apply to a supranational authority. In other words, the Aristotelian argument, which fitted the city, stopped short of the Empire: the one was the outcome of nature and reason, the other merely of force. To provide a rational justification of the universal Monarchy was the task that Dante set himself in his later days, the enterprise "maxime latens et ab omnibus intemptata" which he prided himself on having achieved. He did not think it required a similar enterprise to prove that life in the city is rational and natural, as is shown clearly enough by his answer to Carlo Martello.

If then both the *Convivio* and the *Monarchia* bear witness to Dante's wholehearted allegiance to the Aristotelian and Thomist notion of the State, it must be noticed, however, that on one point their evidence seems to contradict the conclusions so far stressed, viz. that the city was and remained to Dante the fundamental and "typical" form of human association. The reference is in fact not to the city alone; like St. Thomas, Dante in the *Convivio* (IV. iv. 3) and in the *Monarchia* (I. v. 8) breaks away at one juncture from the Aristotelian argument, or, to speak more exactly, both Dante and St. Thomas correct or extend that argument in one very important and substantial respect. The end of *bene sufficienter-que vivere* is achieved not only in the *civitas*, but also in the *regnum*. *Civitas et regnum* is Dante's version of πόλις. The difficulty is a serious, though not an insurmountable one, as least from a theoretical angle. The extension of the Aristotelian notion of the State to square with the new and different types of political organization of contemporary Europe is a common feature of medieval political theory: the relevant point is that the essence of that notion, with its stress on the autonomy and autarky of the political unit, is fully grasped and maintained. Both cities and kingdoms are to Dante "typical" forms of human association, "States" in the Aristotelian sense. In the language of the *Commedia* the two expressions, *città* and *regno,* are used as equivalent even in a larger sense, to describe any kind of human fellowship and organization.[4]

However, in this particular context, Dante's mention of the *regnum* raises one further problem which has recently been the object of much discussion among students of Dante's political thought. It has been maintained, notably by the Italian historian Francesco Ercole, later supported by the great Dantist Michele Barbi, that Dante conceived of the whole of Italy as a *regnum,* in fact, as a "true, autonomous and unitary State on its own." Should this be so, it is clear that the *regnum Italicum* would constitute, as it were, a mediating element in Dante's theory and allegiance, between the emphasis laid on the city on one side and on the Empire on the other. At any rate the municipal element and the cosmopolitan spirit would not constitute the two opposite poles of Dante's experience. In and between them the national spirit must be taken into account, as a powerful factor in the formation of Dante's personality.

I cannot here enter into a detailed discussion of this highly controversial point. I shall limit myself to saying that, in my view, as well as in that of many other scholars—some of them in this country—who have examined Ercole's theory critically and historically, the evidence to support Dante's recognition of a *regnum Italicum* is anything but convincing. This does not in any way imply a denial that Dante had a clear notion of the national unity of Italy. It is in fact extremely interesting to see that notion emerge in one of the first works composed by the poet in his exile, the *De Vulgari Eloquentia,* which is on that score certainly relevant to the student of his political theory. Italy was to Dante a well-defined unit, with her clearly marked geographical features and boundaries, her language, her common customs and civilization. Italy was the object of his passionate love, and in outlining the structure and the function of the Empire he certainly reserved a privileged place to the *giardin de lo 'mperio,* this *nobilissima regio Europe.* But this is a long way from conceiving of Italy as a political unit of the same quality and category as the *civitates et regna*—the city-states and the territorial kingdoms—which provided the basis of Dante's notion of the State.

We are thus brought back once again to what I have ventured to call the *civic* element in Dante's conception of politics. I have tried to assess it by means of a brief survey of the biographical and cultural factors that may have contributed to determine it. But one last factor must be mentioned if we want to have the whole picture clearly before our eyes: it is the factor which, after all, gives Dante's political theory its peculiar historical significance, by showing that the poet did not derive his conceptions merely from nostalgic reminiscences of the past or from his

---

[4] Thus, for example, in *Inf.* i. 124-8; iii. 1; viii. 68-69; xxxiv. 28; *Purg.* i. 4; xiii. 94-95; *Par.* i. 23; xxxi. 25. In these cases, however, the words are clearly used only in a metaphorical sense, and *città* is certainly more reminiscent of the Augustinian *civitas* than of the Aristotelian πόλις.

meditation over philosophical text-books however up to date, but from his exact assessment of historical evidence, even though that assessment became more and more negative with the passing of the years.

Dante, in fact, is important as a witness of the rise of that Italian city-state which deeply influenced the political destinies of Europe. I have no intention of repeating what historians of political thought, from Gierke onwards, have said often and brilliantly on this subject. But there would be no purpose in stressing Dante's notion of the *civitas* as a counterpart to his notion of *imperium*—his "Guelfism" as against the usually accepted view of his "Ghibellinism"—unless we kept in mind that he lived at a time when a new and far-reaching doctrine was sweeping Europe: the very doctrine that Dante spent his later years in trying to confute. We now call it the doctrine of national sovereignty: but it was not yet called by that name in Dante's day. Indeed, it was not simply the *civitas* that formed the background of Dante's reflection on politics. It was the *libera civitas,* the *civitas superiorem non recognoscens* and thus *sibi princeps* or sovereign. The attribute which had once been the Emperor's was now claimed by cities and kingdoms; it had been claimed by the King of France, as it was later to be claimed by the King of England. The Guelf cities of Italy were not behind the European courts in clamoring for the spoils of the Empire.

Whether or not the proud assertion had already been couched in the appropriate legal terms is less important than the fact that, in the vindication of state-sovereignty, Florence had been at once a forerunner and a champion. "Nunquam Comune Florentie fidelitatem fecit alicui imperatori . . . quia semper vixit et fuit liberum." "The Commune of Florence has never given allegiance to any emperor: it has always been free." The answer given by the Florentines to the Vicar of Rudolph of Habsburg in 1281 was a clear statement of policy. It is this policy which Dante himself upheld during his term of office as a Florentine magistrate. Now the liberty of the city was impugned from a different side. It was a Pope —and that Pope was Boniface—who attempted to curb the will of the Commune. He claimed the right to do so because of the vacancy of the Empire and in the name of his newfangled *plenitudo potestatis.* The quarrel in which Dante found himself so deeply involved may at first have been nothing more than one of those typical "jurisdictional" quarrels which fill the records of medieval chanceries. It was soon to become a test-case not only for the loyalty of the Guelf city to the interests of the Papal Curia, but for the very principle of communal independence and sovereignty.

Thus, even though the occasion of the final clash may seem trivial, we are made to realize the greatness of the issues through Dante's own greatness. "Dante Alagherii consuluit quod de servitio faciendo d[omino] pape nichil fiat." Few documents relating to the poet's life have a more dramatic quality than the record of the meeting of 19 June 1301. Dante's reticence on the real causes which brought about his misfortunes cannot but strike us. He preferred to single out one man and one man only as the hidden hand behind the evils that befell him.

> Questo si vuole e questo già si cerca,
> e tosto verrà fatto a chi ciò pensa
> là dove Cristo tutto dì si merca. . . .
>
> *(Par.* xvii. 49-51.)

This is determined, nay is already contrived and will soon be accomplished, by him who meditates it in the place where Christ is bought and sold all day.

At an earlier date, however, he had clearly indicated that "tutti li mali e l'inconvenienti miei dall' infausti comizi del mio priorato ebbono cagione e principio." [5] Such words seem to sound very much like the recognition of an error. With the sad wisdom of posterity, we are usually only too keen to repeat that Dante's failure as a politician was the occasion and cause of his achievement as an artist.

It was certainly also the occasion and cause of a momentous change in his outlook on politics. That change was to lead him to certain conclusions which have been linked to his name ever since. Dante's political theory is neither the epitaph of the medieval Empire, nor the first act of rebellion against Scholastic transcendence. It is, much more simply, a reflection on the existing situation and a warning against its dangers. It is a recognition of the inadequacy of the *civitas* to secure the peaceful enjoyment of the "good life." It is perhaps for this reason that we, of our generation, are better placed than our fathers were to appreciate and understand Dante's message as a political thinker. For we too live, like him, in a period of crisis; we are witnessing the end of what he saw in its beginning. We too are learning that "patriotism is not enough," and that the road which Europe chose to take in the century of the poet does in fact, as he clearly foresaw, lead to an abyss. But I must not let myself be carried away by this kind of reflection. Let me conclude this lecture with a summary of my argument.

The *civitas*—the city-state—is to my mind the first constituent element of Dante's theory of politics. We must take our start from it as the basis on which the rest of the edifice is built. Yes, the true city with its towers and spires rising high in the sky is the proper place for man to live. But the existence of other cities and kingdoms, of different ways of life; above all the presence in man of the *libido dominandi,* and of the ravenous

[5] "From this Priorate sprung his exile, and all the adverse fortunes of his life, as he himself writes in a letter, the words of which are these: 'All my woes and all my misfortunes had their cause and origin in my ill-omened election to the Priorate . . .'" (Bruni).

she-wolf in the world at large—all this cannot but make the benefits of political life extremely precarious:

> con ciò sia cosa che l'animo umano in terminata possessione di terra non si queti, ma sempre desideri gloria d'acquistare, sì come per esperienza vedemo, discordie e guerre conviene surgere intra regno e regno, le quali sono tribulazioni de le cittadi, e per le cittadi de le vicinanze, e per le vicinanze de le case, [e per le case] de l'uomo; e così s'impedisce la felicitade (*Conv.* IV. iv. 3).

And inasmuch as the human mind rests not in the limited possession of land, but ever, as we see by experience, desires to acquire more territory, needs must discords and wars arise betwixt kingdom and kingdom. Which things are the tribulations of cities, and through the cities of districts, and through the districts of households, and through the households of man; and thus is felicity impeded.

Dante was not a passive victim of misfortune. He drew a fruitful lesson from it. The words of his implacable opponent must have rung in his ears when he was taking the road to exile—to discover Italy and the world, but never to set foot again in his beloved city. "Quis errata corriget per civitates et loca provincie Tuscie, et relevabit oppressos, si ad nos non possit recursus haberi?" "Who shall redress iniquity in the cities and dwellings of the Tuscan province, and comfort the oppressed, if recourse is not granted to us?" Thus had Pope Caetani warned the Florentines on the eve of the *infausti comizi*. Dante's notion of *imperium* was to prove an indirect tribute to the cogency of Boniface's argument. It was a rejection of the Papal claim to supreme jurisdiction. But it was also a vindication of the necessity of some such jurisdiction if the world was to be saved from anarchy, and the blessing of civic life to be assured.

The Metamorphoses of the Circle

by Georges Poulet

There is a famous definition of God which, during the centuries, has played an important part, not only in the thought of theologians and philosophers, but also in the imagination of poets: *Deus est sphaera cujus centrum ubique;* God is a sphere of which the center is everywhere and the circumference is nowhere.

It is in a pseudo-hermetic manuscript of the twelfth century, *The Book of the Twenty-four Philosophers,* that this phrase appears for the first time.[1] It is one of the twenty-four definitions of God set forth by an equal number of masters in theology. They themselves, as well as the author of the book, remain anonymous. The twenty-four definitions follow one another in an order whose coherence one must grasp. In particular, the first three definitions are linked with one another in the closest possible manner. Here is the first: *Deus est monas monadem gignens et in se reflectens adorem;* God is a monad which engenders a monad and reflects in Himself His own ardor. The second definition is that of God being a sphere, of which the center is everywhere, and the circumference nowhere. The third presents itself as follows: *Deus est totus in quolibet sui;* God is complete in every part of Himself.

One sees the tie that unites these three propositions. If God as the Father begets an image of Himself, Who is the Son, the love that has made Him create this image of Himself returns it to Him identical. The Father reflects Himself in the Son, the Son reflects Himself in the Father, and this reciprocity of love is nothing more nor less than the Third Person of the Trinity, the Holy Ghost. The cycle is complete. The infinite activity that binds the three Persons constitutes an immense sphere, at every point of which the same plenitude can be found. In the divine

"The Metamorphoses of the Circle" (Original title: *Introduction*). From *Les Métamorphoses du cercle* (Paris: Plon, 1961) by Georges Poulet. Copyright © 1961 by Librairie Plon. Translated by Carley Dawson and Elliott Coleman in collaboration with the author. Used by the permission of Librairie Plon.

[1] *Liber XXIV Philosophorum,* ed. Clemens Baeumker, *Beiträge zur Geschichte der Philosophie des Mittelalters,* 1928, pp. 207-214; cf. on the whole history of the infinite circle the important book of Dietrich Mahnke, *Unendliche Sphaere und Allmittelpunct,* Halle, 1937; cf. also E. Jovy, *Études pascaliennes,* vol. VII and Marjorie Hope Nicolson, *The Breaking of the Circle,* Northwestern University Press, 1950.

sphere, which has no circumference, every point is identical with every other point, every moment is identical with every other moment. God is wholly Himself in whatever part of His Being or His existence that one may consider; or more precisely, there is in God no division of parts, no succession of moments in time, but an absolute simplicity and an absolute simultaneity. One can therefore say that in God the immensity of the circumference can be found again in the unity of the central point, or that the totality of His Being is present in whatsoever fraction of time or space one may arbitrarily distinguish in Him.

In other terms, the infinite sphere can be interpreted as a figuration of the divine immensity, but it can also be interpreted as a figuration of that other divine attribute, eternity. From this point of view, it is nothing else but a metamorphoric transposition of another celebrated definition of eternity, that of Boethius: *Aeternitas est interminabilis vitae tota simul et perfecta possessio;* Eternity is a perfect and simultaneous possession of a limitless existence.[2]

In defining eternity in this way, Boethius was doing nothing more than to repeat the words of a long succession of philosophers; from Parmenides, who affirms that the Absolute Being (represented by him in the form of a sphere) is "altogether present in the Now";[3] to Plotinus, for whom eternity is "a life that persists in its identity always present to itself in its totality . . . like a point in which all the lines meet."[4] Invariably the definitions of eternity conjoin with two terms and two notions which are contradictory, and which only the divine life can reconcile: *omou pan, totum simul, trestout ensemble, insieme tutto, allemittenander, altogether at once,* one of these terms expressing the totality of time, the other, on the contrary, the absence of time or instantaneousness. Eternity is a *Nunc Stans,* an eternal moment, a simple point of duration, but one in which all the points of the circle of this duration find themselves present and conjoined.

This double quality of eternity is clearly explained by Saint Bonaventure in a text that has equal reference to the definitions of Boethius and to *The Book of the Twenty-four Philosophers:*

> If one says that eternity signifies a measureless existence, one must reply that one does not thereby exhaust the meaning of the word "eternity"; because

---

[2] *De Consolatione,* Lib. V, Prosa vi; cf. also Lib. IV, Prosa v, where Boethius compares the peripheral mobility of Fate with the central fixity of Providence.—All the commentaries of the Middle Ages on these texts are important, and particularly that of John Scotus Erigena (*Saeculi noni auctoris in Boetii Consolationem Philosophiae Commentarius,* ed. E. T. Silk, American Academy in Rome, 1935). See especially the following sentence: "*Nam, ut a centro circulus sic ab aevo deducitur tempus; et idem est in tempore aevum quod est in circulo centrum. . . . Nihil est enim aliud aevum quam contractio totius temporis praesentialiter habita in conspectu omnia videntis.*"

[3] νῦν ἔστιν ὁμοῦ πᾶν.

[4] *Enneads,* III, 7.

this means not only interminability, but also simultaneousness; and if, on the one hand, by the mode of interminability one must understand an intelligible circumference, without beginning and without end; on the other hand, by the mode of simultaneousness one must understand simplicity and indivisibility which are the modes of the center; and these two things are affirmed concerning the Divine Being at one and the same time, because He is at once simple and infinite; and so it is that one must understand the circularity in eternity.[5]

As an infinite circumference, eternity, therefore, is the vastest possible circle of duration; as the center of this circumference, it is the fixed point and unique moment which is simultaneously in harmony with all the circumferential points of this duration.

Therefore he who wishes to hold in mind these two contradictory properties of divine eternity must in some manner project his own mind in two opposite directions. He must expand his imagination beyond measure. He must also contract it in the extreme. He must identify himself with the immense circumference that embraces all duration, but also with the central point that excludes all duration. He must transport himself simultaneously both toward the circumference and toward the center.

It is this double movement of the mind that we see represented in Dante's *Divine Comedy.*

In Canto XIV of *Paradise* Dante makes use of the following image:

From the center to the circumference, and likewise from the circumference to the center, the water moves in a round vase, according as it is smitten from without or from within.[6]

As the water in a receptacle flows indifferently either toward the periphery or toward the center, the soul of the poet moves toward a God Who encompasses everything, as well as toward a God Who is at the center of all things. This dual character of an absolute centrality and an absolute circularity, which the Dantean Godhead possesses, manifests itself in a series of passages that finally culminate in the beatific vision of God in the form of both a circle and a point. God, says Dante, is *il punto A cui tutti li tempi son presenti*, a point at which all times are present;[7] *Ove s'appunta ogni Ubi ed ogni Quando*, to which all When and

[5] *Quaestiones Disputatae, De Mysterio Trinitatis*, q. 5, art. I, 7-8, *Opera Omnia*, ed. Quaracchi, vol. V, p. 91.
[6] *Paradiso*, XIV, 1-3.—On the centrifugal and centripetal movements in the *Paradiso*, and the conversion of the one into the other, cf. Karl Witte, *Dante-Forschungen*, 1879, vol. II, p. 181; H. Flanders Dunbar, *Symbolism in Medieval Thought*, Yale University Press, 1929, p. 88; Herbert D. Austin, "Dante Notes," *Modern Language Notes*, XXXVIII, 1923, p. 140; and Allen Tate, "The Symbolic Imagination," *Kenyon Review*, Spring 1952, pp. 257-277.
[7] *Paradiso*, XVII, 18.

all Where are focused.[8] An evident rapport links these two passages of
the *Paradise* to a chapter in the *Vita Nuova* where the god of Love appears to Dante and says to him: "I am the center of a circle to which all
points of the circumference are equidistant; you are not";[9] probably
signifying by these words that, differing from Dante whose thought is
limited to the present moment, the divine thought, center of all moments, comprises the future as well as the past. This is the identical
doctrine of Saint Thomas Aquinas:

> Eternity is always present to whatever time or moment of time it may be. One
> can see an example of it in the circle: a given point of the circumference,
> even though indivisible, nevertheless cannot coexist with all the other points,
> because the order of succession constitutes the circumference; but the center
> that is outside the circumference is immediately connected with any given
> point of the circumference whatsoever.[10]

> Eternity resembles the center of the circle; even though simple and indivisible,
> it comprehends the whole course of time, and every part of it is equally pres-
> ent.[11]

It is, without doubt, to these two passages that another Schoolman of
the period, Pierre Auriol, refers when he writes:

> There are those who use the image of the center of the circle, in its relation
> to all points of the circumference; and they affirm that this is similar to the
> *Nunc* of eternity in its connection with all the parts of time. By which they
> mean that eternity actually coexists with the whole of time.[12]

From these texts it follows that for Dante, as for most of the thinkers
of his time (Duns Scotus is the only exception), the position occupied by
the central point of the circle represents not only the unity and fixity of
divine duration, but the multiplicity of simultaneous rapports that it
holds with the peripheral and mobile duration of creatures. Eternity is
not simply the pivot around which time turns; it is also that point where,
like the rays of the circle, the events of the past and the future converge

---

[8] *Paradiso*, XXIX, 12.

[9] *Vita Nova*, XII: "*Ego tanquam centrum circuli, cui simili modo se habent circum-
ferentiae partes; tu autem non sic.*"—Cf. on this passage G. Boffito, *Bollettino della
Societa Dantesca*, N.S., 10, 1902, p. 266, and Charles Singleton, *Romanic Review*, April
1945; contra, Enrico Proto, *Rassegna critica della Letteratura Italiana*, 1902, pp. 192-
200, and J. E. Shaw, *Italica*, June 1947, pp. 113-118.

[10] *Summa contra Gentiles*, Lib. I, chap. lxvi.

[11] *Declaratio quorundam Articulorum*, op. 2.

[12] *Commentarii in Primum Librum Sententiarum Pars prima*, Rome, 1596, p. 829.
—Cf. also Gilles of Rome, *Defensorium sive Correctorium Corruptorii Operum Divi
Thomae*, Cordova, 1702, p. 10.—Contra, cf. Duns Scotus, *Lib. I Sententiarum*, Dist.
39, qu. unica.

and unite in the consciousness of God. This is what the Neo-Platonist Proclus was one of the first to explain, in a passage with which the Middle Ages were familiar:

> If the center could have a knowledge of the circle, this knowledge would be central and essential. Thus simple knowledge, which is that of Providence, indivisibly perceives all the parts, small or great.[13]

This passage may well have been in the mind of Gerson when he wrote:

> Let us imagine a center endowed with a cognitive force similar to that of the angels, and each ray endowed with the same power. It will follow that every ray comprehends all the points in its course, not only insofar as they are successive stages of the latter, but also as definite objects of knowledge.[14]

Eternity is therefore the cognitive center where, in the unity of divine omniscience, the entire succession of times coexists. "At the center," says Dionysius the Areopagite, "all the lines from the same circle make only one; this point possesses in itself all these lines not only merged one with another, but also with this starting point from which they emanate." [15]

But if all things coexist in God, it is not only because they are thought by Him and merged in Him. God is not uniquely a center of knowledge; He is also a center of force. When Dante describes the divine Point to which all times are present, he adds that from this point "light radiates" and "heaven and all nature depend." [16] This dependence is specifically ontological. Heaven, all nature, the whole of creation in its spatial and temporal unfolding, have existence only because everywhere and always the action from a creative center causes them to exist. Doubtless this creative action is essentially spatial, since every place in the universe is at the receiving end of its action. But it is also temporal, since every new moment is also the effect of this continuous creation. God possesses time not solely by His omniscience, but also by His omnipotence. He is present in all times by the double exercise of His cognitive power and

---

[12] *De Decem Dubitationibus*, ed. Cousin, vol. VI, p. 82.—The Greek text of Proclus is lost; this translation is from the Latin by William of Moerbeke.—Cf. Pierre Courcelle, *Les Lettres grecques en Occident*, p. 289.

[14] Jean Gerson, *Tractatus super Magnificat, Opera Omnia*, ed. Ellis du Pin, The Hague, 1728, vol. IV, p. 438.

[15] *De Divinis Nominibus*, cap. v: "*Et in centro omnes circuli lineae secundum primam unitatem consubstitutae sunt.*" (Translation by John Scotus Erigena)—Cf. all the commentaries on this passage, especially Saint Maximus, Georgius Pachymerus, Saint Dorothy the Archimandrite and the Abbot of Verceil.—Maurice de Gandillac has seen very clearly the importance of the theme of the circle in the work of Dionysius. Cf. his edition of *Oeuvres de Denys*, Aubier, p. 40.

[16] *Paradiso*, XXVIII, 16: "*Un punto vidi che raggiava lume*"; id., 41-42: "*Da quel punto/Depende il cielo, e tutta la natura.*"

His creative power. In one way as in the other, His radiating action immediately and simultaneously attains to all the points of duration as to all those of space. In Dante's poetry, exactly as in Neo-Platonic thought, God is a Point that infinitely enlarges Itself, a radiating seat of energy which diffuses Itself concentrically, universally:

> *E si distende in circular figura*
> *in tanto, che la sua circonferenza*
> *sarebbe al sol troppo larga cintura.*

> And it spreads forth in a circular figure
> so far that its circumference
> would be too wide a girdle for the sun.[17]

But of all the significations that Dante attributes to the divine Point, perhaps there is none more profound than that by which he assimilates it to the Trinity. God is a unique center of activity, but this activity is the same one which brings about the generation of the Word, and the procession of the Holy Ghost. Twice in his final stanzas of the *Paradise,* Dante makes allusion to the mystery of the Trinity; the first time under the form of a triple arrow shot from a bow of three cords; and in the final lines of the poem, precisely under the form of the divine Point which dilates and which in dilating produces three circles. This image has a long tradition behind it. Long before, one of the masters of Saint Augustine, the rhetor Marius Victorinus, had made use of it in a writing destined to refute the heresy of Arius. In order to describe the Logos, identical to the one and yet distinct from it, Marius Victorinus had imagined a sphere of which the diameter was so small that the circumference coincided with the center. "In this case," he wrote, "the extremities and the center are one within the other; . . . what exists simultaneously, without distance, constitutes the first sphere, perfect, unique of its kind; all the other spheres merely attempt to approach it." [18] Likewise, in certain chiastic passages of Saint Augustine, one can see a verbal representation of the circular movement by which the Son is found in the Father, and the Father in the Son: *"In principio erat verbum, et verbum erat apud Deum, et Deus erat verbum."* [19] These variations on the famous passage of the Gospel according to Saint John have no other purpose than to form a circle of words equivalent to the spiritual circle constituted by the Trinity. Besides, it is in no other way that Cristoforo Landino, in the fifteenth century, explains the episode of the third circle in the final passage of the *Divine Comedy:*

---

[17] *Paradiso,* XXX, 103-105.

[18] *Adversus Arium,* lib. I, 60; Pl. 8, c. 1085.

[19] Cf. H. Leisegang, *Denkformen,* 1928; M. F. Rauhut, *Revista de Filologia hispanica,* I, 235 seq., and Leo Spitzer, "Le Style circulaire," *Modern Language Notes,* LV, 1940, pp. 495-499.

The poet, [he says,] expresses here a unique essence in the Three Persons by means of the circular figure. Many centuries before, Hermes Trismegistus had so defined God as a perfect sphere, in as much as the knowledge of God is the knowledge of Himself. Consequently this knowledge proceeds from self to self, like the circle, without beginning and without end.[20]

But the best illustration of the triple circle of the Trinity is found in the writings of the German mystic Heinrich Suso:

> It is said by a wise teacher that God, as regards His Godhead, is like a very wide ring in which the center is everywhere and the circumference nowhere. Now imagine the following image: If a heavy stone is thrown with great force into a sheet of still water, a ring is formed in the water. And of itself this ring makes another, and this other, a third. . . . The three circles represent the Father, the Son, and the Holy Ghost. In this deep abyss, the divine nature in the Father speaks forth and begets the Son. . . . This spiritual and superessential begetting is the plenary cause of all things, and of all souls that come into existence.[21]

In the center and divine circle one must therefore see in the first place the representation of the internal action of the Trinity, but one must also see a prefiguration of the external movement, no less circular, by which this divine activity spreads Itself outward, in order to surround Itself with a new series of circles, which are those of creation. Creation is the common work of the Three Persons; the mystery of their operations perpetuates itself everlastingly. From this point of view, every point in space, every point of time, becomes the eternal place and moment where the Father begins once again to engender the Son, and the Son lovingly to reflect Himself in the Father. Any place and moment of time form the seat and center of the Divinity. Such is the constant doctrine of the Middle Ages: "Everywhere is the center of Thy power," Saint Bonaventure says to God.[22] No one affirms this doctrine with greater insistence than Master Eckhart, in the works in which the two celebrated definitions of God as a monad and a sphere are ceaselessly interwoven one with another, to signify that in every moment and in every place, God constitutes Himself the center of all moments and all places. To the two first definitions of God taken from *The Book of the Twenty-four Philosophers,* Eckhart is fond of adding the third, the one according to which *Deus est totus in quolibet sui;* God is fully in every part of Himself. Already, in

---

[20] Cristoforo Landino, Commentaries on the Divine Comedy.

[21] *Vita,* ed. W. Öhl, *Deutsche Mystiker,* p. 151.—In this passage Suso draws his inspiration from Eckhart (*Predigten,* 50, ed. F. Pfeiffer, p. 165). On Eckhart, Suso, and the German mystique of the circle see especially the excellent book of Maria Bindschedler, *Der lateinische Kommentar zum Granum Sinapis,* Basel, 1949.

[22] *Commentaria Sententiarum,* 1. I, dist. I, p. 1, art. I, q. 1; cf. also *Hexaemeron,* col. 6, 8.

his *Itinerarium Mentis,* Saint Bonaventure had said something approaching it:

> Because God is eternal and absolutely actual, He enfolds all durations and exists simultaneously in all their moments as their center and circumference. And because He is infinitely simple and infinitely great, He is wholly within all and without all; and it is for this reason that He is an intelligible sphere of which the center is everywhere and the circumference nowhere.[23]

But in Eckhart these two formulas: *Deus est totus in quolibet sui, Deus est simplicissimus et maximus, ideo totus intra omnia et totus extra omnia,* are fused together and take on a more radical significance. *"In Divinis,"* says Eckhart, *"quodlibet est in quolibet et maximus in minimo."* [24] "In divine things, everything is in everything else and the maximum is in the minimum." This formula was to become the basis of the philosophy of Nicolaus Cusanus. It was to have an immense influence on Leonardo da Vinci and Giordano Bruno. But one can already see an application or a prefiguration in the poetry of Dante. At the very end of the *Divine Comedy,* when he is describing the moment when he fixes his look upon the divine Point, Dante adds:

> *Un punto solo m'e maggior letargo*
> *che venticinque secoli all impresa*
> *che fe'Nettuno ammirar l'ombra d'Argo.*[25]

> One moment only is for me a longer lethargy
> than twenty-five centuries were to the undertaking
> that made Neptune admire the shade of Argos.

No doubt the extraordinary beauty of these lines is owing, in the first place, to the force of the metaphor. Even when distended beyond measure in its duration, the most glorious undertaking of which mankind had remembrance is nothing by comparison to the instant where, in spite of time and forgetfulness, one remembers having seen God. But by a most bold and unusual play of words, Dante in this passage deliberately confounds two points and two instants. *Un punto solo* is evidently, here, the Italian expression *un punto di momento,* an instant of duration. But it is in this point of human duration that it has been given precisely to Dante to apprehend the divine Point, the point of eternity. Consequently when he arrives at the end of his long periplus, Dante arrives at a point that is at once divine and the point at which he apprehends the

[23] *Itinerarium Mentis ad Deum,* cap. V, 8.
[24] Text given by Denifle, *Archiv für Literatur-und-Kirchengeschichte des Mittelalters,* vol. II, 1886, p. 571.
[25] *Paradiso,* XXXIII, 94-96.

divine. The final object of the poem is no longer an object around which one can turn and toward which one tends; it is an object one possesses, a point with which one coincides. And if one coincides with it, that is because it is no longer now an exterior and remote object. The divine Point is the very center of the soul; it is God interiorly possessed in a human moment.

One can therefore see here in Dante the veiled but striking expression of a doctrine that precisely in the same era of time acquires in the mystic writers its whole force. God is a point, because He is a center, not only of the universe, but of the soul. The synderesis, *l'apex mentis,* the *Seelengrund,* the *Fünkelein,* all these expressions profusely employed by the mystics, signify that the maximum is in the minimum, the infinity of the divine sphere is in the infinite minuteness of the center, and that this center is indeed that of the soul. Because God is an immense sphere of which the plenitude is contained in a center everywhere present, the soul is a center that contains this sphere. Such is the unanimous tradition of mystics from Eckhart to Madame Guyon.

For example, Harphius, the great intermediary between German mysticism and Spanish mysticism, writes as follows:

> The soul is called spirit with regard to what there is most intimate and most elevated in its powers; for the powers of the soul are united in the mind as in their source, and it is from this source that they expand outward, as sun rays do beyond the circle of the sun, just as it is into this source that they flow back. This center is situated in the soul, and in it shines the true image of the Trinity; and it is so noble that no suitable name may properly be found for it; and one cannot speak of it except by circumlocutions.[26]

Thus the movement by which the soul approaches God is a centered motion that takes place in the interior of the soul itself. This is explained by another mystical writer, this time of the seventeenth century, the Englishman Peter Sterry, in terms that irresistibly make one think of the movement—at first eccentric, and then concentric—followed by Dante in his poem:

> There is a Fountain of life, where endlessly springs up in an unconfined Circle, in a bottomless depth, forms of glory innumerable, one within another. . . . The Soul circles round this Deep of the Divine Mind, but as one Spirit encompasses another without circumscription, extension or distance. Yet the Soul, without confinement or adequation, contains in its Unity and Center this glorious Deep of the Divine Mind . . . as the Unity of its Unity, the Center of its Center.[27]

[26] Henricus Harphius, *Theologia mystica,* lib. II, pars 5, col. 2.
[27] *A Discourse on the Freedom of the Will,* London, 1675, p. 93.

So it appears that Dante's journey, like all mystical journeys, is an inward one. Its final goal is a God in which the soul sinks itself because it sinks into itself. French mystic Pierre Poiret exclaims:

> O divine eternity, call us back from our dispersion amidst passing temporal vanities, and gather us into the still center of the heart where we can give place and attention to the all-powerful and ineffable operations of Thy manifestation, of which one moment is worth more than all the duration of time.[28]

The still tranquil center of the heart is reached by Dante in a moment which is at one and the same time the final moment of his journey and of his poem. All his voyage, all his poem, constitute only the succession of movements by which his mind finally accedes to a place and to a moment where there is no longer either movement, succession, or dimension. Then the extreme of grandeur coincides with the extreme of smallness. "The eternal center," says Jakob Böhme, "and the Birth of Life, and Substantiality, are everywhere. Trace a circle no larger than a dot, the whole birth of Eternal Nature is therein contained." [29]

Moreover this final coincidence of eternity with the moment of vision and the immense sphere of God with the narrow sphere of the creature, is foreshadowed in the final lines of the *Divine Comedy,* in the passages which celebrate the most striking example of this conjunction of the immense infinite with the infinitely small. Just before the final vision of the poem, Dante makes Saint Bernard pronounce the eulogy on the Mother of God. *"Nel ventre tuo si raccese l'Amore."* [30] Love rekindled in the Virgin's womb is the immense sphere of the divinity mysteriously reappearing in the narrow sphere of a human body. The Incarnation, also, is a manifestation of the maximum in the minimum, and the infinite in the finite. It is of this geometrical paradox that one of Dante's inspirers, Alain de Lille, sings, in a hymn that dates from the end of the twelfth century:

> *Sphaeram claudit curvatura*
> *Et sub ipsa clauditur.*
> *In hac Verbi copula*
> *Stupet omnis regula.*[31]

[The arc encloses the sphere and is enclosed within it. In this joining of the Word every rule is confounded.]

One of the most beautiful examples of this inscription of the divine sphere in the sphere of humanity is found in the *Roman de la Rose.*

[28] *Œconomie divine,* Amsterdam, 1687, vol. VII, p. 387.
[29] *De Triplici Vita Hominis,* cap. VI, 45.
[30] *Paradiso,* XXXIII, 7.
[31] Alanus ab Insulis, *Opera,* Migne, Pl. 210, col. 578.

Just after having defined eternity in the same terms as Boethius, as

> Possession of life that by the end cannot be seized,
> Altogether at once, without division,

Jean de Meung introduces in his poem an episode of primary importance. Profoundly different from divine eternity that possesses at once all the elements that constitute it, human existence moves from moment to moment, without any of them ever attaining plenitude. Everything changes, everything perishes, nothing endures. Alone, in creation, forms remain. But again what will guarantee their permanency? To answer this question, Jean de Meung recalls first a famous passage of the *Timaeus*: that where the demiurge, addressing the inferior divinities whose mission is precisely that of maintaining the permanence of forms, reminds them that they themselves have no permanence, and that it is from Him alone that they obtain their stability:

> Par nature mourir pourriez
> Mais par mon veuil ja ne mourriez.
>
> By nature could you die
> But by my will never will you.

The only fixity that there is in the universe is therefore finally hanging on divine good will. Human reason cannot go further. Vainly it tries to find in itself some grounds for belief that God's benevolence toward His creation will always endure. Consequently, to escape the anguish into which he is thrown by the thought that a new divine decree could hand over the world to the most radical vicissitude, one must lift oneself up to the contemplation of revealed truths and remind oneself that the good will of God was manifested once and for all, in the most extraordinary manner, in the mystery of the Incarnation. This reveals to man that he is firmly tied to the eternal will. For eternity has incarnated itself in time and the infinite sphere within the boundaries of the human sphere. Such is the assurance the Virgin possesses:

> Car el sot des qu'el le portait,
> Dont au porter se confortait,
> Qu'il iert l'espere merveillable
> Qui ne peut estre terminable,
> Qui par touz leus son centre lance,
> Ne leu n'a la circonference. . . .
>
> For she knew as soon as she carried him,
> Whose carrying was comforting,

> That he was the marvelous sphere
> That can never be terminated,
> That midst all places its center throws,
> Whose circumference is in no place. . . .

Then, linking to the mystery of the Incarnation the mystery of the Trinity that precedes and announces it, Jean de Meung sets, as it were, within the symbol of the circle, the symbol of the triangle, in a way typical of all emblematists of the Middle Ages:

> Qu'il iert li merveilleus triangles
> Dont l'unité fait les treis angles.

"Whose oneness equals three angles." Finally the two symbols appear, completely merged one within the other:

> C'est li cercles trianguliers,
> C'est li triangles circuliers
> Qui en la vierge s'ostela.[32]

> This is the triangular circle,
> This is the circular triangle
> That within the Virgin found its home.

This recalls a Latin hymn attributed to Philippe de Grèves:

> *Centrum capit circulus*
> *Quod est majus circulo,*
> *In centro triangulus*
> *Omni rectus angulo,*
> *Sed fit minor angulus*
> *Unus de triangulo,*
> *Dum se mundi figulus*
> *Inclusit in vasculo.*[33]

---

[32] *Roman de la Rose,* ed. Langlois, Société des anciens textes français, 1914, vol. IV, pp. 254-256.

[33] *Analecta Hymnica Medii Ævi,* Leipzig, 1886, vol. XX, p. 88.—The analogy between the divine circle and triangle is found in numerous texts and emblems of the Middle Ages and Renaissance. Cf., for example, the circle inscribed in a triangle in the corners of which are the letters of the tetragram JEVE, in a text of Garnier de Rochefort, quoted by Clemens Baeumker, *Beiträge zur Geschichte der Philosophie des Mittelalters,* XXIV, 1926, p. 35. In it Garnier de Rochefort mentions the first definition of God in the *Book of the 24 Philosophers:* "*Spiritus Sanctus est ardor Patris et Filii; monas gignit monadem et in se suum reflectit ardorem.*"—We should also remember this passage of Gerson's in the *Tractatus super Magnificat,* which connects the first two

[The circle contains the center which is greater than the circle. Its center is triangular and straight in every angle. Yet, of the triangle on angle will become the less when the Potter who shaped the world encloses himself in a little vase.]

What is striking in these two poems is the metaphysical paradox that situates the infinite in the finite; but there is also the ethical paradox that places the ultimate of grandeur in the ultimate of humiliation. From this point of view, the spectacle of the incarnated Christ is no different from that of the Christ descended into the lowest parts of creation, that is to say, Hell. In one case as in the other, the mind finds itself in the presence of grandeur reduced to the most exiguous dimensions. When, in the first part of his *Divine Comedy*, Dante was describing his own descent into Hell, he could not but have thought of that other descent to the narrowest and most foul place in the universe. Saint Bonaventure writes:

It is not only on the surface of the earth that the Christ came; it is in its profoundest center, "in the entrails of the center and in the heart of the earth" that He worked for our salvation; for, after His crucifixion, His soul descended into Hell and restored the voided celestial thrones. It is in this profound center that salvation lies, for he who draws away from the center of humility is lost.[34]

definitions of the same book: "*Unitatem Dei per unitatem centralis puncti posse manudici. Hinc est ex Philosophis Dei descriptio, quod est sphaera intelligibilis cujus centrum est ubique, circumferentia nusquam.—Unitatem divinam gignere unitatem, et in se suam reflectere unitatem per amorem spirativum, triangulo intelligibili perfecte circulato.*" (*Opera*, ed. Ellis du Pin, vol. IV, pp. 443-444.)

The same identification of the circle and the triangle is found in a passage from the *Prisons* of Marguerite De Navarre whose importance has been demonstrated by Abel Lefranc (*Grands Écrivains de la Renaissance*, pp. 170 ff.):

> D'extérieur en l'intérieur entre
> Qui va par moi, et au milieu du centre
> Me trouvera, qui suis le point unique,
> La fin, le but de la mathématique;
> Le cercle suis dont toute chose vient,
> Le point où tout retourne se maintient.
> Je suis qui triangle très parfait
> Le tout-puissant, sage et bon en effet. . . .

Finally, in his *Orbis Sensualium Pictus* (1658), Comenius reproduces the figure of the circle inscribed in a triangle with the word *Deus* on the side. In his *Theologia naturalis* (Verona, 1779, p. 34) Christian Wolf comments on this emblem as follows: "*Comenius pingit triangulum cum circulo inscripto. . . . Circulus designat aeternitatem, triangulum circumscriptum Trinitatem in unitatem. . . .*"

[34] *In Hexaemeron*, col. 1, 24. *Opera omnia*, ed. Quaracchi, vol. V, p. 333.—Cf. Etienne Gilson's excellent commentary on this passage, *La Philosophie de Saint Bonaventure*, Vrin, 1924, p. 222.

Descended into the womb of a virgin or into the womb of the world, the Christ is that Immensity that renounces Its celestial expanse, the sphere reduced to a "center of humility."

Perhaps the most beautiful passages on this center of humility and the incarnation of the circle are to be found, in the seventeenth century, in the writers of the Counter-Reformation:

"We adore," writes Bérulle, "an infinite God, but One Who has made Himself finite, and is bound, Himself, into the circumference of human nature." [35]

Johann Scheffler similarly says:

> When God lay hidden in the womb of a Virgin,
> Then the Point contained the Circle.[36]

One of the most impassioned poems on the incarnation of the circle is that of the English Jesuit Richard Crashaw, *In The Glorious Epiphanie Of Our Lord God*. It is a hymn sung by the three Magi who, from different regions of the earth, have converged toward that central place where the Savior of the universe was born:

> To Thee, thou Day of night! thou east of west!
> To thee, the world's great universal east.
> The Generall and indifferent Day.
> All circling point. All centring sphear . . .
> O little all! in thy embrace
> The world lyes warm, and likes his place.
> Nor does his full Globe fail to be
> Kist on Both his cheeks by Thee.[37]

There is no trait more characteristic of the baroque imagination than this intercrossing movement by which the immensity of the universe becomes a toy in the hands of a child, while the smallness of the child becomes the immensity of a God Who embraces the world.

But the image of the God Who embraces the world should recall to us also another aspect and perhaps the most important of our theme. For the doctrine of the Incarnation, as well as that of the Trinity, both imply a God Who is not content with being the center and the circumference of the universe, but Who, from His center, animates and peoples in the most fecund way the space that His circumference contains.

This aspect of the theme is admirably described in a Spanish poem

---

[35] Cardinal De Bérulle, *Opuscules de piété*, ed. Rotureau, Aubier, 1944, p. 184.

[36] Angelus Silesius, *Cherubinischer Wandersmann*, bk. III, 28.

[37] Richard Crashaw, The Poems, ed. L. C. Martin, Oxford: Clarendon Press, 1927, p. 255.

dating from the beginning of the seventeenth century. The author is the conceptist Alonso de Bonilla:

> God is the original circumference
> Of all spherical figures,
> Since rings, orbs, circles and altitudes
> Are included at the center of His essence.
> From this infinite center of knowledge
> Issue immense lines of creatures,
> Living sparks of the pure light
> Of this inaccessible omnipotence.
> Virgin, if God is the center and the abyss
> From which emerge such exterior lines,
> And if Thy womb includes God in it,
> Thou art the center of God's own center,
> So much so, that at the issuance of Thy womb,
> God is a line issued out of Thy center.[38]

Center that is prolonged in the line, circle begot from the radiating center. Long before, the Pythagoreans had insisted on the generating force of the point. For Plotinus the center is "the father of the circle." [39] For Scotus Erigena it is "the initial universal point." [40] So also the Jewish Cabbala and Arabian thought make of the central point the starting point from which the world has developed. All medieval philosophy of light is a long commentary on the spherical diffusion of every luminous point. "*Omne agens multiplicat suam virtutem spherice.*" [41] This phrase of Grosseteste is applicable to all activity, but, first of all, to God. God is a light propagating Itself, a force that multiplies and diffuses Itself. None has better described this phenomenon of Divine expanding creation than Master Eckhart:

> There is a reflection and a conversion of God within and upon Himself, and an installation and a fixation of God in God. But there is also a seething up and an overflowing of God out of Himself. . . .[42]

Therefore it is easy to perceive that precisely from Eckhart on this is no longer a static God, settled in Himself, Who fascinates all intellects; this is, on the contrary, a dynamic God, seething and overflowing. In

---

[38] Alonso de Bonilla, *Neuvo Jardin de Flores Divinas*, Baeza, 1617, Biblioteca de Autores Espanoles, vol. XXXV, p. 45.

[39] *Enneads*, VI, 8, 18.

[40] *De Divisione Naturae, Opera*, Migne, PL., 122, c. 625.

[41] Robert Grosseteste, *De Lineis angulis et figuris*, ed. L. Baur, *Beiträge zur Geschichte der Philosophie des Mittelalters*, IX, 1912, p. 64.

[42] *Expositio Libri Exodi*, Die Lateinischen Werke, ed. Kohlhammer, vol. II, p. 22.

other terms, about the time of and throughout the Renaissance, what increasingly absorbs the attention of theologians and philosophers is less the spectacle of a Divinity considered in Itself, than that of His action on the world. Following Nicolaus Cusanus, Ficino, Pico, Patrizzi, Campanella, and above all, Bruno in Italy; Charles de Bouelles, Pelletier du Mans, Ramus, La Boderie, and Yves de Paris in France; Paracelsus, Kepler, Böhme, Kircher, and Leibniz in Germany; all the Platonists of the Cambridge School; and all the poets called "metaphysical" in England; all return, no less indefatigably than the Scholastics of the Middle Ages, to the emblem of the circle and the center; but what strikes them in this image is the circle perceived as a dilation of the center. The divine reality is no longer situated at two extremes, in an invisible circumference and within an ineffable central point; it is everywhere present and moving in the cluster of activities that It projects in every direction around Itself. As Robert Fludd later writes:

> So that from God all things did flow and spring, namely out of a secret and hidden nature to a revealed and manifest condition, from an unknown estate into an evident and known existence; from a pure Archetypal simplicity into a real type or similitude; from a radical fountain into a Sea, and from a mere point into a circle or circumference; verifying that saying of the wise Philosopher: God is the center of everything, whose circumference is nowhere to be found.[43]

This universal explication and manifestation of the divine in nature haunts the imagination of the men of the Renaissance: "God overflows everywhere," [44] says Pontus de Tyard. And Ronsard:

> Dieu est partout, partout se mêle Dieu . . .
> Car Dieu partout en tout se communique. . . .[45]
>
> God is everywhere, everywhere God mingles . . .
> For God everywhere, in all things, communicates Himself. . . .

Finally, Ramus:

> God fills everything with His perpetual power, and nowhere and never is He filled up. Thus a certain philosopher has rightly said of Him: God is a sphere of which the center is everywhere, and the periphery nowhere.[46]

[43] *Mosaical Philosophy*, London, 1659, p. 133.
[44] *L'Univers ou Discours des parties et de la nature du Monde, Second Curieux*, ed. John C. Lapp, Cornell University Press, 1950, p. 144: *"Car Dieu est substance, puissance et action, qui surpassent et de qui dépendent toutes autres substances, puissances et actions. D'où prit source l'opinion des poètes qui ont chanté tout être plein de Jupiter, c'est-à-dire Dieu être épanché partout et particulièrement et généralement."*
[45] *Le Chat* (1573).
[46] Pierre Ramus, *Commentarii de Religione Christiana*, Frankfurt, 1583, t. I, cap. III.

After all these texts one can see what a profound transformation the symbol of the infinite sphere underwent at the time of the Renaissance. This is no longer transcendence, but divine immanence which is placed in strong relief. God, being the center everywhere, is everywhere a diffusive and repletive force. To employ Henry More's expression, every place and every moment appear as "a reiteration of the divine center." [47] "The divine center is in every place," says Marsilio Ficino, "as the virtue of God, distributed in His creatures, is in every minute particle of the universe." [48]

God, infinite center, is not a contracted God, limited to the center; He is a God Who diffuses Himself from this center; the English philosopher Cudworth writes:

> Wherefore although some novelists make a contracted idea of God, consisting of nothing else but will and power, yet His nature is better expressed by some in this mystical or enigmatic representation of an infinite circle, whose inmost center is simple goodness, whose radii and expanse are all-comprehending immutable wisdom, and whose exterior periphery or infinite circumference is the will or omnipotent activity by which everything outside of God is brought forth into existence.[49]

Father Mersenne says the same thing: "God is an indivisible center whose irradiation expands over the periphery of all things." [50]

But if every point of the universe thus reveals itself as a center from which God irradiates Himself, it follows that man can also place himself in every one of these points to contemplate from around about himself the magical spectacle of this divine irradiation. "The soul is a kind of center," says Giordano Bruno.[51] It is a center, not alone as the mystics believe, because in it God has His favorite dwelling-place, but because this divine place of residence is also the converging place for all cosmic phenomena. "The whole universe surrounds man," says Paracelsus, "as the circle surrounds the point." [52]

---

[47] Letter to Descartes of the 5th March 1649: "*Hanc autem repetitionem centri divini, quae mundum occupat, ulterius productam, infinita par est extra coelum visibile spatia secum expandere.*"

[48] *Tractatus de Deo et Anima vulgaris* (1457), Supplementum Ficinianum, ed. Kristeller, Florence, 1937, vol. II, p. 147.

[49] Ralph Cudworth, *A Treatise concerning eternal and immutable morality*, bk I, ch. III, 8.

[50] *Quaestiones in Genesim*, Paris, 1623, col. 57.

[51] *Articuli adversus Mathematicos, Opera Latine Conscripta*, Florence, 1889, t. I, pars 3, p. 60: "Considerate vim omnem circuli esse in centro. . . . Anima centrum quoddam est, quae etiam est circulis se ipsum movens."

[52] *Explicitatio totius astronomiae, Opera*, Geneva, 1658, vol. II, p. 649: "Ad centrum omnia contendunt: et homo est centrum totius mundi." Cf. also *Astronomia Magna, Opera*, vol. II, p. 567: "Homo a mundo cinctus est, sicut punctum obitur a suo circulo."

This new central position occupied by man has nothing in common with the median position occupied by the earth in ancient cosmology, now disappearing. There is no more any question now of a fixed point, the lowest of all placed at the center of the finite and finished world. What is now in question is any point, since it is in any point that thought can place itself to contemplate the cosmic spectacle and the operations that God accomplishes in creation. In whatever situation man may place himself, in whatever moment that he thinks, he is always able to discover himself in the center of an infinite universe which God develops around him so that he shall be conscious of this very universality. "I have placed thee at the center of the world," says God to man in a celebrated discourse by Pico della Mirandola "so that thou shalt more conveniently consider everything that is in the world." [53] "The soul is the center of nature," [54] says Marsilio Ficino. And Charles de Bouelles: "Man is a nothing facing the all . . . , so that he shall become the eye of everything, the mirror of nature, detached and separated from the order of things, placed far from everything to be the center of everything." [55]

The soul, like God, is therefore a center of infinite information. But it is also, like God, a center of force. The mystical doctrine of the synderesis transforms itself into a doctrine of psychic diffusion: "From the depths of thy being," says the Spanish mystic Juan de los Angeles, "from the center of the point of thy soul thy powers proceed in a manner no different from that by which the rays come from the sun." [56] Cudworth was to say the same: "This is an ever bubbling fountain in the centre of the soul, an elater, or spring of motion. . . ."[57] There is in the soul a "secret centrality" that manifests and develops itself by a "free dilation." [58]

But how to imagine this "free dilation," unless as the movement by means of which man profits by every moment and every place in such a way as to enfold in his gaze the universe which the divine force has disposed precisely around this moment and this place? Everywhere is the center of the divine activity. Everywhere, too, is the center of the activity inherent to the soul. Neither one nor the other has limits. "The soul will become an immense sphere," exclaims Campanella.[59] "My Soul

---

[53] *De Hominis Dignitate, Opera*, Basel, 1601, vol. I, p. 208.

[54] *Theologia Platonica*, l. III, cap. II: "Merito dici (anima) possit centrum naturae, universorum medium, mundi series, vultus omnium, nodusque et copula mundi."

[55] Carollus Bovillus, *Liber de Sapiente*, ed. Klibansky, Leipzig, 1927, p. 353.

[56] Juan de los Angeles, *Conquista del Espiritual y Secreto Reino de Dios* (1595), Nueva Biblioteca de Autores Españoles, Madrid, 1912, vol. I, p. 45.

[57] *A Treatise of Freewill*, ed. Allen, London, 1838, p. 28.

[58] Henry More, *Antimonopsychia*, strophe 34.—Speaking of the soul, More says: "central depth it has, and free dilation." A little later, still discussing the soul, More uses such expressions as "hidden centrality" and "central energy."

[59] *Poésie*, ed. Gentile, Scrittori d'Italia 70, 1915, p. 42:

is an infinite Sphere in a Centre," proclaims Thomas Traherne.[60] The infinite sphere has now become the symbol, not only of God, but of man. The infinite sphere is nothing now but the field encompassed by human consciousness. At this point we can stop and consider the road traversed. In passing through the ages, the great emblem of the center and the sphere has singularly changed in meaning. Now it no longer is exclusively applicable to God, but also to man. It is man who, equally with God, discovers himself to be center and infinite sphere. Even more, it is every moment, every place where man finds himself, that constitutes itself as the ever-renewed center of this infinite sphericity; for every place and every moment offer to man a new point of view. As he places himself therein, he perceives around him each time a universe no less infinite than the universe glimpsed in the preceding moment or in the next place. So much so that the world, being composed of an infinity of places and moments, is an infinity of worlds, all infinite, which the human consciousness apprehends everywhere and always. Such is the richness that relativist thought discovers in the cosmos. This richness appears to it as a manifestation of the Divine Being. But let the figure of God, as will happen a century later, withdraw itself to the horizon of thought, let the variety of the world appear in itself, stripped of all theological signification, then the symbol of the center and the sphere will reduce itself to a simple perspective diagram. Man in the eighteenth century will no longer embrace within his gaze the sphere of God, but the sphere of scientific knowledge. The divine encyclic will become a simple encyclopedia.

L'anima si faria un'immensa spera,
che amar, saper e far tutto potrebbe
in Dio, di maraviglie sempr'altera.

[60] Thomas Traherne, *Centuries of Meditations*, ed. B. Dobell, London, 1908, p. 136.

The Recollection of the Way

by Charles Williams

Of all this experience Dante says (*Par.* XXXIII, 58-63): "I was like one who sees in a dream, and when the dream is gone the passion stamped (*impressa*) by it remains, and the other comes not again to mind; even so my vision has almost entirely disappeared, but the sweetness born of it distills still in my heart." Wordsworth said something similar of the early Romantic sense (*Prelude*, II, 312-22):

> the soul
> Remembering how she felt, but what she felt
> Remembering not. . . .

The vision or communication disappears, but the consciousness of the passion remains. It was then to Wordsworth a mood of "shadowy exaltation," and perhaps, in many, some such recollection is all that remains of the "stupor," especially during that period which has been called here "the death of Beatrice." We may complete the quotation from the English poet:

> The soul
> . . . retains an obscure sense
> Of possible sublimity, whereto
> With growing faculties she doth aspire,
> With faculties still growing, feeling still
> That whatsoever point they gain, they yet
> Have something to pursue.

This is applicable to the whole *Commedia,* until the last Canto. There, in the last four lines, there is a return, almost in so many words, to the simile used in that famous dream of the *Vita.* The dream occurred after Beatrice had refused him her salutation; Love said: "I am as the center of a circle to which all parts of the circumference are equal, but with you it is not so." In the *Paradiso* she had again turned from him, and after that he had seen all, and he wrote:

> All' alta fantasia qui mancò possa;
>   ma già volgeva il mio disiro e il *velle*,
>   sì come rota ch' egualmente è mossa,
> l'amor che move il sole e l' altre stelle—

Power failed the high imagination; but the Love which moves the sun and the other stars rolled my desire and my will, as if they were a wheel which is moved equally.

The final line is known everywhere. But the final line has a subordinate verb, and not the chief verb of the sentence. The important thing to Dante was not so much that Love moved the sun and the other stars, as that Love rolled his own desire and will. It is clearly more convenient for us to recollect the sun and the rest rather than our desire and will; that is why the last line is so popular. But it is the desire and will which, in the poem, are fully in the Empyrean; the sun and the other stars are (literally) below that heaven, and (allegorically) they are lesser states of that heaven.

It is the simile of the equally rolling wheel which recalls the earlier circle simile. For now, to Dante as well as to Love, "all parts of the circumference are equal"; with him "it is so." This distinction between the two states, as was said of the Salutation, has been the whole purpose of the journey. The wheel which is he rolls in the Empyrean; that is, in the world of substance. His motion is a motion in true substance; indeed, his desire and will are the motion; that is, he is himself the motion. This is now his function, for which he was created—to be exactly that perfect motion in substance, and this is the chief statement in the last four lines. Nevertheless, the sun and stars have their poetic place; they ease the imagination from the single flash—"fulgor"—in which it perceived *how* the Image of Man "came together with the circle—"

> come si convenne
> l' imago al cerchio, e come vi s' indova—

"and how it in-dwelled there." They allow the mind to relax (if such a word may be used of such a state) toward the creation. The eyes of Beatrice are permitted to turn again toward the gyres of the eternal and roseal City.

The operative word of the last line is "move—moves." The sun and stars are in movement, engaged on their similar functions. They too are movements in substance. As was explained to Dante, all the heavens are, in fact, one heaven. He has to know them separately, but they are all one, only known in distinction by their "feeling, more or less, the eternal breath." All then are seen in that simultaneously understood City, with all their times and places; all the small roses and all the mighty are in this Rose. If Dante—say rather, if Beatrice—had been able to look back —or rather, considering the last line of the poem, if they were able to follow that returning Way—But, of course, they were; it was precisely this which the freedom of the City granted them; the wheeling desire and will looked out on the sun and the other stars. The second Iris derived from the First; our Image was fixed in it; the eyes which see that Image deepest are the eyes—"da Dio diletti e venerati—loved and venerated by God"—of Mary, of her from whom the Image in the Iris is derived, as she herself is imaged by every soul in heaven. It is therefore that the other images can now be seen, beginning with Eve, herself the mother of all lives, between whom and Mary is a great interchange—for "the wound which Mary closed and anointed she who is so beautiful at her feet opened and thrust" (*Par.* XXXII, 4-6), in which exchange both have a complete joy; so that the shapes of all who wound and all who heal here courteously rejoice together. Between all the human images the golden bees of the angelic creation fly, and the introduction of that other creation adds a strangeness and a touch of "stupor," and consequently an added exaltation to the whole; for even here the human perfection is in relation to some quite different perfection; humanity itself is not self-enclosed. In that state it becomes again possible to talk "of every *when* and every *where*—ogni *ubi* ed ogni *quando*" (*Par.* XXIX, 12), for here was the state in which Dante first saw, reflected in the eyes of Beatrice, the point from which "depende il cielo e tutta la natura—from which heaven and all nature hangs." He saw it reflected in her eyes before he turned to see it in itself, and this therefore is the moment of the opening downwards of that reflection which is the principle and cause of all the images, which indeed is what makes things images, and that not only of things toward God but of things toward each other. The full working out of this possibility has to be seen (in God) below this. Beatrice—that is, not only Beatrice but every relationship according to proper vocation —"imparadisa—in-paradises" the mind (*Par.* XXVIII, 3), which has already been "innamorata—in-amoured" (*Par.* XXVII, 88). This is possible to each of that great crowd who have been seen "triumphing" in Christ; but not before they are seen as a whole. It will be remembered that Dante could not bear the full heavenly smile of Beatrice until after he had seen Christ glorious in his saints—a figure of profound significance, for it was the earlier subdued smile of Beatrice which had brought him to Christ and his saints; and here again is a continual exchange of power between one image and all the other images. This certainly is the principle—discovered or undiscovered—of every love-affair, by which (now) is meant every affair of love.

That celestial power, in such continual exchange, moves always toward earth as always up from earth. The ladder of the great contemplatives is just below that Saint John whose glory blinds Dante, though in the Earthly Paradise it was Saint John who had seemed to Dante to be in trance, with closed eyes. I suppose a small additional image might be borrowed there from poetry—say, from the *Commedia* itself; for a line which seems to us great but of which we do not understand the full significance will lie vibrating but quiescent, whereas when we do understand something of the significance it seems to have relevancies of all kinds, and we are defeated by it in quite another way. Such pause and progress in exploration is the paradisal counterpart of the sleeping and waking in the *Purgatorio*. In hell there is no progress, only insignificant monotony. The descent from and in that blinding power leads contemplation to the great eagle of earthly justice, and so to the cross of the courageous and of the families. This is the heavenly knowledge (in the eagle) of all commonalty, of all proper balance—the "I" for the "We" and the "We" for the "I"—and (in the cross) of time and transition, and of exile. So that, this way, the idea of exile has a double meaning, for the temporal exile of Dante is the result of the act of the self-exiled from heaven. It is the topmost note—and the first in this descent—of immediate personal suffering from sin; those above know—like Adam our lord and father—that they were sinners, and denounce sin on earth, but this is the prophecy of sin on earth shooting direct arrows, and the salt bread and hard stairs express it. As for the families and the history of Florence, there is the tale of physical derivation in time. Birth, in itself, had been known above; giving birth was the function of the God-bearer, but that was single, and it was "the cause and occasion" of all the rest. This is the spectacle of the rest. The eagle of justice and the cross of courage are, respectively, humanity seen simultaneously and humanity seen sequentially; they are complementary.

Below these are the wheels of pure light which are the heaven of the sun, and of the philosophical intellects of the City. There are two great stages of ascent in heaven, as there are two great pits of descent in hell. The wise and accurate doctors of this stage correspond to the false pollution of Geryon, as the ladder of the contemplatives above corresponds to the abyss of the giants below—the giants are even less intelligent than Geryon, just as the contemplatives are wiser even than the doctors. But though we can say "below" in one case, we cannot rightly say "above" in the other. Hell is a funnel; heaven is a rose. The narrowing inorganic rock of the one is the chosen antitype of the intensifying organic heart of the other. The wheels of the doctors mark a sudden change in Paradise, more intense than that only from one heaven to another. Descending knowledge, issuing downwards from those wheels, finds itself in a heaven already touched with the shadow of earth. The three heavens of this lowest order need to be touched by it with a particular tenderness, for they have in them a marked insufficiency of their own. This must, theologically, be true of all the heavens; only, in the poem, it is made spectacular here. Below the heaven of the doctors Dante has not once worthily forgotten Beatrice; insofar as he ever did forget, it was of the nature of sin. But sin here, as the heaven of Venus sings, is known only as an occasion of glory; "sin shall have worship in heaven," as the Lady Julian said. Lovers, citizens, nuns, are the symbols of the three grades. And then, still sinking, and issuing from the lowest, the sweetest and most childlike of the heavens, the descending knowledge—memory—is aware of two suns, but that one in which all paradise dances is lost behind the other, the lower, sun; and suddenly there is landscape—a great forest, trees, earth, streams, men and women walking. One might certainly imagine that here too, as in another wood of which somewhere we heard (in a nightmare—forgotten all but the soul's "how she felt") were three creatures—something like a leopard, gay and dangerous (the first three heavens and their "spotted vanity"), and something like a lion strong and noble (the second three heavens and their universal intellect and proportion), and a third not at all like a wolf, but a two-natured existence, whose craving for souls is greater than that of any wolf's for food. The Sacred Griffin moves in its own forest, the paradise of earthly function; a pageant plays itself which can be seen when it breaks out of the air to welcome or threaten a mounting soul, but for the rest is known only to the air and the recesses of that primal wood.

All this while the human memory, as it sinks, has been aware of the eternal Images—of the God-bearer, of Beatrice, of Adam, of the three apostolic lords, of the City above and the City below, of teachers and poets and friends, of lovers and nuns; rather, has been accompanied by them. But now, it recalls how, in a whirl of accusation, the most constant of the Images had appeared. She was one whose eyes once reflected the point beyond all points, and also the two Natures of the Griffin. But the human memory recollects that once it did not understand that. It is blessed enough now to be able, with the *Convivio*, "to bless the times past, and well may it bless them." It says: " 'Had I not passed by such a way, I should not have had this treasure; I should not have had means of joy in the City to which I approach,' and therefore blesses the way it has gone." Especially it blesses the great master who before Beatrice came and when Beatrice disappeared was all that was not Beatrice, all that was not the direct point of experience, all the offices of others that served its own *vita,* and its *vita nuova*. It sees all the degrees of that new life on earth and after, how arch-natural, and how natural. If it recollects its sins, it recollects, with them, its purifications; if it recollects its own lack of love and courtesy, it recollects, with that, the love and courtesy of others; it is fulfilled by others, as (it may dare to hope) in some way, known or unknown—what does that matter?—it is a fulfillment of others. At least, before the purifications, it can still for ever acknowledge its debt—"tu duca, tu signore, et tu maestro," "la gloriosa donna della mia mente." Dante himself called both Virgil and Beatrice light—"O degli altri poeti onore e lume—O honour and light of other poets"; "O luce, O gloria della gente humana—O light, O glory of the human race."

But in that light it sees also something else—the whole opposite of itself which it might have become. It sees the little vile side-paths through the wood, opening before those who walk in a coma of themselves, and oblivious of those shining natural "membra—members" which were more beautiful than anything else in all Nature and all art. It sees the valley where "la gloriosa donna" does not come, and Virgil hardly except as a faint ghost, though certainly there it did turn to that ghost of poetry and found recollection and "salute." It sees the great sad gate, which can only properly be understood by those who know Paradise, for it is the light of Paradise which has engraved itself over the gate. Within, are those who know the worst—"the expense of spirit in a waste of shame." Shakespeare, in his darkest play, wrote that

> the worst is not
> So long as we can say, This is the worst.

It is perhaps a note of Dante's different greatness that the souls here can both feel the worst and say that it is the worst; their extreme consciousness, without intellect, is itself the pain. But into this "low hell" there is no need to go again. It is, all of it, without intellect, however enormous it may seem to those in it, and yet also very narrow for most—and very small to the redeemed, no more than a little snake slipping for a moment out of a rocky cleft into a grassy valley. The soul looks back rather to its real beginnings, its birth and its re-birth—its re-birth as particular to each soul as its birth, but for Dante, as for many, the experience of the natural eyes of a laughing girl in a city street.

Those eyes are named all through the *Commedia*. In the *Convivio* (IV, ii) it was said that Philosophy contemplated herself "when the beauty of her own eyes is revealed to her. And what else does this say but that the soul in philosophy not only contemplates truth, but also contemplates its own contemplation and the beauty of it . . . ?" In the *Commedia* this act of knowing is the subject throughout; so it had been, in a lesser way, in the *Vita*. In the *Commedia* Beatrice is a poetic image; being in a poem, she cannot well be anything else, though of course her relevance, like that of any other poetic image, may extend outside poetry. The most extreme supporters of the femininity both of Beatrice and of the Lady of the Window never supposed that in the poem Beatrice could be anything else, however great and wide a relevance they may suppose her to have outside. The allegory of her is (Dante said) at least fourfold, perhaps multifold. She is, in the whole *Paradiso*, his way of knowing, and the maxim is always "look; look well." Attention is demanded of him and her expositions are the result of his attention. She is, in a sense, his very act of knowing. It is in this sense that the *Paradiso* is an image of the whole act of knowing which is the great Romantic way, the Way of the Affirmation of Images, ending in the balanced whole. Indeed the entire work of Dante, so inter-relevant as it is, is a description of the great act of knowledge, in which Dante himself is the Knower, and God is the Known, and Beatrice is the Knowing. To say so is not to lessen Beatrice in herself to a mere quality of Dante, or only in the sense that, had we her *Commedia*, Dante would have been a quality of hers. All images are to excite qualities in us; so, in fact, Virgil taught in his great rationalization of love during the night in Purgatory—Virgil, himself a lesser master of knowing. We have only hints and fragments of her story; it is perhaps preserved for us after we have "condescended" to understand Dante's. Her eyes are his knowing; the beauty and wonder of his knowing deepens with the heavens; they are not in the hells because there is no true knowing in hell; they are not in the purgatories because he is only learning again what he forgot. But they are on earth and they are in heaven. Unsatisfied desire sees itself, in her, satisfied; satisfied desire sees itself, in him, unsatisfied. His actual knowing, even so, is a reflection; the Two-Natured is reflected in it, and the final Point Itself. Those eyes yield, in the end, to the eyes of the God-bearer. Then the Knower begins to know after a quite other manner, about which nothing can be said. It is, in a way, astonishing (but blessed) that this great poet should have said so little in the ordinary speech of Christians; he omits so much that any small Christian versifier would have put in. The God-bearer appears intensely, but how little! how little, in so long a poem, our most courteous Lord himself! But then she is the primal motion in substance, the motion being an exchange in unity—"figlia del tuo figlio." After that, in the poem, the Knower knows altogether, or remembers how once he did know altogether, "because I feel my joy increase." He hears still the running of the wheels of desire and will, the ever-humming speed of "il ben dell' intelletto."

Beatrice is his Knowing. To say so is not to reduce her actuality nor her femininity. The reason for the insistence on her femininity is simple —it is that this is what Dante insisted on, and that we ought perhaps to take Dante's poetry as relevant to our own affairs. Perhaps also we ought not. But if we ought, then the whole of his work is the image of a Way not confined to poets. That Way is not only what the poem is "about"; it is (according to it) what Love is "about." It is what Love is "up to," and the only question is whether lovers are "up to" Love. Were they, the *Vita* and the *Paradiso* would be the only way. The complex art of this knowledge is certainly not confined to romantic love of the male-female kind. Wherever the "stupor" is, there is the beginning of the art. Wherever any love is—and some kind of love in every man and woman there must be—there is either affirmation or rejection of the image, in one or other form. If there is rejection—of that Way there are many records. Of the affirmation, for all its greater commonness, there are fewer records. "Riguarda qual son io"—we have hardly yet begun to be looked at or to look.

Chronology of Important Dates

1265? Dante is born under the sign of Gemini (middle of May—middle of June).
1283? Dante's father dead and Dante becomes of age. He is married shortly therafter to Gemma Donati.
1289 June 11, the Battle of Campaldino against Arezzo, in which Dante takes part.
1290 June 8, the death of Beatrice. Dante begins his philosophical studies.
ca. 1292-3 The *Vita Nuova* is written.
1294 Spring, Dante meets Charles Martel in Florence.
1295 Dante enters political life.
1300 Jubilee year proclaimed by Boniface VIII.
1300 Easter, the fictive date of the journey in the poem.
1300 June 15, Dante becomes Prior of Florence.
1301 At the approach of Charles of Valois, Dante sent on an embassy to Boniface VIII.
1302 January 27, the first sentence of exile against Dante reaches him in Siena.
1302 March 10, Dante is permanently banished from Florence under pain of death.
1304-7? *De Vulgari Eloquentia* and the *Convivio*.
1310 The Descent of Henry VII into Italy. Dante's epistle to him. *De monarchia?*
1313 Death of Henry VII. Birth of Boccaccio.
1314 At least the *Inferno* completed.
1315 Florence offers to repeal his sentence on condition that he acknowledge his error, but Dante refuses.
1315-16? Dante in Romagna.
1316? Dante in Ravenna.
1320 Dante lectures at Verona on the *Quaestio de Aqua et Terra*.
1321 September 13 or 14, death of Dante in Ravenna.

Notes on the Editor and Authors

JOHN FRECCERO, the editor of this volume, is Professor of Italian and Curator of the Dante and Petrarch Collections at Cornell University. He is the author of several studies on Dante.

ERICH AUERBACH (1892-1957), the author of *Mimesis*, was one of the foremost critics of our time. His studies on Dante and the Middle Ages have had a profound influence in both Europe and America. At his death he was Professor at Yale University.

LUIGI PIRANDELLO (1867-1936), Italy's greatest dramatist, was an essayist and critic as well.

T[HOMAS] S[TEARNS] ELIOT'S (1889-1965) classic essay on Dante contributed to a revival of interest in the Italian poet's works throughout the English-speaking world.

GIANFRANCO CONTINI occupies the chair of Romance Philology at the University of Florence and is the director of *Studi danteschi*. He is internationally known as a critic of the "Hermetic" school and as a medieval philologist.

BRUNO NARDI is the author of several books on Dante and medieval philosophy and is responsible for the re-evaluation of Dante's philosophy in our time. He is Professor of Philosophy and the founder of the review *L'Alighieri* in Rome.

KENELM FOSTER is an English Dominican who has lectured at Cambridge University. His study of the last cantos of the *Purgatorio* (*God's Tree*) is his best known contribution to an historical understanding of Dante's poem.

RENATO POGGIOLI (1907-1963) was Professor of Slavic and Comparative Literature at Harvard University before his tragic death last year. His last published studies were devoted to Dante and the pastoral tradition, and at his death he was a member of the Council of the Dante Society of America.

LEO SPITZER (1887-1960), one of the most widely acclaimed critics of this century, was the master of stylistic criticism, which he applied to a vast range of languages and literatures in hundreds of articles. At his death he was Professor Emeritus of Romance Languages at the Johns Hopkins University.

CHARLES S. SINGLETON'S *Essay on the "Vita Nuova"* and his two volumes of *Dante Studies* have established him as the world's leading critic of the *Divine Comedy*.

He is at present Professor of Humanistic Studies at the Johns Hopkins University.

ROBERT E. KASKE is an outstanding American medievalist and has written numerous studies on Chaucer, Langland, and other topics in Old and Middle English literature. He is Professor of English at Cornell University.

ALESSANDRO PASSERIN D'ENTRÈVES is Professor of the History of Law at the University of Turin and was formerly Serena Professor of Italian at Oxford. He is the author of many works of political history and of *Dante as Political Thinker.*

GEORGES POULET's *Studies in Human Time* and *The Interior Distance* are acknowledged to be among the most original contributions to contemporary criticism. His most recent work, *The Metamorphoses of the Circle,* is not only critical but also constitutes an essay in the history of ideas. He now occupies the chair of French Literature at the University of Zürich.

CHARLES WILLIAMS (1886-1945) was a novelist, translator, and poet, as well as a Lecturer at Oxford. His deeply personal book on Dante, *The Figure of Beatrice,* has had great influence in England, particularly among Anglo-Catholic writers and students of the poem.

Selected Bibliography

A new edition of Dante's works by the *Società Dantesca Italiana* is in preparation. A text, translation, and commentary by Charles S. Singleton is about to be published by the Bollingen Foundation. Both of these publications will doubtless be indispensable and will supersede earlier ones. In the meantime, the standard edition is still that of Michele Barbi *et al., Le Opere di Dante* (critical text of the Società Dantesca Italiana, 2nd ed., Florence, 1960), while the most useful prose translation is that by J. D. Sinclair with facing Italian text (Oxford). Verse translations generally sacrifice fidelity for the sake of English prosody, but some occasionally manage to translate Dante's poetic tone effectively. Among these, John Ciardi's translation of the *Inferno* (Mentor Books) is worthy of praise, while for the *Purgatorio* and the *Paradiso* the translation of Dorothy Sayers, completed by Barbara Reynolds (Penguin Books), is recommended, especially for its excellent notes. Below is a list of works to which the reader may wish to refer for guidance in the vast field of Dante bibliography.

Auerbach, Eric. *Dante, Poet of the Secular World,* trans. by R. Manheim. Chicago: University of Chicago Press, 1961.

―――. "Figura." In *Scenes from the Drama of European Literature,* trans. by R. Manheim. New York: Meridian Books, 1959.

Barbi, Michele. *Life of Dante,* ed. and trans. by P. Ruggiers. Berkeley: University of California Press, 1960.

Cosmo, Umberto. *A Handbook to Dante Studies,* trans. by David Moore. Oxford: Blackwell, 1950. An excellent guide for the student as well as the specialist, to which one may refer for all essential bibliography.

Curtius, Ernst Robert. *European Literature and the Latin Middle Ages,* trans. by W. Trask. New York: Pantheon, 1953.

Eliot, T. S. "Dante." In *Selected Essays.* New York: Harcourt, Brace, & World, 1932.

Fay, E. A. *Concordance of the Divine Comedy.* Boston: Dante Society of America, 1888. A new one is in preparation under the auspices of the Dante Society and the direction of Ernest Hatch Wilkins.

Gilson, Étienne. *Dante and Philosophy,* trans. by David Moore (Harper Torchbooks). New York: Harper and Row, 1963.

Koch, Theodore W. *Catalogue of the Dante Collection presented by Willard Fiske to Cornell University,* 2 vols. and Supplements. Ithaca (N.Y.): Cornell University Press, 1898-1921. The standard bibliography of printed books in the field.

Moore, Edward. *Studies in Dante* (in four series). Oxford: Clarendon Press, 1896-1917.

Reade, W. H. V. *The Moral System of Dante's Inferno.* Oxford: Clarendon Press, 1909.

Singleton, Charles S. *An Essay on the Vita Nuova.* Cambridge: Harvard University Press, 1949.

────── *Commedia: Elements of Structure* (Dante Studies I). Cambridge: Harvard University Press, 1954.

────── *Journey to Beatrice* (Dante Studies II). Cambridge: Harvard University Press, 1957.

Toynbee, Paget. *A Dictionary of Proper Names and Notable Matters in the Works of Dante.* Oxford: Clarendon Press, 1898. A new edition of this indispensable work is being prepared by Charles S. Singleton.

The following journals should also be consulted for their periodical critical bibliographies:

Studi Danteschi (Florence)
Deutsches Dantejahrbuch (Germany)
Annual Report of the Dante Society (Cambridge, Mass.)

Finally, the most useful line-by-line commentary now in print is Hermann Gmelin's *Kommentar* to his translation in three volumes: *Die Göttliche Komödie.* Stuttgart: E. Klett Verlag, 1954.

TWENTIETH CENTURY VIEWS

Forthcoming Titles

The poetic reputation of Dante Alighieri, as John Freccero reminds us in his introduction to this collection of critical essays, remains undisputed seven hundred years after his birth. But, despite the immediacy of his poetry, no writer presents greater difficulties to the twentieth century mind.

The Divine Comedy confronts modern readers—most of whom can no longer accept the premises on which Dante's works are founded—with one of the central critical problems of our time, the relationship of poetry to belief.

The essays in this volume examine this problem and others in relation to crucial episodes of *The Divine Comedy*—the passion of Francesca and Paolo, the suicide of Pier delle Vigne, the allegory of the Car of the Corrupted Church, and the approach of the poet to his beloved Beatrice in Paradise—placing these episodes, and the entire poem, against the cultural background of medieval thought.

Representing an unusually wide range of critical opinion, these selections include an article by Luigi Pirandello, a new translation of one of Italy's most famous and most difficult critics—Gianfranco Contini—as